When Your Rabbit Needs Special Care

Traditional and Alternative Healing Methods

SANTA
MONICA
PRESS

When Your Rabbit Needs Special Care

Traditional and Alternative Healing Methods

Lucile C. Moore
Kathy Smith

Published by:

 Santa Monica Press LLC
P.O. Box 1076
Santa Monica, CA 90406-1076
1-800-784-9553
www.santamonicapress.com
books@santamonicapress.com

Printed in the United States

The information contained in this book is intended to help you provide care for your rabbit; however, this information is not intended for diagnostic or prescriptive purposes. The examples provided were helpful in each particular case, but a veterinarian and/or alternative practitioner qualified to treat rabbits should be consulted for your specific concerns. Although the author researched the topics in this work, the advent of new procedures—as well as future changes to those treatments considered standard at the time of publication—will render some information obsolete and further emphasizes the need for consultation with a rabbit-knowledgeable vet. The author, contributors, editors, distributor, and publisher are not responsible for any use or misuse of the information in this book, and are not liable or responsible to any person or group with respect to any loss, illness, or injury caused or alleged to be caused by the information found in this book.

Santa Monica Press books are available at special quantity discounts when purchased in bulk by corporations, organizations, or groups. Please call our Special Sales department at 1-800-784-9553.

ISBN-13 978-1-59580-031-2
ISBN-10 1-59580-031-X

Library of Congress Cataloging-in-Publication Data

Moore, Lucile C., 1952–
 When your rabbit needs special care : traditional and alternative healing methods / Lucile C. Moore and Kathy Smith.
     p. cm.
 ISBN 978-1-59580-031-2
 1. Rabbits—Diseases—Treatment. 2. Rabbits—Health. 3. Rabbits. I. Smith, Kathy, 1954- II. Title.
 SF997.5.R2.M66 2008
 636.932--dc22
                              2007041438

Cover and interior design and production by Future Studio
Cover photo by Velly Oliver

CONTENTS

PART I: Traditional Healing Methods

PART II: Alternative Healing Methods

ACKNOWLEDGMENTS

Kathy Smith, who generously contributed several pieces and chapters to this book, wished to thank those who shared their time and knowledge with her:

I would first like to thank Lucile Moore for the opportunity to collaborate on this wonderful project. We both want to thank all the bunny angels—especially King Murray, Dante, Stormy, Houdini, and Buster—who made sure everything fell into place as it was meant to.

A special thanks to Dr. Noella Allan, my wonderful veterinarian, who always makes time for me whether I have a sick rabbit who needs her care or a writing project that would benefit from her collaboration and review. I would also like to thank Dr. James K. Morrisey and Dr. Christine Eckermann-Ross, both of whom also found time in their busy schedules to answer my e-mail questions.

Finally, I would like to thank the communicators, rescuers, and caregivers who shared their experiences and gave permission for their stories and/or photos to be included in the sections I wrote: Vineeta Anand, Meg Brown and Greg Wait, Dawn Baumann Brunke, Joanna Campbell, Brenda and Jim Holden, April Jones, Janie Landes, Jeanette Lyerly, Kim Meyer, Deborah Miles-Hoyt, Molly Sheehan, Kerry Stewart, Suzanne Trayhan, and Evonne Vey.

PREFACE

Most books on house rabbits are written as a result of the author's personal experience with a rabbit companion. This book is no exception. I first conceived the idea of writing about disabled buns after my experiences with a rabbit who required constant specialized care. He inspired me to write an article about caring for special-needs rabbits, which appeared online, and I then planned to expand the topic into a book. I also discovered that even my healthiest rabbits require occasional special care, if only for a short time after a spay surgery or when recovering from a digestive upset brought on by stress. I hope that this book, with tips from many people who have cared for rabbits affected by everything from obesity to permanent paralysis from a fractured spine, will help others who face giving daily specialized care to their rabbits.

My focus in this text is on how to actually provide home care to rabbits with medical problems. But it is my intent to include enough medical information on each disease or condition that you will be able to understand what is happening and discuss it with your veterinarian. Only then can you make the best choices and provide the best possible care to your rabbit companion. It is beyond the scope of this book to include all the diseases and conditions that could possibly affect your companion rabbit, so I have for the most part chosen to include those that you are most likely to encounter.

Rabbit care and medicine, after years in its dark ages, is progressing rapidly. Periods of swift increase of knowledge in any field are exciting, but there are also instances where not everyone is going to agree, and when it may be difficult to provide one "right" answer. Many differing points of view may have validity; opinions are often based on personal experience, and what is successful in one case may not be in another.

In addition to opinions from veterinarians and alternative health care professionals, views of the rabbit caretakers in whose hands rest the actual daily tasks involved in giving special care to rabbits are included. Again, what hints they have to give others striving with the same care issues are based on their own personal experiences as they struggle to give the best possible care to the companion rabbits they love. Their perspective may be entirely different from that of the professionals.

Rabbits are intentionally referred to as "he," "she," and "who" in this book, because those of us who share our lives with animal companions think of them in this way. For the same reason, I chose to use the word "symptom" instead of the more technically correct "sign" when referring to the visible manifestations of disease in rabbits.

I am aware not all veterinarians will agree with my decision to include the tables of medications. My reasons for including them were: 1) The information is widely available on the World Wide Web and in publications, usually without the warnings I give; 2) Not all readers are fortunate enough to live where they have access to a veterinarian experienced with rabbits, and even the best vets may occasionally make errors in writing prescriptions. I recommend that a person always compare a prescription to the range of doses given in a formulary. If there is a question, a quick phone call to the vet's office can resolve any discrepancies and possibly save the rabbit's life.

I owe thanks to many people for their help in creating my share of this book. First and foremost, I owe thanks to Amy Spintman, board member and educator, San Diego chapter of the House Rabbit Society, owner of Cats & Rabbits & More, founder and moderator of the Disabled Rabbits Weblist. Without her encouragement and the inspiration provided by the lives of her special-needs rabbits, especially Bijou, along with the stories and pleas for help from members of the Disabled Rabbits Weblist, this book would never have come to be.

Secondly, I owe a great debt of thanks to Debby Widolf, manager of rabbits at the Sanctuary of Best Friends Animal Society. It was at her suggestion the chapter on triage for large-scale rescues was included. Despite her busy schedule, Debby also took on the task of reading through my completed manuscript and offering comments and suggestions. Thanks also to Shelley Thayer, Rapid Response Project Specialist at Best Friends Animal Society, and to Sandi Ackerman of Washington, who graciously added her knowledge and perspective on large-scale rescue.

Lezlie Sage, certified interfaith chaplain and adoption program administrator at Best Friends Animal Society, willingly tackled the difficult issues of euthanasia and recovery from grief at my request.

I was thrilled when Kathy Smith, author of *Rabbit Health in the 21st Century* and *King Murray's Royal Tail*, informed me she was interested in contributing to this project. Many thanks to Kathy for her multiple contributions, especially for writing several of the chapters for Part II, and for reading over my material and offering her comments and suggestions. Warm thanks also to writer Jodi McLaughlin for her many informative contributions and to author Nancy Furstinger for sending a piece on her 15-year-old rabbit, Cupcake.

Several supporters of various chapters of the House Rabbit Society (HRS) encouraged me in this effort. I owe special thanks to the following for the stories and photographs of their rabbits they allowed me to use: Kim and Terry Clevenger of the Kansas City, Missouri, Chapter; Margo DeMello, development director of the national organization; Donna Jensen, HRS member and former chapter manager who fosters rabbits in the Bay Area of California; and Maria L. Perez, manager of the Las Vegas chapter.

Members of other rabbit organizations were also generous with their time and expertise: Stephen F. Guida, volunteer with Brambley Hedge Rabbit Rescue; Patti Henningsen, volunteer with Friends of Rabbits and her own Bright Eyes

Sanctuary; Rebecca Kintner, volunteer with Bunny Magic Rescue; and Barbara Yule, founder of the North Texas Rabbit Sanctuary.

Thanks to the following veterinarians for their generosity in giving their time to answer my questions on various aspects of rabbit medicine by telephone, e-mail, and/or letter: Drs. Mark Burgess, Bill Guerrera, Susan Keeney, William Kurmes, James K. Morrisey, Jamie Sulliban, and Jason Sulliban. (The fact that they answered questions for me in no way implies they agree with all the information presented in this book.) Special thanks to Dr. Kurmes for meticulously going through my entire part of the manuscript searching for any medical errors.

I am grateful to the expert practitioners who contributed to my alternative methods of healing chapters: Chandra Moira Beal, George Belev, Marnie Black, Anita DeLelles, and Greg Wait.

I also owe thanks to the many rabbit caregivers (some members of organizations such as the HRS, some not) who gave me permission to share their care tips or photos so that others might benefit: Betsy Bremer, Meg and Buster Brown, Shannon Cail, Marion Davis, Melissa Epperson, Alexandria Fenner, Laura and Peter Franco, Becky Hawley, Jennifer Heaton, Morgan Heller, Jen Hendricks, Stacey Huitikka, Arlette Hunnakko, Ronie Lawrence, Karen Cole Leinenkugel, Delores Lowis, Jeanette Lyerly, Joe Marcom, Rachel Marek, J. Medawar, Joseph Nobile, Missy Ott, Suzanne Pani, Angela Percival, Susan Robbins, Theresa Romaldini, Lynn Sagramoso, Sharon, Julie Sherwin, Renee Stratton, Dawn Stuart, and Joanne Wilcox. Your love for and devotion to your rabbits is always evident!

Special thanks to Dave Stewart for his constant encouragement and support during this project. How many people would leave work and drive over 500 miles to pick up a rabbit to get him to a vet in time?

Finally, I owe thanks to the many wonderful rabbits who have shared and do share my home: FBR (Fierce Bad

Rabbit) Bunnyman, Muffy, Sweetie Pie, Timothy (Mr. Tim), Anthony, Funny Face, Binky, Snugglebiter, Angel-bunny (aka Beulah), Magic, Pixie, Fuzzy Wuzzy Fuzzbug, Rapunzel, Dolly Doodle, Phantom Elvis, Ruby, Siegfried, and Roy.

Lucile C. Moore, PhD

INTRODUCTION

Mr. Tim:
An Introduction to
Special Needs and Special Care

The baby rabbit was barely visible on the bottom of the hay-filled box at the back of the barn. As my eyes adjusted to the dim light I could see that his tiny body was shaking. He appeared so small, so delicate; I was afraid even to touch him. I looked at my friends, my questions in my eyes.

"I was going to euthanize him because he has a lot of congenital abnormalities," Sharon explained to me. "But my husband fell in love with him and begged me to find him a home. I couldn't trust just anyone to give him the special care he needs, so I thought of you."

Sharon carefully lifted the tiny rabbit from the box and handed him to me. For some reason I held the frail body as I would rarely hold a rabbit—upside down, cradled in my arms. His trembling stopped immediately and he relaxed against my chest with a visible sigh. My heart contracted and a fierce protectiveness filled my being.

"Did you see that? Did you see how he looked at her with instant total trust?" my friend Dave marveled. "He knows he is safe now. He knows he has found a home."

That was my introduction to the world of special-needs rabbits. For the next several years, my life would revolve around the tiny little tortoise Holland Lop. Answering his needs would fill my every day, and his incredibly strong spirit would dominate that of every other rabbit in my home. He lived three wonderfully happy years, and when he died, he died in my arms. For his burial, I wrapped him in a hand-stitched velveteen heart quilt given to me for that purpose by a friend who understood the magnitude of my loss. A lock of my hair rested on his breast.

This book is dedicated to you, Mr. Tim, and to all those

human companions who meet the difficult and rewarding challenge of caring for special-needs rabbits.

Mr. Tim was a true special-needs rabbit; a rabbit who required special care every day of his life. But any rabbit can become a rabbit that requires support for a short time. The bun might become ill, break a limb, have serious digestive troubles, or simply live long enough to develop some of the infirmities of old age. Occasionally, a rabbit may not come through a routine surgery as expected and suddenly require special care. Nor is a physical problem necessary for a rabbit to require extra support. Sometimes rabbits need special care because of emotional problems stemming from early mistreatment.

Usually the need for special care is temporary, lasting only long enough for the rabbit to recover from a transitory condition. Sometimes, though, the need is permanent. Most caretakers of permanently disabled rabbits don't set out to become caretakers. A perfectly healthy rabbit may become a disabled rabbit in an instant if the spine is severed in a cage accident or from mishandling. Other times, rabbits have serious congenital problems that may not show up until months or years have passed.

Any rabbit may require special care at some time.

Most of us can cope with a temporary need to give a rabbit extra care if we are able to find the information to help us do it correctly. Sometimes all it takes is a day or so of monitoring a rabbit's temperature and food intake, and adding a light blanket to the cage for warmth. Or we may need to give an oral medication for a few days. We can probably even cope—though we may be a little more hesitant—if we find we need to administer subcutaneous fluids for a week.

Providing such care for the life of the rabbit is a different matter entirely. If you are suddenly confronted with having a rabbit that requires lifelong special care, one of the first questions to ask yourself is whether you will realistically be able to

Peanut is a permanent special-needs rabbit.

take on the commitment. Caring for a permanently disabled rabbit requires a great investment of time, money, and emotion. If you have cared for a healthy house rabbit, quadruple or quintuple the time you spend on it for an estimate of the amount of time it will take to care for a severely disabled house rabbit. Does your job and family life permit such an investment? Can you take the emotional upheaval of caring for a permanently disabled rabbit? Many such rabbits experience widely varying ups and downs that can be hard to take. Just when you feel the rabbit has turned the corner, he/she slides back down—over and over and over again. Finally, do you have the financial resources to provide permanent special care to a rabbit? Special daily supplies and food are often required, not to mention veterinary costs and medications.

If you can't answer the above questions in the affirmative, you may want to think before taking on the care of a severely disabled rabbit. The twin necessities of earning money and caring for one's human family may simply make such a commitment impossible for many, however much they may wish to take it on. If your current circumstances don't allow you to take on such care and you find yourself with a rabbit requiring special assistance, contact your local

House Rabbit Society (HRS)[1] chapter or rabbit rescue organization. They may be able to find someone who can.

But if you do answer in the affirmative, prepare yourself for a life-changing experience. Caretakers often develop remarkably close relationships with their special-needs rabbits. Donna Jensen, who became a member of the House Rabbit Society (HRS) in 1992 and has fostered rabbits with special needs ever since, comments, "Nothing is more special than caring for them. It is very rewarding, and I always say it is an honor to serve. They really, really want to be here, so you say 'Yes, I will do this for you.'"

Maria Perez, manager of the Las Vegas chapter of the House Rabbit Society, sanctuaries 16 medically compromised rabbits. "The most rewarding thing is that I learn something of value from *them* every day," Maria states. "They indeed never cease to amaze me." Although she loves all the rabbits who come to her, it is evident that one, Chloe, holds a special place in Maria's heart. "The veterinarians say that she is a miracle—with all of the adversity she has overcome and medical challenges, yet she remains the happiest soul I have ever known. She is my life coach. 'It's OK Mom, tomorrow is another day,' she'll whisper when I'm blue. She is a joy to my heart each and every day."

Stephen F. Guida, a volunteer with Brambley Hedge Rabbit Rescue, has shared his life with several rabbits need-

Intrepid Chloe enjoys life despite her special needs.

1 The House Rabbit Society is an all-volunteer, non-profit organization dedicated to rescuing abandoned rabbits and educating the public about rabbit care.

ing special care. "I have received so much from caring for my special-needs bunnies," Steve comments. "For one, the complete and total trust they place in you is very beautiful and heart-warming. The love they show every time you care for them is something that never grows old. Curiously, my special-needs bunnies have always seemed to be my happiest bunnies, taking such complete joy in a simple brushing, a pat on the head, a scratch on the ear, or something that any 'normal' rabbit would not think twice about."

Lucile C. Moore, PhD

PART I

TRADITIONAL HEALING METHODS

CHAPTER 1

BASIC CARE I

Lucile C. Moore

Most of the time spent in giving special care to a rabbit will be in providing the essentials. Rabbits must be kept:
- Clean and dry
- Groomed
- Comfortable
- Hydrated
- Fed
- Pain free

Creating a safe, comfortable, and clean environment for the rabbit requiring special care is the first necessity. This may be a relatively simple task in the case of a rabbit recovering from a spay surgery, or it may be a difficult challenge, as in the case of a rabbit that has a broken spine or head tilt. In either situation, location is the first concern. The rabbit may be disinclined or unable to move much on his own, so care must be taken to ensure his personal space will be safe and comfortable. The rabbit should be in a spot where he is not too near a heat source, cold draft, or fumes. An area where the rabbit will be able to watch some activity is preferable, as you do not want the rabbit to feel isolated, but too much noise or activity could be stressful.

Rabbits needing special care are not unlike humans

who are ill; things that might not stress them at other times may when they are not feeling well. Loud noises could be stressful, so be sure the bun is not too close to a television or radio. Another possible source of stress to an ailing rabbit is the presence of other animals. Although many rabbits get along well with household cats and dogs, this is learned behavior. When a rabbit is ill, he may become stressed by the presence of these "predators." Do not assume because of your affection for the cat and dog members of your family that this cannot happen.

It is always necessary to keep a rabbit's space clean, and this is even more critical for the rabbit needing special care. For general cleaning, the best choice is white vinegar or a dilute solution of an iodophor such as Betadine®, Vetadine®, or Vanodine®. Iodophors are good, inexpensive, general-purpose disinfectants with bactericidal properties. They are safe for cleaning areas where rabbits live as well as their food and water dishes and bedding. Follow dilution instructions carefully, as their effectiveness depends upon it. A dilute solution of chlorine bleach (one part bleach/ten water) can also be used, and is an effective disinfectant, but you will need to keep the rabbit away from the fumes and not return him to his pen until surfaces are thoroughly dry.

Where transmission of a disease is a concern, you may need to keep a rabbit in a separate room and observe strict sanitation. Wash hands thoroughly before entering and immediately after leaving the room and have a footbath at the door to step in on your way in and out. Fold an old towel in the bottom of an inexpensive plastic dishpan, and pour in enough of a rabbit-safe disinfectant to wet the towel. Then simply step into the dishpan before entering and exiting the room.

Bedding

If your rabbit requires special care only temporarily and is not incontinent, the only change you may need to make to his bedding is to add a soft towel or blanket for extra comfort. Rabbits who are still recovering from anesthesia and rabbits who have had areas of fur shaved off for surgery may need a light blanket over them or bunched around them to help conserve body heat.

Bijou relaxes comfortably in her donut bed.

Bedding for rabbits who are permanently incontinent, paralyzed, or suffering from other debilitating disabilities requires more ingenuity. Some caretakers of paralyzed rabbits use large cat beds (not cedar-filled, as the fumes from the shavings could have negative effects on rabbits), line them with a puppy pad or diaper, and place a soft towel or piece of synthetic sheepskin on the top. These beds have the advantage that they can be carried from room to room, and allow the caregiver to keep the rabbit with them most of the time. However, they may not be feasible with larger rabbits or rabbits who have not lost all their mobility.

Depending upon the particular disease or condition the rabbit has, manufactured housing can provide a safe, easy-to-clean living space. A rabbit cage on a high wheeled base with a top opening can be very useful for providing intensive nursing, as can a rabbit "condo" with a hinged top (Appendix III).

Many caretakers of rabbits who have lost their mobility create a space for them by placing layers of bedding in an area set off by indoor pet fencing or in a purchased baby crib or playpen. The size of the pen needed will vary according to the size of the rabbit, but in general, a space about three feet by four feet is adequate for one rabbit who has lost mobility. The perimeter can be made from baby gates or a small-animal exercise pen. You will need to be able to access the pen easily, as you will be replacing the bedding and tending to the rabbit frequently.

A waterproof barrier such as a piece of plastic or a bed pad for incontinent persons is placed on the floor of the pen. The next layer can be a piece of egg crate foam or sheets of large plastic bubble wrap. Both of these will help to prevent the formation of pressure sores, which is always a concern in rabbits with limited mobility. Next, a puppy piddle pad, diaper, or incontinent pad for humans adds another waterproof barrier. Absorbent towels, old T-shirts, or synthetic sheepskin makes a comfortable and absorbent top layer. The hands-down favorite faux sheepskin with members of the Disabled Rabbits group on Yahoo! is that from Palace Pet Beds™. This comes in various sizes and colors, and caretakers who use it claim it can withstand repeated washings. Less expensive alternatives for faux sheepskin include "sheepskin" mattress covers that can be cut into pieces for use as bedding, and synthetic sheepskin of varying thicknesses that can be purchased by the yard at fabric stores.

Other beddings that can be used in creating an area for special-needs rabbits are dog-crate liners and inexpensive carpet samples that can be used until they are soiled and then thrown away.

Paralyzed rabbits will also need to have something in their pen to rest their head on. It is important to keep the front quarters of the rabbit elevated and in a more natural position. This can help prevent lung problems and usually makes the rabbit feel better both physically and mentally. A purchased donut bed can provide this support for a paralyzed bun, or you can make your own supports by rolling up soft cotton fabric, mattress pads, or towels.

Toys

Rabbits needing special care are as intelligent and curious as any healthy rabbit, and will need toys and other items to provide stimulation. Donna Jensen, a former HRS chapter manager who has fostered literally hundreds of special-needs rabbits over the past 15 years, always has plenty of toys within reach of her special buns. She prefers soft stuffed

Tootsie rests among an assortment of toys.

toys, as these will not be injurious if the bun falls over them, and the rabbits can also use them as props on which to lean. One of Donna's favorite toys is a ladybug that plays music when the center is pressed—one of her special rabbits actually learned to press the ladybug to make it play a tune!

Soft, bunny-safe stuffed rabbits can perform double duty: as toy and as companion. I was skeptical of this at first, until I rescued a tiny, nervous Polish rabbit who had a broken leg. I did not have a gentle rabbit I could bond her to, but disliked having her alone, so I decided to try a "bunny buddy," a soft, cotton-filled rabbit shape I purchased from a business associated with a shelter (Appendix III). My little Polish rabbit loved her "buddy," and snuggled, licked, mounted, and threw it around her cage. It truly did keep her from feeling too lonely until her leg healed and I could bond her to a real rabbit companion.

Companion Rabbits

When the particular disease or condition requiring special care in a rabbit allows it, a rabbit companion or "nurse bunny" can be very effective in raising the spirits of the special care rabbit. If the special-needs rabbit is already bonded to another rabbit when he becomes affected, the bonded rabbit will often

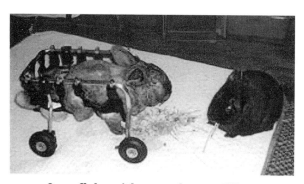
Snowflake with nurse bunny Elliot.

naturally assume this role. If a special-needs rabbit is adopted by himself, it may be worthwhile to get in touch with your local rabbit rescue group. They will often be able to guide you toward a likely match, and even allow you to try the pairing before committing to adoption.

Food and Water

If your rabbit needing special care is recovering from a surgery or gastrointestinal problem, changes in your feeding and watering arrangements may be minimal, although they may need to be coaxed to eat (Chapter 2). Rabbits that have had dental surgery or other mouth surgery may need to have pellets softened in water and often prefer a bowl for water instead of a sipper bottle. Should the rabbit refuse to take either, you will need to coax him to drink. Adding a few drops of fruit juice (without added sugar) may encourage some reluctant buns to take liquids. In other instances, giving the rabbit a couple of tablespoons of undiluted fruit juice (again, without added sugar) can encourage him to begin drinking on his own again. Syringe feeding may be necessary temporarily (Chapter 2).

Many permanently disabled rabbits are able to eat on their own, but they may need assistance in reaching the food. Dishes can be placed next to the rabbit at feeding times, held up to their face, or a special eating area can be set up. Kim Jackson Clevenger created a special feeding area with supports for her special-needs rabbit, Tiffy. When mealtime came, Kim could place Tiffy at her "feeding station," as Kim termed it, where Tiffy could eat in comfort (Chapter 6).

While there is little argument that good grass hay should comprise the bulk of a companion rabbit's diet when that is possible, what other foods are acceptable to give rabbits, ill or otherwise, is an issue not all experts agree upon. Some veterinarians prefer to see house rabbits on a "natural" diet consisting strictly of grass hay and fresh greens (Chapter 3). However, such a diet does not truly mimic the diet of wild rabbits, and other vets point out that rabbits receiving no commercial pellets at all could be at risk for developing acquired dental disease (Chapter 7) and bone disorders such as osteoporosis (Chapter 9). A diet of grass hay with some fresh greens and a very small amount of a good timothy-based or high-quality alfalfa commercial pellet (1–2 tablespoons per 2.5 pounds of rabbit) may be a safe compromise. However, it should be remembered that not all rabbits are the same. One rabbit may be unable to eat hay because of a physical impairment, and another rabbit may be unable to tolerate greens, even when they are introduced slowly into the diet.

It can be a real challenge to tempt a rabbit with low appetite to eat. Rabbits needing special care can be very picky (and very stubborn) about what foods they will or will not eat, making the task of feeding them even more difficult. Shannon Cail describes the foods her nine-year-old special-needs rabbit companion Bailey would eat:

> Bailey decided that the only things he was going to eat were Critical Care®, cilantro and kale, and of course his treats of cranberries and banana chips. He would no longer eat pellets, no matter what pellet mush recipe I tried, and he hardly ate any hay.[1]

Many veterinarians who treat rabbits suggest tempting anorexic rabbits to eat with a teaspoon or so of canned

1 Cail, Shannon. 2006. An Extraordinary Journey: A Rabbit's Fight for Survival Against the Odds. *Rabbit Tracks* 3: 2–4.

pumpkin or an oatmeal/fruit baby food preparation (without added sugar) such as Gerbers® Tender Harvest™ line. Other veterinarians argue that even small amounts of grain, fruits, or high-carbohydrate vegetables such as carrots or squash should be avoided. They feel that these high-carbohydrate foods have too great a potential to disrupt the bacterial balance of the rabbit's digestive tract, especially in the cecum (Chapter 3).

However, it should be noted that feeding a healthy rabbit and coaxing a seriously anorexic rabbit to eat are two very different situations. Saunders and Davies, in *Notes on Rabbit Internal Medicine,* respond to the concerns some vets have that giving anorexic rabbits foods too high in simple sugars may contribute to enterotoxemia. They comment that avoiding hepatic lipidosis by providing a rapidly available source of energy may be critical and note that deaths in such cases are "nearly always being due to hepatic lipidosis, and rarely to enterotoxaemia."

Giving rabbits fruit is a particularly controversial subject, even among highly qualified rabbit specialists, because of its high sugar content. Some believe all fruit should be avoided. Others feel small amounts are fine to give rabbits. In an article titled "Rabbits, Geriatrics, and Chronic Disease," Harvey writes, "Since fructose is easily digested in the rabbit's small intestine, it is unlikely to cause carbohydrate overload in the caecum and is a safe calorie source." She further comments that small amounts of banana or apple can be useful in disguising medications.

There is no argument that *large* amounts of high-carbohydrate foods such as fruit are unhealthy for your rabbit and may predispose him to serious gastrointestinal disorders. But whether or not to give your rabbit *small* amounts of fruit is a decision you will need to make for yourself in consultation with your veterinarian. I give the equivalent of one tablespoon of fresh fruit per 2.5 pounds of rabbit to my rabbits daily, both those who are healthy and those who are receiving special care.

Grooming

Many rabbits requiring special care will not be able to groom themselves or may not feel well enough to do their normal grooming, so you will need to do it for them. This can often be a challenge, especially with the long-haired breeds. In fact, you will probably find that a surprising amount of the time you spend giving a rabbit special care will be spent on grooming-related tasks.

Fur

Fur will need to be kept combed and clean. Short-haired rabbits are relatively easy to brush and comb, but long-haired breeds can be a real problem. First you will need the proper tools for your bun's type of fur. I have an assortment of grooming tools, from flea combs and combs with teeth of varying length to slicker brushes and baby brushes. My favorite grooming aides are a comb with rotating teeth for combing out snarls in woolly fur, and a combination tool that has a soft brush on the front, a metal slicker brush on the back, and two combs in the sides. Try different kinds of combs and brushes until you find the one that works best for your rabbit's fur.

Grooming rabbits with long woolly fur can be stressful to both rabbit and caregiver. Try to reduce pulling by holding the base of the fur with the fingers of one hand while you comb or brush it out with the other. Rabbits' skin is sensitive, and if it hurts too much, the rabbit is going to resist or become stressed. If mats are present, it is sometimes easier to trim them out than to comb them out, but be sure to use grooming scissors with rounded ends so you don't nick the rabbit's tender skin. Groom a small area at a time, reward your rabbit with a safe treat such as a bit of parsley, and do another section of fur later. Another trick that works for some is to massage the rabbit while you comb and brush. This helps the rabbit relax, and can even turn the session into a pleasant one! Jodi McLaughlin, CMT, suggests doing a "brush massage":

One of the handiest tools for disabled bunnies is a soft bristle baby brush. You can use the brush to gently massage and "scratch" the outside and all around the base of bunny ears. A lot of people find it more comfortable to "brush massage" instead of using their hands and fingers for TTouch® techniques. You can make small circles on the outside and inside tips of the ears, down the neck, across the hips, and especially on the disabled feet! But start slowly on the feet because you are in effect giving a reflexology session and too much too soon can elicit a healing type crisis, or just over-stimulate the bun. Brushing the disabled feet also activates the proprioceptor response. You may notice bun attempting to flex and extend the toes or legs of rarely used extremities. Use a light touch. Try sweeping the brush up over the loin area and down the tail too. Watch the reaction on bun's face when you use the brush. Bunnies love it! It may not take off a lot of fur, but it is great for stimulating the circulation and offering a wonderful sensation for our disabled furbabies. Use only a soft bristle baby brush; other brushes are too harsh for bunny massage.

Grooming severely disabled buns who are in pain and discomfort from other conditions may be especially difficult. If grooming becomes excessively stressful to the rabbit, you may need to balance the need to groom with the need to optimize the rabbit's overall health and mental condition. I have had permanently disabled rabbits where I felt I was doing more harm than good by trying to keep them entirely mat-free. Although the rabbits looked a bit like unkempt waifs at times, I felt it was the best choice for their particular cases.

Many rabbits needing special care will be unable to access their cecotrophs. Watch for them, collect them promptly, and feed the whole ones to the rabbit. Uncollected cecotrophs will become smeared on the rabbit and bedding and generally make a mess, smell, and attract flies. If any do become mashed on the rabbit's fur, clean them off carefully with a soft cloth dampened with warm water. Shampoos especially formulated for rabbits can be purchased from rabbit supply businesses (Appendix III).

Any urinary incontinence in your rabbit will require that you clean the hindquarters to try and prevent urine burn (see section later in this chapter) and discourage flies. Flystrike is a danger of which many rabbit caretakers are either unaware or underestimate. Barbara Yule, founder of the North Texas Rabbit Sanctuary, summarizes the risk:

> Most people have no idea that rabbits can suffer from flystrike, medical name "myiasis." Flies are attracted to rabbits (or other animals for that matter) that have urine or feces on or near them, or in some cases may simply smell of illness. Many older rabbits suffer from flystrike because they are unable to keep themselves totally clean, possibly because of arthritis, obesity, or illness. The fly will lay hundreds of tiny white eggs in the fur close to the tail or the genitals. After a few days the larvae hatch and they will eat into the flesh of the rabbit. Often, the caretaker of the rabbit is unaware that this is happening until the rabbit is seriously ill and going into toxic shock. It is a horrible, painful way to die. If you find white eggs or larva on your rabbit, consider it a dire emergency and go immediately to a rabbit-savvy veterinarian for proper treatment.
>
> Setting your rabbit outdoors (for any reason) is an open invitation to flystrike. Indoor rabbits are at risk if windows are un-

screened or some other occurrence allows flies into the house that could allow them to have access to the rabbits. It is wise to check your rabbit carefully if there is any exposure. The best treatment is truly prevention. Do not keep or put your rabbit outdoors. Be sure if your rabbit has dirty butt or urine stains that you treat the cause which could be obesity, a bladder infection or something more serious that needs medical treatment. Know your rabbit's habits. This will help you identify changes in diet and behavior. Each week, when you brush your rabbit, do a quick health check and check for dirty butt or redness around the tail and genital area.

Nails

As with any rabbit, you will need to keep a special-needs rabbit's nails trimmed. Untrimmed nails can be a cause of ulcerative pododermatitis and will be prone to catching on objects and even being pulled out. A variety of styles of clippers are available from rabbit supply businesses. Hold the rabbit in your lap and cut each nail to about a quarter inch out from where you see the vein. For darker nails it can help to look at the nail through the beam of a flashlight or lamp. For those rabbits with very dark nails, you will need to guess how far back to cut the nails. Try clipping a tiny bit at a time. If you should cut too far and the nail bleeds, apply a bit of styptic powder, cornstarch, or flour to the end of the nail.

Ears

Many special-needs rabbits will be unable to use their feet to clean their ears, so this is another task you will need to do for them. Lops, even those not needing special care, often have difficulty keeping their ears clean on their own. Ears that have not been cleaned may itch and irritate the rabbit, and over time the buildup of wax and debris may lead to otitis and eventual hearing loss.

There are several ear cleaning products available, including Novalsan® Otic Solution and Zymox® Otic Solution. You can use a cotton-tipped swab for the outer ear canal, but your little finger covered with a soft piece of cloth or tissue may be safer for anything you need to remove from deeper inside the ear. (Never attempt to dig too deeply in the ear, it is likely to harm the rabbit.)

Eyes

Watch your rabbit's eyes for any buildup of secretions and remove them with a soft clean cloth or sterile gauze pad dampened in warm water or a sterile eyewash such as Opticlear™ or TheraTears®. Remember *not* to clean the eyes with your unwashed, uncovered finger—you might introduce bacteria or a virus into the rabbit's eye. If a rabbit's eyes run constantly, he may have dacryocystitis or another condition you will need to have addressed by your vet (Chapter 8).

Scent Glands

The scent glands on either side of the genitals may become a bit stinky and "gunky." If they appear brownish, take a moistened cotton swab and clean out the wax-like buildup.

Incontinence

A variety of conditions may cause a rabbit to be temporarily or permanently incontinent. Incontinent rabbits present several difficulties to the rabbit caregiver. Urine and feces cause the fur to mat, attract flies, and lead to urine burn. Urine burn is extremely painful to the rabbit, and may eventually cause the rabbit's fur to fall out.

Temporary incontinence can be dealt with several ways. It may be enough simply to limit the rabbit's space for a few days, do some extra mop-ups, and change the top layers of bedding frequently so the rabbit is always clean and dry. A careful trim of the fur on the hindquarters can help prevent urine and feces buildup.

Permanent incontinence can be more difficult to deal with. A different litter box style can help in some cases. Joseph Nobile uses a special litter box with a low front for his rabbit Snuggles, whose hind legs are paralyzed. Snuggles is able to pull himself in and out with his front legs. Joseph made a special ½' × ½' vinyl-coated mesh stand to fit inside and covered it with an E-Z Feet floor mat. This allows urine and droppings to pass through, and keeps the bunny warm and dry.

Snuggles in his special litter box.

Some caretakers address the problem by having the rabbits' hindquarters shaved. This may be the best answer for rabbits who are paralyzed or have difficulty assuming the proper stance for urination because of arthritis or other degenerative disease. Donna Jensen, who has cared for many rabbits with incontinence, takes her special-needs bunnies in once a month for what she calls "sanitary shaves," and finds it a great help in keeping her buns clean and free from urine burn. Remember, because of rabbits' sensitive skin, you should have the shaving done by an experienced person. Don't attempt it yourself.

Baths

Although completely bathing a rabbit is not usually recommended, many rabbits requiring special care will need to have their hindquarters bathed occasionally. There are several ways to give these "butt baths," as caretakers refer to them. One way is to put the rabbit on a slanted dish drainer by the sink and pour warm water over the hindquarters from a bowl or with a retractable sink hose. Rabbit-safe shampoos are available from many rabbit-supply businesses (Appendix III) and can be used if desired. Try

Diego, wrapped carefully after his bath.

to complete the bathing quickly, and dry the bun by pressingly gently with an absorbent towel and blowing with an electric dryer set on low and held a minimum of 15 inches away from the rabbit. Caretakers usually find rabbits tolerate these "butt baths" quite well, seeming to understand the care done for their comfort.

Diapers

Diapering incontinent rabbits is another way to reduce urine burn. You might expect the rabbit would fight to get the diaper off, and a few do, but many caretakers who use diapers claim their rabbits leave them alone. Perhaps the rabbits realize they are given more space to roam while they have them on and are not dribbling urine everywhere!

Purchase a diaper that will lie flat. Don't buy the smallest diapers—many caregivers report that smaller ones don't work as well unless the rabbit is a dwarf breed—and cut a slit in the middle for the tail (not everyone does this). Pull the diaper around the rabbit, being sure the tail comes out the slit, and close the tabs over the stomach or chest, wherever the diaper comes to on the rabbit. Jodi McLaughlin shares the diapering technique she has developed for her special-needs rabbit, Diego:

> The Little Swimmers® have no Velcro tabs
> and slip on very easily, but then you must get

a diaper safety pin to tighten the top band. These are very, very easy to slip on if you place bun's two front feet on the edge of a table, dangle the hind legs, and slip them into the diaper together, then thread each leg into the proper hole and pull the whole thing up around the waist.

The other diaper we like is Huggies® #2, they fit snug and work for his four-pound body. With traditional diapers like these, I fasten the outside leg of the nappy first, then thread that leg through, then I flop him over and thread the other side around and tighten that one. Usually I have to retighten the first leg hole again. I make sure it is snug enough that only one of my fingers can fit between the diaper edge and the belly area. I don't always cut a hole for his tail and I change the nappies every four hours or so.

Expressing the Bladder

If you have a paralyzed rabbit, your veterinarian may tell you that you will need to express, or empty, the rabbit's bladder. Nor are paralyzed rabbits the only rabbits who may need to have their bladders expressed. Any rabbit whose mobility is limited will have a tendency to collect sludge in the bottom of his bladder. This is not always removed by the rabbit's normal urination, and over time this sludge will irritate the bladder, cause bleeding, and predispose the rabbit to other urinary disorders. Expressing the bladder will help to remove the sludge. Another reason to express a rabbit's bladder is to reduce inappropriate urination. Older rabbits, in particular, may begin to urinate anywhere anytime, and caregivers may feel it necessary to cut back on the rabbit's freedom for this reason. A better solution can be to express the rabbit's bladder three times a day and continue to let bun have the run of the house.

Arlette Hunnakko, who expresses her older bun's bladder daily, describes the procedure she has developed for her arthritic rabbit Cocoa: (*These instructions are provided as a review for those who have previously been instructed on how to express a rabbit's bladder by a veterinary professional. Bladder rupture is possible if an obstruction is present.*)

I first position Cocoa with his hind legs in a squat under his abdomen as naturally as possible. This helps with the bladder's muscle contraction. I then place my hands between the end of the rib cage and the hip bones with my fingers spread and reaching beneath the hips downward encompassing the bladder. I then press my fingers together gently, starting with slight pressure, then increasing the pressure gently.

With fingers in position just inside the hip bone and between the thighs, I gently increase pressure on the bladder by pressing my hand/fingers toward each other. When a bunny is ready to urinate, his tail will lift and he will pee. With some practice, one can distinguish the feeling of a full and relieved bladder. Sometimes a bunny needs to move/walk around a bit to encourage the urine to flow.

Urine Burn (Urine Scald)

Urine dribbling and subsequent urine scald over the rabbit's genital area is a common problem with older rabbits, obese rabbits, rabbits with chronic illnesses, and paralyzed rabbits. Diapers and/or expressing the bladder may help prevent urine scald, as may frequent "butt baths." But sometimes urine scald occurs despite your best efforts to prevent it, or a rabbit may come to you already having urine burn. In minor cases, the skin is simply a bit reddened from the irritation. In worse cases, the fur will fall out and ulcers may be present, and in the worst cases of urine scald, tissue death may occur. Maria Perez, manager of the Las Vegas chapter of the HRS, had an obese rabbit come to her who had such terrible urine scald that the rabbit had to be hospitalized for two weeks.

Minor cases of urine burn are usually treated with a gel, cream, or powder. First clip away any soiled fur, clean the area with an antiseptic such as ChlorhexiDerm™ Flush, Betadine®, or Clenderm® Solution, and then apply a topical treatment. Remember that almost anything you put on your rabbit may be ingested (unless physical disability prevents it), so any topical medication must be something that will not harm your rabbit if ingested in small amounts. Some antibiotic-containing creams—if ingested in large enough quantities—can cause intestinal dysbiosis (Chapter 3), so caution should be observed.

The following products have been recommended for urine burn by veterinary professionals in practice or in texts. Some of them contain antibiotics and others contain zinc, either of which may rarely have negative side effects on a rabbit if ingested in large enough amounts. If you decide you would rather not risk a preparation containing antibiotics or zinc, read the labels before purchasing.

- Aloe vera gel
- Bactoderm® (mupirocin) ointment
- Bactroban Cream®
- Bag Balm®
- Calendula gel
- Cornstarch
- Domeboro™ (powder)
- Gentocin® spray
- Germolene® ointment
- Neo-Predef® powder (available by prescription from your vet)
- Neosporin® (not Neosporin Plus)
- Oxyfresh pet gel with aloe vera and oxygene®
- Panolog® (neomycin sulfate)

- Rescue® Remedy cream
- Silvadene® Cream (available as Flamazine® in Canada)
- Zymox® topical cream

If the rabbit is permanently incontinent, preventing urine burn will be difficult. Some people have found 3M™ Cavilon™ No Sting Barrier Film to be helpful. This is an alcohol-free liquid that is sprayed on, and was designed specifically to protect skin from urine and feces. It dries quickly, creating a film that protects the rabbit's skin while still allowing it to breathe.

Collasate™ (3M™) post-operative dressings are also recommended by veterinarians for some cases of urine burn. These dressings are made of collagen in a gel form. When applied and then air-dried, they adhere to the wound and help to prevent bacterial infections while also soothing the site. They do not harm the rabbit if licked off, but are usually left in place by the bun.

One severe case of urine burn was successfully treated by applying Zymox® ointment and oxygen therapy (applying 100% oxygen to the affected area for 15 minutes, 4–5 times a day). For serious cases of urine burn in rabbits who are suffering from degenerative diseases that don't allow the proper stance for urination to be assumed, amputating the tail may be recommended by your veterinarian.

Mobility

When a rabbit loses his mobility, it can be partially restored by using slings or carts. Restoring a bit of mobility to a rabbit can do wonders for the rabbit's spirits. Often the rabbit *wants* to move. Ronie Lawrence wrote about her rabbit, Bun Bun, who had lost the use of her hind limbs:

> When I put her to bed at night, I placed her in her Tupperware box that was sideways on the floor, so it was like a little house for her. This

box was the only thing she knew of, as home, so I wanted her to keep it. But now in the mornings, she was no longer in her box, but elsewhere in the room. The little determined girl had started dragging her body out of her box in the middle of the night to see what else was out there to do!

OK, so this girl wanted to move. Fine, I work with animals every day. I could help her with that. So I got a towel and placed the little woman in a towel sling. We do this in the Vet world all the time to assist sick animals to get back on their feet. We started at one end of the hallway, I lifted and supported her hind end, and off she went!! She was motoring down the hallway!! Front legs worked fine!! She was elated!! Her little lop ears swung back and forth, looking and listening to her surroundings as we walked!! She tired easily and plopped her front end down for a rest every few feet. But in a minute or so, she'd pop back up, wait for her hind end to be supported, and started motoring again!! She was a mobile bun again! Now we made her *walk* to the room we were sitting in. No more pitiful paralyzed bun. We made her walk and she wanted to walk.[2]

Slings

Many caretakers of disabled buns find, as did Ronie Lawrence, that slings help their special-needs rabbits get needed exercise and also improve their spirits. Donna Jensen, who fosters many special-needs rabbits, uses a long scarf, finding the length and softness make an ideal sling. Arlette Hunnakko used her ingenuity to create a sling for her arthritic rab-

[2] Lawrence, Ronie. 2005, 2006. Just Look for the Sparkle. Pts. 1 and 2. *Wisconsin House Rabbit News* 12(4): 6; 13(1): 3–4.

bit Cocoa from a pillowcase. Slings can also be purchased from some pet supply stores and makers of carts for disabled animals (Appendix III).

Cocoa is ready for a walk in his pillowcase sling.

Carts

Several companies make carts that fit rabbits, including K-9 Carts and Doggon' Wheels (Appendix III). Not all rabbits will adapt to using carts. Margo DeMello, development director of the House Rabbit Society, offers a few hints as to which rabbits might be more likely to adapt to their use from her own personal experience:

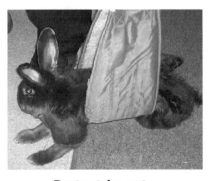

Buster tries out a manufactured sling.

> I've had a half-dozen paralyzed rabbits over the last ten years who have been able to use a cart (mine were purchased from Doggon' Wheels, and I have a small and a large cart) to provide mobility for them.
>
> Rabbits who have been disabled for a long time prior to getting the cart, or older rabbits or rabbits who were otherwise extra-compromised did not take to the cart well, and could not use it to move around at will. But younger, stronger rabbits whose only disability involved their rear legs generally took to the cart very well, if not immediately. I gen-

erally trained them on a carpeted floor, because a smooth floor was too difficult for them to get their footing. Once they got proficient using the cart, they could generally roll on any type flooring.

Hopper

When we bought our first cart, Hopper, who had suffered spinal cord damage before coming to me, was not strong enough to use it. My husband created a set of training wheels to fit on the front, acting as surrogate front legs (the cart is designed to substitute for usable back legs with wheels in the back). Even still, he could not move more than a few inches on his own, but I still had him use it most days for a little while, because it seemed to me that he needed relief from laying on his side all day.

On the other hand, Mrs. Bean and Pippin were two rabbits who avidly used

Pippin

their carts, rolling all around the house with them. Mrs. Bean even used to go on vacation with us, rolling around hotel rooms in her cart. Another rabbit who was able to use a cart successfully was Lulu, a black rabbit who arrived at my house without the use of her rear legs, and with her boyfriend Gus, a big New Zealand with a head tilt. Lulu could not only use her cart to get around, but she would crawl onto Gus's back in the cart and drape over him to rest.

Lulu rests on friend Gus, cart and all.

Caregiving

It is relatively easy to give special care to a rabbit that is temporarily ill. Most of us can fit the extra time into our schedules for a few days. Providing such care to rabbits who are permanently disabled is more difficult. Much as we love our rabbits, the never-ending daily care may become burdensome at times, particularly if we forget to care for ourselves in caring for our rabbits. Kathy Smith, the author of *Rabbit Health in the 21st Century,* offers her advice on avoiding caretaker burnout.

Avoiding Caregiver Burnout
Kathy Smith

Long term care of an ill loved one (human or animal) takes its toll on the caregiver. It is important to recognize signs of caregiver burnout:
- Extreme fatigue
- Irritability (especially "impatience with the patient")
- Feelings of "I can't do this any more" or "I can't do anything right"

There are many steps caregivers can take to reduce burnout.

Take Care of Your Body
- Eat well
- Get adequate rest
- Exercise
- Take vitamins
- See your doctor regularly
- Remember to take *your* medications

Don't think you don't have the time/energy/money to take care of *your* health. You cannot afford not to!

Surround Yourself with Supportive Friends
Seek out others—in your community or online—who understand the importance of your rabbit. Your vet or local rescue group may know someone who has dealt with similar medical conditions. Talking to animal-loving friends, even if they are not "rabbit people," is another great source of comfort.

Identify at least one person you can open up to about your fears and frustrations as a caregiver. Having such feelings does not mean you should give up, nor does it make you a bad caregiver. It means you are human. By discussing these feelings openly with a supportive friend, you face them and help dispel their negative energy.

Ask for help. Don't be afraid to say to friends, coworkers, or your vet, "Do you know anyone who can help with . . . ?" Help and support often come from unexpected sources. You have nothing to lose—if you don't ask, the default answer is "no."

Accept your limitations. Real friends understand that this is not the time for you to take on new obligations. Give yourself permission to say "no" to energy-draining activities. If you can, limit contact with people who don't understand your dedication to your rabbit.

Make Time for Activities That Bring You Joy
Pamper yourself. Schedule time for whatever is therapeutic for *you*. Anything that leaves you feeling relaxed and supported qualifies: massage, Reiki, counseling, hairdresser appointment, manicure/pedicure, lunch with friends, a bubble bath, movies, reading, music, baking, etc. . . .

Embrace activities that truly feed your soul. These may include prayer, yoga, meditation, volunteer work, or simply communing with nature.

It is *not* selfish to focus on yourself. Anything that improves the quality or quantity of *your* energy also benefits your rabbit.

Be Realistic About Your Role
Many caregivers hold the unrealistic belief that it is their fault (or their vet's) if their rabbit does not recover. Recognize that even in human medicine, not every problem can be "fixed." Talk frankly with your vet to ensure you fully understand your rabbit's prognosis. Then, focus on enjoying your time together. View each day as a gift, not a given.

Don't second-guess decisions you and your vet make about treatment options. Trust that you made the best decision you could with the information and resources available, even if the result is not what you hoped for. There is no guarantee that a different choice would have been better.

If possible, make a conscious decision to let go of the illusion that you can control the outcome of your efforts. If you believe in a Higher Power, consciously surrender life-and-death responsibility to that Power. You can then focus fully on *your* role—providing love and comfort to your rabbit.

Spend Quality Time with Your Rabbit
Because of the time and energy spent attending to their physical and medical needs, ill rabbits often develop incredibly deep bonds with their caregiver(s). Equally important to an ill rabbit's well-being is the time you spend simply being with them in a loving, nurturing way. Seek activities that fit both your needs and those of your rabbit. This may include snuggling, petting, playing, or simply relaxing with your rabbit. The positive energy created during shared quality time is important to the healing process and can help prevent burnout.

Although Myrrh was here only nine months, we found a daily routine that nurtured us both. During his rescue and transport to me, Myrrh demonstrated that he enjoyed being held. Knowing this, I started a nightly ritual of holding him on my lap and giving him a full-body massage. After a while, I realized I could share the benefits of the massage I was giving. As I massaged him, if I focused on the same part of my body, the tension evaporated. It was a wonderfully relaxing, deeply bonding experience and will always be a treasured memory.

Myrrh

CHAPTER 2

BASIC CARE II

Lucile C. Moore

I n addition to keeping your rabbit safe, comfortable, and clean, you may, at times, need to administer pain medications, antibiotics, other therapeutics, food, and fluids. *Instructions on medical procedures in this chapter are provided for those who have previously received instruction from a veterinary professional but wish to review the procedure before attempting it at home.*

Pain Control

Pain control is basic when giving special care, whether the rabbit is in temporary pain while recovering from a neuter procedure or has constant pain from arthritis or another degenerative disease. Most caretakers are familiar with the signs of severe pain:
- Tooth grinding
- Remaining hunched in corner of cage or room
- Failing to eat and drink

However, caretakers will also learn to recognize more subtle signs of less severe pain in their rabbits:
- Not wanting to move as much
- Muscle tremors

- Body tension
- Increased respiration
- Irritability, impatience, or aggression
- Excessive licking and chewing

Each caregiver will learn to recognize the signs of pain in their rabbits and how to take steps to decrease it, whether it is by providing a more comfortable surface for the bun to rest on or by giving medications for pain. There are three basic kinds of pain medication that may be prescribed by your veterinarian: narcotics, steroids, and non-steroidal anti-inflammatory drugs, commonly known as NSAIDs. Acupuncture and acupressure have been found to be of great help in giving their rabbits relief from pain by several caretakers. Alternative methods are discussed in detail in Part II.

NSAIDs

The non-steroidal anti-inflammatory drugs (Appendix I) are most often prescribed for alleviating pain in rabbits, especially long term. They do have possible side effects, including damage to the kidneys or GI upsets (e.g., ulcers). However, rabbit caretakers must balance possible side effects against the necessity of controlling pain in their rabbits. Any rabbit on pain medication should be monitored closely, and if negative side effects appear, the dose can be reduced or the medication changed. Remember, possible side effects from a medication are just that, possible. They will not necessarily occur.

Recommended dosages of pain medications for rabbits are usually on the conservative side. Some rabbit veterinarians now believe that rabbits can tolerate higher doses for longer time periods than was at first thought. However, this is something you should always discuss with your veterinarian or a consultant if you believe the amount that has been prescribed is not giving adequate pain relief to your rabbit. Do not increase doses in your rabbit without such consultation.

Narcotics (Opiates)

These pain medications (Appendix I) may be a bit more effective than NSAIDs, but in general, their effect does not last as long. They are often used for more intense pain, such as that during or immediately after surgery, or for fractures. Theoretically, they can depress the respiratory and/or gastrointestinal systems, so many vets observe caution in their use. However, there are many cases where their greater ability to relieve pain is extremely helpful.

Steroids

Corticosteroids (Appendix I) have anti-inflammatory/pain-relieving effects, but are generally not prescribed for rabbits as often as the other pain relievers. They can also depress the immune system, and could possibly allow subclinical infections to become clinical. Steroids should not be given at the same time as NSAIDs.

Antibiotics

It was not that many years ago that few rabbit-safe antibiotics (Appendix I) were in use. Now it seems there are new ones every day. At the time of this writing, fluoroquinolones (e.g., Marbocyl®) in particular appear to have promise in treating many infections in rabbits. Injectible penicillins, particularly bicillin, have been found to be useful treating abscesses. At the same time, some professionals believe that a few of the old standbys, such as enrofloxacin (Baytril®), may have been overused. They are being reported to be less successful in treating some infections than before.

It is important to remember that treatment with antibiotics will have the best possibility of being successful only if culture and sensitivity testing are done. Dr. Bill Guerrera, a veterinarian who frequently treats rabbits, comments:

> There are some really great antibiotics out there. Here I would stress that there is no "cure all" and the goal of treatment is to choose the anti-

biotic that is safe and effective against what you are treating. So the important thing is to know what we are treating and what it is susceptible to. We must do more culture and sensitivities to decrease causing antibacterial resistance.

Always give the full course of antibiotic the veterinarian prescribes for your rabbit unless otherwise instructed. Failure to do so may allow the bacteria to become resistant. Report any suspected side effects to your vet immediately. Never forget you know your rabbit best, and speak up if you have questions or concerns.

Food

Coaxing a rabbit to eat when he does not feel well can be difficult, but it is necessary. A rabbit must eat frequently or face gastrointestinal complications that can lead to eventual death. If your rabbit is reluctant to eat, first try coaxing him. Some rabbits will eat pellets or hay that is held in a caretaker's hand when they won't take it from a dish

If that doesn't work, try offering a special treat, such as a sprig of parsley or cilantro. (Remember that any foods a rabbit is not used to eating may cause digestive problems if too much is consumed.) If that also fails to tempt your rabbit to eat, some experts recommend offering a teaspoon or so of plain canned pumpkin or an organic baby food preparation— without added sugar or onion—of fruit, oatmeal, or carrots (see Chap-

Sometimes a reluctant rabbit can be coaxed to eat by hand-feeding him.

ter 1 regarding giving anorexic rabbits fruit and grains). Sometimes if the rabbit will eat a small amount of baby food on his own, it then encourages him to eat some of his regular pellets or hay afterwards. Baby foods and/or canned pumpkin should not be used as a primary food source or be given long-term; they are far too high in carbohydrates.

Because rabbits needing special care can be such picky eaters, some owners devise their own "convalescent foods" that their rabbit will eat. In order to coax her rabbit, Oreo, to eat, Alex Fenner concocted a mixture that contained necessary nourishment and still tasted good. Her husband dubbed it "Oreo's Oil":

Oreo

> I ground up oat hay and mountain hay in a coffee grinder— not too fine. Then I added a sprinkling of Critical Care®, and just enough water and a tiny bit of apple juice for taste and texture. He was gobbling this stuff up. I'd give it to him up to four times a day, or as much as he would want.

If all the above tips for coaxing a rabbit to eat fail, it may be necessary to syringe-feed the rabbit. Critical Care® is a supplemental food (available in two flavors) that can be given by syringe, and American Pet Diner makes another called Critter Be Better®. (Individual rabbits may find one or the other more palatable.) If you are unable to obtain either of these, you can grind the rabbit's regular pellets in a food processor or coffee grinder. Combine the supplemental food or ground pellets with enough water that the mixture will go through the feeding syringe. (Note: Any pellet or food ground finely enough to go through the tip of a syringe has most likely lost its ability to stimulate gut action in the same manner as long indigestible fiber.) The size of the feeding syringe you will need depends upon the size of the rabbit, but you will need a larger syringe for food than those you might use to give oral medications.

Take from 2–4 cc at a time (the actual amount will depend upon the size of the rabbit), place the tip of the syringe into the rabbit's mouth at an angle—if it goes straight in it increases the possibility that the rabbit will get some in the respiratory tract—and squeeze the food in. After the rabbit swallows, refill the syringe and repeat the process. The amount to give will be suggested on the supplemental food package, and for ground pellets give about 20 ml per kg (approximately 2.20 lb. of rabbit) at a session, up to three times a day. Frankly, both you and the rabbit are likely to be covered with the food at the end of the meal, so have a soft damp cloth ready to wipe the rabbit's face and neck area off when you are finished.

Water and Fluids

It is always necessary for rabbits to drink large amounts of water. It is very important that rabbits not become dehydrated, as their delicate digestive systems will not operate correctly unless they have adequate water. Furthermore, dehydration may be difficult to recognize in rabbits. Some experts report that "tenting" the skin as one might with a cat does not work as a test of a rabbit's hydration, because fluids may be pulled from the gastrointestinal system, giving skin an appearance of elasticity when the rabbit is actually dehydrated. Watch your rabbit's water bottle or water bowl, and if it does not seem to be emptying as fast as usual, your rabbit may be becoming dehydrated. Another sign of dehydration is dull or dry eyes.

If an ill rabbit or one recovering from surgery is reluctant to drink water, first try offering the water in a different way (Chapter 1) and coax the rabbit to eat a few high-water-content greens, such as leaf lettuce (not iceberg). Rinsing the lettuce in water before feeding it can also help. If those methods do not work, you can syringe-feed water just as you do food. Take up a few cc in the syringe, insert at the side of rabbit's mouth, and squeeze the water in.

If the rabbit repeatedly fails to take liquids, you may need to ask your vet about giving subcutaneous fluids. This means that fluids are injected into the space between a rabbit's skin and muscle, where they are absorbed into the bloodstream. This will only help if a rabbit has not become seriously dehydrated. Once a rabbit becomes too severely dehydrated, the fluids will not be able to be absorbed this way, and the vet will need to give them intravenously.

If your veterinarian feels a single time of administering subcutaneous fluids is all that is likely to be needed, he/she will probably do it at the clinic or hospital. However, there are many situations in which the rabbit may require administration of sub-Q fluids every day or every other day. In those cases, your vet may ask if you would be willing to be instructed in administering them yourself. You may be reluctant at first—it is not unusual for a caretaker to resist poking their much-loved furry companions with needles! But the knowledge that it will help their rabbit is usually enough to persuade even the reluctant to give it a try.

Always receive personal instruction from a veterinary professional before attempting to administer fluids on your own. And be aware that there are some conditions under which giving rabbits sub-Q fluids is not a good idea. Rabbits with breathing difficulties or heart conditions can be made worse if fluids are administered subcutaneously.

The fluids you are given will most likely be lactated Ringer's solution (LRS) in a bag, although plain saline may be preferred for some conditions, such as kidney failure. Along with the bag, your vet will have given you needles and a drip set (venoset) or lines of tubing with clamps that connect the bag to the needle, if one is not already connected to the bag.

The color of the cover on the needle will indicate its size, although not all companies use the same colors. The number will also be printed on the cover. The higher the number, the smaller the needle. Fluids will usually be given to rabbits with 14–20. Sometimes a rabbit will be small enough or sensitive enough that numbers 22 or 25 are used, but it will take a longer time for the fluids to drain with a smaller needle. (Some rabbit caretakers report that older male rabbits often develop tough skin that is difficult to pierce and may require a smaller needle.) About 100 ml of fluid per 2.20 lb. of the rabbit's body weight are needed each day for maintenance, but less may be prescribed if the rabbit is drinking some on his own.

1) Before beginning, check your bag of fluids. Take off the outside plastic protective covering and look at the fluids. If they are cloudy, they may be contaminated, so throw the bag away. If they look good, first warm them a bit by placing the bag in a bowl of very warm water for a few minutes, keeping the end with the port above the water. *Do not microwave fluids.*

2) Dry the bag off and find the seal on the port at the end that you will need to pull off in order to attach the drip set. (Hold the bag so the open end is up or they will leak all over.) Pull the seal off (this may take a strong tug). Take off the bit of tubing that protects the sharp pointed end (often white) of the drip set, being careful not to touch the point. Insert the sharp point on the end of the drip set into the port on the bag, and close the drip set clamp.

3) Hang the bag above the place you will give the rabbit fluids. If you are giving them on the floor, you can hang the bag over a door using a clothes hanger. They should not be hung so high you can't see the drip chamber or reach the valve on the dripset.

4) Attach the needle, leaving the cap on.

5) Open the two clamps on the drip set: roll the white roller clamp up and push the other clamp so the wide end is over the tubing. This will allow the fluid to push the air from the tubing. Drops of fluid will also now be visible in the drip chamber. If the chamber should fill completely up so you can't see drops, turn the chamber over and squeeze so that some of the fluids go back into the bag. Close the clamp.

6) Hold the rabbit and make a tent of the scruff by pulling it up with your thumb and forefinger. (You can also give fluids in the loose skin over the chest, but most people find it easier to administer them in the scruff.) Uncap the needle and insert it inside the tent you have made. Holding the needle in place with one hand, open the drip set clamp with the other. If you have inserted the needle properly, the fluids will be going in the rabbit; if not they are likely to be running down his fur. This

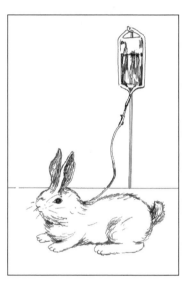

Fig. 2.1

probably means you have stuck the needle though the skin and out the other side (easy to do at first). If you find you have done this, simply pull the needle back a little until the fluids are going in under the skin. Check the drip chamber to see if the fluids are running through at a good rate. If not, make slight adjustments to the position of the needle under the skin until they do (see fig. 2.1).

7) Watch until the desired amount of fluids has gone in, and turn the valve off, take out the needle, and squeeze the area gently with your fingers. If a small amount of fluids

leak, this is nothing to worry about. If there is blood as you remove the needle, this probably means you hit a small venule or capillary. It will not harm the rabbit. Return your rabbit to his home area.

8) Change the needle and throw the old one out in a heavy plastic container, such as an empty dish-soap bottle.

Amy Spintman, board member and educator in the San Diego chapter of the HRS, and owner of Cats & Rabbits & More, has given fluids to rabbits many times. She offers the following tips:

I hook the fluids around the top of a clothes hanger which I hang from the chandelier over the dining room table. Depending on the rabbit, I may need to put up some barriers so she/ he doesn't try to take off. I sit down at the table and cuddle with them as they get their fluids, which helps to keep them somewhat distracted. When they start getting restless, it's usually a sign they've had enough and most of the time, it matches the amount I was planning to give.

I store the fluids in the refrigerator, and warm them up beforehand by soaking them in a large pan of hot water. While the fluids are being administered, I keep part of the tubing in hot water so it gets warmed up a slight bit more before it goes into the bunny.

My vet gave me a tip when having to give fluids or shots regularly to a bunny. So that you don't always give it at the exact same spot, picture a clock around the scruff area. When you give the first shot, inject it at 12:00. For the next shot, do it at 2:00, then 4:00, etc.

The most important part of giving shots and medicine to a rabbit is confidence!

When I was less experienced, the bunnies would squirm, I would squirm, and we all wound up frustrated and pissed off! But with experience and confidence, the rabbits don't fuss anymore and medicating them is usually a quick and easy process.

If your rabbit requires sub-Q fluids on a regular basis, here are a couple of problems that can develop. What are termed "sterile abscesses" can form. Dr. Bill Guerrera, a veterinarian with extensive rabbit experience, discusses the term:

Sterile abscess is an oxymoron. Abscess means infection is present. What does develop is inflammation. Most of the time, these will resolve when the inciting trauma is discontinued. They can develop into secondary abscesses and require treatment, but that is extremely rare. To prevent these reactions make sure the injection is deep into the sub-Q and not in the dermis, and use a new needle with each injection.

Another problem that can develop from frequent injections is that the skin may become resistant from the small adhesions that develop where the needle is stuck in, making it increasingly difficult to insert the needle. The area may also vascularize, or develop more tiny blood vessels, making it more difficult for you to give fluids without hitting a capillary. Giving the injections in different spots can help prevent these problems, although they may not entirely prevent their occurrence.

Jodi McLaughlin, certified in animal and human massage, offers the following hint for needle sensitivity:

One thing you can do to help with adhesions and sensitivity from regular needle sticks is skin rolling. Rabbits usually love this massage technique and it can be done directly down the spine, the only massage technique that is safe on top of the spinous processes. I skin roll across the shoulders, lower neck, and loosened skin on the hips too.

Roll bunny's loose skin between your thumb and index and middle fingers, just like rolling a cigarette, only continue to move over new areas. This technique is also considered a TTouch® or Myofascial Release technique. It will free the tiny adhesions caused from needles as well as stagnant circulation. It feels very good and is easy to do. Try to do skin rolling after sub-Q fluids.

Using a Butterfly Catheter (or Scalp Vein Set) to Administer Fluids

Some caregivers have found it easier to give fluids to their rabbit companions with a butterfly catheter, or scalp vein set (used for human infants). Meg Brown had to give fluids to her rabbit companion, Buster, and discovered using the butterfly catheter was a much less stressful experience for Buster. She describes the process step by step:

Supplies you will need:
Bag of lactated Ringer's
60-ml sterile syringe
18- or 19-gauge sterile
   needle
Alcohol wipes
Butterfly catheter
   (aka scalp vein set)
   with 20-gauge needle
   attached
Tall mug of hot water

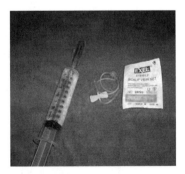

Butterfly catheter setup

1. Use alcohol to clean the bladder of the lactated Ringer's bag before using. Draw 50–60 ml of the fluid into

the syringe, using a large gauge needle.

2. Open the butterfly catheter package and replace the needle with the catheter.

3. Place the full syringe, plunger side up, into a tall mug of hot water, to heat the fluid. Be sure the tubing and needle of the catheter are hanging over the side of the mug, not in the water, which is not sterile.

Drawing LRS into syringe.

4. In approximately two minutes, check the temperature of the LRS by squirting a little on your wrist.

5. When warm, kneel down with the rabbit between your legs, head facing out, toward your knees. If you have a very small rabbit, it may help to put a towel in back of him, near your feet, so he doesn't scoot out behind you. You can secure the rabbit in another way, if kneeling is not comfortable for you. Just be sure he is held securely.

6. "Tent" the skin behind the rabbit's neck.

7. Insert the needle at an angle. You should be able to feel the needle enter the rabbit's skin. It is not necessary to push it in any further.

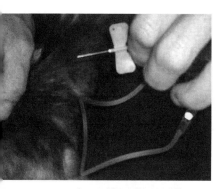

Inserting butterfly catheter.

8. Begin to depress the plunger. It may be somewhat difficult to do, especially if your hands are small or not very strong. The tubing is long enough to allow you to push the end of the plunger into the floor or table, at least until it gets down lower. You can also ask a second person to push the plunger for you. You might find that administering 40–50 ml is enough and easier to push in.

9. It takes approximately 40 seconds to aminister 55 ml of lactated Ringer's.

10. The butterfly catheter must be safely discarded and a new one used each time.

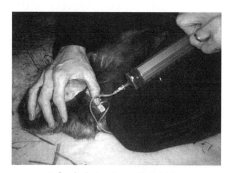

Administering fluids by butterfly catheter.

11. This method is more expensive than simply using the bag of LRS, tubing, and a needle. But, we have found it to be quicker, easier, and much less stressful for our family, so it is well worth it.

Administering Medications

Medications prescribed for your rabbit may be administered by intravenous injection (IV), intramuscular injection (IM), subcutaneous injection (SC or SQ), intranasally (IN), or by mouth (PO). The vet will give any that must be administered intravenously, but caretakers will fre-

Giving liquid medications.

quently be instructed to give additional medications to their rabbits at home. Perhaps the easiest to administer will be those prepared in a palatable oral suspension, often flavored like apple, watermelon, or banana. These are given orally in a small syringe, and many of the rabbits like the odor and flavor so much you will have no difficulty getting the medication down the rabbit. Other times, the vet may ask that you put a less palatable medication on a favored food in order to disguise it. Rabbits will often take these medications when they are put on a half-teaspoon or so of an organic baby food preparation (without added sugar or onion) of apples, peaches, bananas, oatmeal, or carrots.

At times, care of a rabbit will require that medication be given under the skin, or subcutaneously. Your veterinarian, veterinary nurse, or other professional will always instruct you in the proper procedure before you are given the medicine to take home. After you have done it a few times, you will increase in confidence and skill, and the whole procedure will be much easier on you and your rabbit! Following is a review of the procedure:

1) Prepare the syringe. Sometimes, veterinarians will send the medications ready in small syringes with needles attached, so all you have to do is have it at hand. Other times you might be given an empty syringe and need to draw it from a bottle of medication. Draw carefully so the

medication goes to the precise number line for the dose your veterinarian prescribed.

2) Place the rabbit in a safe place (an upholstered chair seat is a good choice) and tent the skin of the rabbit's scruff with the thumb and finger of your non-dominant hand.

3) Take the syringe with your dominant hand and hold it with the mm measure marks up so you can see how much medication is going in.

4) Firmly insert the needle at a 90° angle parallel to the skin and pointing toward the rabbit's head (see fig. 2.2).

5) Inject the amount you have been instructed to give. Watch to be sure the medication is

Fig. 2.2

going in the rabbit and not on his skin. It is easy to puncture through both layers, especially when you first attempt giving subcutaneous injections. If this happens, pull the needle back a little bit until it is going in the space under the skin. It is also possible to push too hard and the needle may come off.

6) Remove the needle and recap it immediately to prevent injuries.

Problems can occur from giving medications subcutaneously, as they can from giving fluids this method. Sterile abscesses may develop, the rabbit's skin may become resistant from the tiny adhesions that form, and the skin may vascularize. See section above on giving subcutaneous fluids for tips on avoiding these problems.

Intramuscular Injections

Rarely, a veterinarian may ask if you are willing to give injections intramuscularly. This is a bit trickier, and your vet will probably not ask you to do it unless the rabbit requires daily medication that can only be given this way. Injections are often done in a hind leg. Placement of the injection is critical, as the sciatic nerve, which travels down the back leg, could be hit by mistake. If your vet asks you to give injections intramuscularly, be sure you understand the instructions well, and if you do not, keep asking until you feel comfortable with the procedure.

1) Find a place where you will be able to hold on to the rabbit securely. Intramuscular injections are painful to the rabbit and he may struggle and bite. If you can find someone to help you and hold the rabbit, that is best. If you must do it alone, try securing him between your body and the elbow of your non-dominant arm while you sit on the floor or a sofa, his head sticking out toward the back.

2) Find the area on his hind leg that is in the quadriceps muscle group (see fig. 2.3) and wipe with an alcohol-saturated cotton ball. (This is only to allow you to see the skin more easily, it does not kill bacteria that quickly.) Tense the skin at the area with the fingers of your non-dominant hand.

Fig. 2.3

3) Insert the needle into the muscle, about half the length of the needle, and then draw back very slightly. If there is any blood, it means you have hit a blood vessel. In that case, redirect the needle.

4) Inject the drug and pull needle from muscle.

5) Recap needle and dispose of it in safe plastic container with lid.

Kathy Smith offers the following tip on needles:
> Most needle syringes have detachable needles, allowing the drug to be drawn up with one needle and injected with a fresh one. There is some risk of popping the needle off while giving the injection, thus wasting a dose by squirting it on the rabbit. Luer lock syringes reduce this risk. Insulin syringes have permanently attached needles, but require the medication be drawn up and injected with the same needle. Your vet can recommend a syringe based on the medication being given and the vial it is dispensed in.

Nebulizing

Nebulizing medications, or delivering them to the site of infection in the form of a fine spray, can be very effective for respiratory ailments in rabbits. Although some veterinarians will prefer to do this to the rabbit themselves in their clinic or hospital, caretakers can purchase the equipment and learn to do it themselves quite easily.

The nebulizing solution, or mix, will be one of a precise "recipe" determined by your vet. It will often include saline, an antibiotic (frequently gentamicin, amikacin, or enrofloxacin), a bronchodilator such as aminophylline, and a medication that loosens mucous (acetylcysteine or bromexine). This mixture is placed in the nebulizer. (The nebulizing unit will have to be purchased, and the cost runs from around $100 to $250 at the time of this writing.) A hose connects the compressor to the nebulizer. The nebulized solution is delivered to the rabbit by placing a mask over the rabbit's face or putting him in a chamber where he is forced to breathe the nebulized medication. Most rabbit caretakers seem to prefer a mask, as rabbits appear to tolerate a mask better than a chamber, and the mask uses less medication. There are rabbits, though, who are stressed more by the mask than a chamber, so you will need to discover which works best for your particular rabbit.

Chambers can be made in several ways. A carrying cage can be put inside a large plastic bag or covered with plastic wrap, or a large plastic storage container with a corner cut out for the nebulizer's mouthpiece to fit through can be used. Masks may be made rather than purchased, and can be fashioned out of pieces of flexible plastic or plastic bottles cut in half. (The hose and mask should be cleaned with a 10% bleach solution or rubbing alcohol after each use.)

Maria Perez, manager of the Las Vegas chapter of the HRS, nebulizes her rabbit, Chloe, who has a slow-growing lung cancer. Maria gives Chloe a nebulizer "cocktail" two or three times a day, and has discovered the least stressful way to do this for Chloe through trial and error. Noticing that rabbits can be stressed by the noise of the compressor, Maria chose a nebulizer that had a long hose. The hose connects to a plastic cylindrical chamber where the medication goes. This cylinder has a beak which Maria places directly over Chloe's nares rather than connecting it to a mask or chamber. Maria stokes Chloe and talks to her while the medication is being delivered, and Chloe stays put until the session ends.

Taking a Rabbit's Temperature

There may be times it is necessary for you to take your rabbit's temperature, such as after a surgical procedure or when a rabbit is suffering from a gastrointestinal disturbance.

However, it can be very stressful to the rabbit, and the need to take the temperature will have to be balanced with the negative effect of stress. *Have a veterinary professional give you firsthand instruction before attempting it yourself, the next time you are at your vet's office.* This is a skill you need to know.

A rabbit's normal temperature may vary several degrees, depending upon the time of year, environment, and stress, but will usually be between 101°F–104°F (38°C–40°C). If it is lower than 100°F or higher than 105°F, you should contact your veterinarian immediately.

Using a glass thermometer is not recommended by some vets because of the risk of it breaking should the rabbit struggle. Digital pediatric rectal thermometers are safer and faster to use. Coat the end of the thermometer with a lubricant such as Vaseline. Restrain the rabbit on the floor or a low sofa or chair with one arm. Some people prefer to hold the rabbit cradled upside down in the "trance" position, but it can also be done with the rabbit right side up. Before trying to insert the thermometer, touch the area with the tip. If you are in the right place, the opening will usually "wink" at you. *Gently* insert the thermometer into the rectum with your free hand. It should slide in easily. If not, adjust the angle slightly. Never force it, because the rectal walls are easily damaged. Speak soothingly to the rabbit while you leave it in (a minute or so for a digital thermometer, longer for a glass thermometer), and then ease it out. If the rabbit struggles too much, do not insist on taking the temperature as the stress could be harmful to the rabbit.

Lab Tests

Since the focus of this book is on care, how to interpret laboratory tests your veterinarian may order for your rabbit is not within its scope. For an excellent, easy-to-understand explanation of such tests in layman's terms, see Kathy Smith's book, *Rabbit Health in the 21st Century.*

Surgery

Care of a rabbit having a surgical procedure should start before the surgery takes place. Question your veterinarian about the procedure: how many times has he/she performed it and what is his or her success rate? Ask what anesthesia will be given, what pain medications will be given afterward, and what kind of stitches will be used (surgical glue or sutures under the skin are less likely to be chewed and come out). Ask where the rabbit will be put during recovery from the anesthesia, and what precautions will be taken to safeguard the rabbit during recovery. (One rabbit was taken in for routine spay surgery, panicked when coming out of the anesthesia, threw herself around the cage where she had been placed for recovery, and went home with a broken back. The rabbit, who had gone in to the vet perfectly healthy, developed a severe infection and other complications from the injury and had to be euthanized less than three months later.) Finally, if your vet asks you to withhold food from a rabbit before surgery you probably have the wrong vet. Rabbits should not fast before surgery (unless it is a short one- to two-hour fast immediately before surgery to remove any danger from any food remaining in the mouth or esophagus being aspirated into the trachea).

Dr. Jamie Sulliban, a veterinarian who is actively involved with the HRS and NSPCA, suggests that if your particular veterinarian is not an expert on rabbits, you should not be afraid to do research and take any good information you find to your vet and ask him or her to read it. Or find another veterinarian in another city with experience with your rabbit's particular disease or condition and ask your vet to consult. If you do this in a tactful manner, your veterinarian should be willing to agree to your request. "You must be an advocate for your rabbit's health," Dr. Jamie advises.

Remember that every surgery carries risk, both from the anesthesia and from complications during the surgery itself. There is always some loss of body heat when the rabbit is under anesthesia because the metabolic rate drops and more of the rabbit is exposed to air, leading to heat loss. Unexpected complications such as sensitivity to various drugs being used can arise, as can many other possible, yet unlikely complications.[1]

Rabbits recovering from surgery will need special care for a few days until they are back to themselves.

- Provide warmth
- Watch for any bleeding
- Coax rabbit to eat and drink
- Watch for signs of infection
- Administer any medications and fluids prescribed by the vet

What stage of recovery your rabbit is in when he leaves the veterinarian's care depends on whether you took him to a clinic or had a procedure done by a veterinarian with a mobile clinic. Some rabbit owners prefer the latter because the rabbit does not suffer the stress of being transported to a veterinary clinic and being around predators (cats, dogs, birds, ferrets) while recovering. If your rabbit's surgical procedure is done by a mobile clinic that comes to your home, you may get the rabbit back while he is still recovering a bit from the anesthesia. Put him in a quiet place where he will not harm himself if he staggers around, and provide warmth by covering him with a light blanket. A slight bit more warmth is often good the first day or so after a surgery, especially if much fur has been shaved off for the procedure. Monitor the rabbit's body temperature closely the first couple of days (see previous section).

You should always ask for pain medication if your rabbit has had a surgical procedure. If the procedure was minor, such as a neuter, the veterinarian may give him enough before releasing him. Often the rabbit will require

---

1 The author of this book has a concern about the trend to neuter rabbits as early as the age of three months. Unless the surgeon is extremely skilled, spays done that young may be incomplete because of the stage of development of the reproductive organs. I recommend keeping rabbits physically separated until spays can be done at four to five months.

pain medication for several days following the procedure. Rabbits do not tolerate pain well. Pain will slow recovery and can have such negative effects on the rabbit's digestion system that it could even lead to death.

Your rabbit companion is likely to be a bit quieter than usual after coming home from an operation, and it is often better if the rabbit is not too active right after a surgery. (After some surgeries, such as spays, it is best if the rabbit is kept away from dominant companions that might mount her or chase her for a few days.) Lynn Sagramoso came up with a unique solution when her mini lop, Joe, underwent surgery for a severe stomach blockage and needed to be kept from running around and pulling stitches loose. She would drag his thick quilt around on their wood floors, giving him a magic carpet ride as she satisfied his desire to move around the house. He came to love his floor surfing, and continued to enjoy it after he was healed!

If a rabbit recovering from surgery is extremely quiet, can't move normally, or sits hunched grinding his teeth, you should contact your vet at once. You may need to coax your convalescent rabbit to eat or drink, and if this fails, syringe-feed him. If he is still reluctant to eat after 24 hours, call your vet.

Watch incisions for excessive bleeding and any development of infection. Occasionally a vessel may be punctured when the rabbit is being sewn up, and it may bleed a fair amount when the rabbit begins to recover and move around. This will not harm the rabbit, but if you see excessive bleeding it is a good idea to call your vet and ask about it. If you see any sign of infection—swelling, pus, and redness—you should always call your vet immediately.

Feces production may slow after surgery, and the droppings may be smaller when they reappear, but if feces do not reappear within a day, call your vet. If there is any diarrhea, mucus, or watery discharge, call your vet immediately.

When You Have Questions About Treatment and Medications

It should be the goal of every person sharing his or her life with a companion rabbit to find a good, rabbit-savvy veterinarian. However, this does not mean you can never question a treatment your veterinarian has prescribed or ask for a second opinion from another vet. Remember, you know your rabbit better than anyone, including the veterinarian, and you may be the first to notice problems with a particular treatment protocol. Rebecca Kintner tells the story of her rabbit, Chance:

> Chance came to me a happy, apparently healthy, seven-month-old boy. He and my rabbit Courage bonded very quickly and were never more than three feet apart. They loved to run and play. Late one evening I noticed Courage was sticking close to me, but Chance was nowhere to be found. When I located him, he was hiding in a small area under the bed. He was very lethargic and his breathing was extremely rapid and shallow. Concerned that he was ill, I held him for a short time. As I set him down in his cage with Courage he began to seize. I allowed him to finish the seizure and then immediately picked him up to check for injury and breathing difficulties. Luckily there were none.
>
> The following morning I called the vet and scheduled an appointment. While waiting for the appointment, Chance began circling and going into head tilt as well as grinding his teeth. The diagnosis was a severe ear infection. He was placed on Baytril® and bicillin. Two weeks into treatment, there was no improvement. The vet then recommended we add chloramphenicol in case the ear infection had been complicated by EC. After several weeks

I saw no improvement. Chance was still not eating or drinking. I decided to get a second opinion. At this point, the second vet removed him from everything for a few days, and then placed him on albendazole, Baytril®, and bicillin. I finally began to see improvement.

The next obstacle came when I found a bump the size of a dime in the area where he was receiving his injections. As I felt around more, I noticed there were several others. Once again he was loaded up and made the two-hour drive to the vet. Upon examination, the lumps were determined to be abscesses. So Chance underwent surgery and had seven abscesses removed. The vet felt that the bottle of bicillin I was using was contaminated. So we got a new bottle and began the Baytril® and bicillin therapy for treatment for abscesses. Things were not going very smoothly, as within 48 hours Chance had rolled and knocked out the sutures in half the incision. So he had to be re-sutured. Also I noticed the masses were beginning again.

The vet recommended we continue the protocol and see if maybe the bumps decreased in size. This was not the case; in fact the opposite happened. They increased in size and were no longer just where the injections were being given. So back to the vet and back to surgery he went. This time he had four more abscesses removed with the biggest being about three inches across. This time the vet decided that he was having a reaction to the bicillin, and changed his meds to Zithromax®. Again Chance knocked out the sutures in the entire incision and had to be re-stitched. The good news was that the Zithromax® seemed to be working, and there were no more bumps beginning. Since the last re-stitch job, we have had no more problems.

I have learned several things from this three-month-long experience:

- When giving sub-Q fluids by yourself, place the rabbit in a top-open carrier. It is incredibly difficult to securely hold the rabbit while inserting the needle. In the carrier, you know the rabbit is safe; he isn't going to jump down or bite. You also have both hands to insert the needle and begin the flow of fluids.
- Mixing chloramphenicol pills in baby oatmeal will decrease the nasty taste and allow you to get it into the rabbit pretty easily.
- Running sutures do not work well on the back and neck areas of a wry-neck rabbit. When the rabbit rolls, the chance of catching a suture on anything is increased. With the running sutures, when one stitch is broken, the rest of the incision is doomed to open as well. Individual tied sutures eliminate the chance of all the stitches coming out.

Chance

- It is possible for rabbits to have negative reactions to medications. Don't be afraid to question your vet about this possibility.
- Trust your gut feelings. You know your rabbit better than anyone. If something doesn't feel right, question it.
- Don't be hesitant to suggest another treatment.

CHAPTER 3

DIGESTIVE AILMENTS

Lucile C. Moore

A nyone who shares his or her life with a companion rabbit will most likely, at one time or another, need to give special care to that rabbit for a digestive ailment. Rabbits' digestive systems are complex, easily upset, and the first thing to show the effects of any emotional or physical stress. The cause of the stress may be something as simple as moving the location of a rabbit's cage across the room, or as serious as a cancerous tumor. Digestive ailments are even more of a problem for permanently disabled buns, because these rabbits are often unable to get the exercise that is so necessary to keep the digestive system functioning optimally.

The precise symptoms of each digestive problem vary, but every person who lives with a rabbit should learn the following signs of a digestive disorder:
- Anorexia (failure to eat)
- Diarrhea
- Reduction or cessation of fecal pellets
- Pain
- Abdominal distention
- Low body temperature (99°F or below)

Just as important as knowing the most common

symptoms of digestive disorders is knowing the measures that can help prevent your rabbit from developing digestive problems. These include:

- Providing constant access to fresh, clean water
- A good diet that is low in carbohydrates and protein and has lots of fiber
- Plenty of exercise
- Frequent, thorough grooming, especially of long-haired breeds
- Preventing ingestion of non-food items such as carpet fibers and plastic

Even if the above preventative measures are followed, rabbit caregivers may face a digestive problem in their rabbit. Most people who have companion rabbits have heard of what is commonly called gastrointestinal stasis (GI stasis). This is also termed gastrointestinal hypomotility, which reflects the fact that it is a slowdown of the rabbit's gastrointestinal tract. There are several other digestive disorders of rabbits that are equally serious. Unfortunately, many rabbit caregivers—and even some veterinarians—are not as familiar with these other disorders as they are with GI hypomotility.

For this reason and others, some veterinarians do not like to use the term "GI stasis." Dr. Mark Burgess, a veterinarian with an exotic animal practice and over 20 years' experience treating rabbits, comments:

Rabbits have a number of stomach and intestinal problems; unfortunately the recent trend is to lump them all under the term "GI Stasis." This is a terribly inaccurate term and should not be used in any educated discussion of rabbit intestinal disease. The original term "Gastric Stasis" was coined for one specific gut problem, that of slowed stomach contractions and blockage (the classic "hairball" disease). Even here, "gastric stasis" was a poor description, as "stasis" means complete lack of movement. Rabbit "hairballs" involve slowed stomach emptying, but complete shutdown only occurs in the most severe cases. Many cases are still eating and producing small amounts of stools until the disease is advanced.

Most rabbit gut problems result from bacterial imbalances occurring in the bowel and cecum, not from blockage of the stomach. Shifts in the gut bacterial population can cause excess gas production and bloating, or improper digestion and diarrhea, or toxin production which can slow the gut and lead to shock, and sometimes complete loss of gut contractions. "GI stasis" means gastrointestinal stasis, or shutdown of the entire digestive system (the proper term for this is "ileus"). Again, while this may occur in the most severe gut disorders, many cases have only a slowing of gut motility, not a complete shutdown (so there is no "stasis").

Some intestinal upsets have normal or even *increased* motility, as can occur with *E. coli.* The toxins from this bacterium have been shown to sometimes stimulate excessive contractions in the gut, hence the owners hearing loud "gurgling" in the abdomen. This noise (borborygmus) results from gas production and increased gut contractions. Diarrhea often is seen during bowel upsets, and this shows us that the gut is moving but isn't processing food properly. We should forget the term "GI Stasis" as it promotes misunderstanding about what is really going on in the rabbit digestive system.

Intestinal Dysbiosis

The term "dysbiosis" means an imbalance. When used in reference to the digestive system of rabbits, it usually means an imbalance in the bacteria of the intestinal tract, when harmful bacteria out-compete "good" bacteria, or certain kinds of "good" bacteria become too proliferate. Symptoms of dysbiosis may include:

- Pain
- Watery or mucoid diarrhea (not always present)
- Lethargy
- Hypothermia (low body temperature)
- Shock

Thanks to devoted nursing, Tonto (right) recovered from a serious digestive disorder.

According to recent printed veterinary conference notes of a presentation by Jerry LaBonde, DVM, "[c]ommon causes are inappropriate diet (low fiber, high carbohydrates, or sudden change in diet), inappropriate antibiotic therapy (clostridial enterotoxemia), and bacterial (*Salmonella, Pseudomonas,* and *Campylobacter* like species)."

Remember that dysbiosis can be a result of gut slow-down and can also be a *cause* of the digestive system slowing down. Dysbiosis is a common and serious condition that, untreated, may lead to complications resulting in the death of your rabbit.

Treatment for dysbiosis may include:

- Fluids
- Syringe feeding
- Antibiotics (used with caution as they may

worsen the condition rather than help it)
- Probiotics (these may compete with more harmful bacteria in the gut and provide some stability to the flora)
- Motility drugs (metoclopramide or cisapride may stimulate bowel contractions and improve motility in the gut, reducing bloating and improving function)
- Analgesics (including Banamine®)[1] to reduce cramping and improve appetite

Home care provided after veterinary care will primarily consist of giving prescribed fluids and medications, and careful monitoring of body temperature.

Gastrointestinal Hypomotility
(also referred to as GI Stasis, Chronic Stasis)
This is a slowdown of the normal movement of the stomach and intestines. It may occur as a primary condition and lead to bacterial imbalances in the gut, or the slowdown may be secondary to a bacterial imbalance (see dysbiosis above). When it occurs as a primary condition, the normal intestinal movement slows, kinds of fiber are no longer separated well, and bacteria begin to multiply. The contents of the gastrointestinal tract become compacted as the rabbit drinks less, painful gas accumulates in pockets, and toxins from multiplying bacteria accumulate. An imbalance of electrolytes (minerals that carry an electric charge) occurs. If the condition goes uncorrected, the rabbit will die. Stress, either physical or emotional, is the usual cause, so rabbit caregivers must be on the watch for symptoms at all times.
Symptoms of gastrointestinal hypomotility may include:

1 Many veterinarians find limited, short-term use of Banamine® effective, but its use may be contraindicated in some cases. See section on disorders of the cecum later in this chapter.

- Anorexia
- Enlarged abdomen
- Gradual reduction in amount and size of fecal pellets
- Pain
- Dehydration
- Weight loss
- Lethargy

Some veterinarians report that in the early stages rabbits may crave high-fiber foods and eat items made of paper and cardboard. Body temperature may be normal or below normal and the rabbit may be alert or lethargic and depressed, depending upon how long the condition has existed.

Treatment and Care
The treatment strategy for gastrointestinal hypomotility is to rehydrate the rabbit, coax him to eat, and promote normal intestinal contractions. Provide a quiet, non-stressful environment. If the rabbit will drink on his own,

Enjoying a daily treat of fresh cilantro.

encourage him, if not, subcutaneous fluids may be necessary. Correct the electrolyte imbalance by giving a little Pedialyte® or adding an electrolyte powder such as KaoLectrolyte™ to the drinking water. Some vets may do a blood screen to check for other diseases (kidney disease, etc.) that may be slowing the gut.

In the past, enemas were sometimes recommended, but most vets no longer advocate them because of the stress to the rabbit. Saunders and Davies, in *Notes on Rabbit Internal Medicine*, point out that enemas also carry a risk due to the thinness of the intestinal and colonic walls in rabbits. Dr. Mark Burgess comments:

> The rabbit gut *likes* the stools hard and dry, a condition that promotes constipation in carnivore intestines. The only time we consider an enema is to directly infuse medications like toxiban into the colon to absorb bacterial toxins, *not* to loosen the stools.

Tempt the rabbit with gastrointestinal hypomotility to eat with hay and fresh vegetables such as leaf lettuce or fresh, aromatic cooking herbs (remembering to use those the rabbit is accustomed to having in his diet—new additions may exacerbate the problem). If the veterinarian thinks it necessary, Periactin® might be prescribed as an appetite stimulant. If the rabbit won't eat at all, it may be necessary for the caretaker to syringe-feed the rabbit three to four times a day (Chapter 2). There are supplemental foods made especially for such feeding, including Critical Care® or Critter Be Better®. Follow the guidelines on the containers for amounts.

Antibiotics may be prescribed in order to prevent bacterial overgrowth, but not all veterinarians recommend this. In cases of gastrointestinal hypomotility, the balance of microflora in the gut is already going to be unstable, so unless there is a real likelihood of a bacterial infection, some practitioners prefer not to prescribe antibiotics. Acidophilus can be given to help restore a healthy balance of microflora. Although it does not naturally occur in a rabbit's digestive tract, there is some evidence it will help in cases of gut slowdown because of its inhibitory affect on *Escherichia coli* and other harmful bacteria. Some caretakers recommend giving Questran®, as it binds bacterial toxins such as those produced by clostridia. Questran® absorbs water, however, and should not be given unless the rabbit is also given additional fluids.

The painful gas that accumulates can be helped in several ways. Children's simethicone (about 1 cc per 5-lb. rabbit, every two hours or as instructed by your vet) is often recommended. According to pharmacological information accessed by Dr. William Kurmes, simethicone works by changing the surface tension of fluid in the digestive tract. This causes foamy gas bubbles to coalesce into larger bubbles that are easier to pass from either end of the tract. Since the rabbit's fermentation chamber is in the large intestine, the gas goes out the back end. (Note: sugar substitutes—malitol, maltitol, mannitol, sorbitol, xylitol—have been found to increase gas production in humans. If the simethicone preparation you purchase contains a sugar substitute and you feel your rabbit's gas problem may be getting worse after administering the simethicone, consult your veterinarian.)

A gentle fingertip massage may also help gas pain, but should only be done if radiographs done by your vet have shown no obstruction. If you are not comfortable giving a massage yourself, the rabbit can also be placed on a massage pillow set on low. Analgesics can help the pain caused by the pressure from the gas on internal organs. Veterinarians usually recommend NSAIDs for gastrointestinal upsets (Appendix I) rather than narcotics because of the theoretical potential for narcotics to slow the GI system further.

If the rabbit will eat timothy hay, this will encourage intestinal contractions, as will exercise. Motility drugs such as metoclopramide or cisapride (available from compounding pharmacies) may be prescribed for GI hypomotility if the rabbit is not in shock and if there is no sign of obstruction. This latter should be verified by X-rays if there is any question of an obstruction being present. Metoclopramide (Reglan®) may have more effect on the upper GI tract and cisapride the lower, although not all veterinarians agree there is a difference, and some veterinarians do not believe either is effective.

Home care for a rabbit with gastrointestinal hypomotility will focus on providing a stress-free environment; monitoring food and water intake; giving simethicone, analgesics, sub-Q fluids, and any other medications prescribed by the vet; encouraging the rabbit to exercise; watching fecal output; and monitoring body temperature. The rabbit's body temperature may fluctuate considerably, so you may wish to check it several times a day. (Ask your veterinary professional to show you how. If your rabbit finds the procedure too stressful, you will need to discuss it with your vet and balance frequent checking of temperature with reducing stress.) If the rabbit's temperature falls below 100°F (37.7°C), the rabbit will need to be warmed. Cover him with a light blanket or place a microwaveable heated corn-filled pillow, SnuggleSafe®, or towel-covered hot water bottle (electric heating pads should not be used) next to the rabbit for about 20 minutes. Recheck temperature, and be careful not to overheat the rabbit.

Prevention
There are a few steps caretakers can take to minimize the likelihood of GI hypomotility. Provide the rabbit with unlimited grass hay and fresh water. (If your rabbit is one of those who is reluctant to drink much water, this may contribute to the development of stasis. Renee

Plenty of grass hay helps keep Diego healthy.

Stratton, who has worked with a highly skilled exotics veterinary team to control the stasis her bunny is prone to develop despite the exemplary care he is given, believes the bunny's reluctance to drink water is a major factor causing the stasis.) Feed small amounts of pelleted food and avoid giving excessive carbohydrates. Firm fecal pellets are desirable, and a sign the rabbit is getting enough fiber. (Soft or rock-hard fecal pellets may be a sign of incorrect diet and developing GI problems.) Be sure your rabbits are given the opportunity to exercise. If your rabbit has mobility problems, try to exercise him by using a sling or cart (Chapter 1).

Acute Bloat and Blockage

Bloat occurs as gas accumulates in large amounts in the gastrointestinal tract. Acute bloat, however, occurs as a result of a physical obstruction or severe ileus. True obstructions are usually high in the gut, near the pyloric opening (at the bottom of the stomach) or within the first six inches of the small bowel. Blockage may occur from ingested material such as plastic; carpet fibers; dried peas, corn, and beans; cat litter; and mats of hair (some hair is naturally present in a rabbit's digestive tract and ordinarily does not cause obstruction, but sometimes hair may form a clump in the stomach, which gets caught in the bowel). Tumors, adhesions, abscesses, and a twisted intestine (rare in rabbits, and more likely to occur in older rabbits or rabbits with paralysis) may also cause blockages. Because of the obstruction, gas and liquids cannot pass normally and begin to accumulate in the stomach, distending it. As it expands, it presses on other internal organs and causes extreme pain to the rabbit.

With severe ileus, the bowel and stomach are completely immobile, sometimes causing severe accumulation of gas and fluid despite no physical blockage. This could be termed a "functional obstruction." Dr. Mark Burgess explains:

> [Functional obstruction] is not a surgical problem, as there is no real object obstructing the gut. Distinguishing between the two conditions can be nearly impossible in some cases. Abdominal X-rays may be useful; if the pattern of dilated gas and fluid accumulation is throughout the entire gut, then the condition is more likely ileus. If the proximal gut (stomach and upper section of small bowel) appear dilated with gas/fluid, and the dilation

abruptly stops and the lower gut seems small and empty, this is more likely a physical blockage requiring emergency surgery. But in many cases, gas pattern and X-ray appearance can be identical in severe ileus or obstruction cases.

According to another veterinarian, functional obstructions can happen occasionally at the pylorus from normal ingested food that is not chewed adequately, as well as in the intestine from the impacted contents that collect when intestinal contractions slow. The latter functional obstructions may occasionally move out on their own, causing periodic episodes of pain and anorexia until they have passed into the colon. (Once in the colon, many of these blockages will no longer be as obstructive, as the colon is larger.) This passage can sometimes be monitored with radiographs. In one case a rabbit who had consumed a large number of fresh willow twigs developed a functional blockage. The blockage was monitored by X-rays, and as it appeared to be moving, albeit very slowly, the caretaker chose to give supportive care (electrolytes, fluids, warmth, supplemental nutrition, and pain medications) rather than risk surgery. In this particular instance, the blockage did finally pass through and the rabbit survived.

Remember that bloat is very dangerous to the rabbit—it is extremely painful, stresses the rabbit, may cause the rabbit to go into shock, and in some cases ruptures the stomach. A rabbit with acute bloat from a complete gastrointestinal obstruction can go from perfectly well to critically ill within an extremely short period of time, and die within 12 to 24 hours of onset of symptoms if there is no successful intervention. *If you see several of the following signs in your rabbit, it is an extreme medical emergency and the rabbit must receive immediate veterinary care to have any hope of survival*:

- Sudden refusal to eat or drink
- Extreme pain (rabbit will often sit hunched, grinding his teeth)
- Loud gurgles and/or sloshing sounds in gut

- Distension of abdomen with tight feel (tympany)
- Abrupt cessation of fecal pellets
- Shock (two signs of shock are body temperature below 99°F and bright pink or grayish-white gums)
- Sudden onset—rabbit was fine one minute, near collapse the next

Treatment

Treatment for bloat and blockage can be very tricky, and the strategy will depend upon the cause of the gas accumulation and the condition of the rabbit. Once a rabbit is in the vet's care, the rabbit will most likely need to be stabilized before any treatment is done. In cases where the rabbit is in critical condition, emergency doses of IV fluids, analgesics, and antibiotics may be given first. *A radiograph should be taken of any bloated rabbit to help pinpoint the reason for the gas accumulation.* The vet will then decide what course of action needs to be taken. If there is still some outflow from the stomach, the condition may be treated without surgery. In non-obstructive bowel bloating, supportive care and motility drugs are given, but if the wrong diagnosis is made and there is an obstruction, the motility drugs will worsen pain and cramping and could cause rupture, especially at high doses. If there is a complete obstruction of outflow, surgery may be necessary. Dr. Mark Burgess prefers an "aggressive but hands-off" approach whenever possible:

> You need to treat rapidly but not stress the rabbit at all. We avoid stress by not doing a blood draw, not stomach tubing them (unless very critical and so bloated we don't have a choice), not handling with heavy restraint of the rabbit . . . but we do get injectable meds in: Reglan®, a dose of Banamine® for cramping and pain, SQ warm fluids to help get body temp up (usually hypothermic if bloated), then

oral probiotics, simethicone liquid to break up gas . . . and put in a heated cage.

In acute cases where the rabbit is extremely bloated and decompression is necessary, many vets feel it should never be done with a needle. The late Barbara Deeb, in the chapter "Digestive System and Disorders" in the *Manual of Rabbit Medicine and Surgery*, warned that attempting stomach decompression with a needle will result in peritonitis and death.

Cases of acute bloat that are caused by a total obstruction of the pylorus or intestine that is completely cutting off outflow will require emergency surgery. This surgery carries high risks, and unless the veterinarian is very skilled and experienced, it is likely to be unsuccessful. However, in most of these cases of total obstruction, the rabbit would die without it. It can be very difficult to distinguish between acute bloat that must be treated surgically and bloat that can be treated medically, even for experienced rabbit veterinarians. Dr. Mark Burgess recounts his experience:

> I've seen one bunny who had nearly identical signs twice, a year apart. The first time we cut him because he seemed tightly bloated and we worried about a blockage; but nothing was in there, he simply had ileus, so we got him on high dose Reglan® and closed him fast. A year later he came in looking the same once again; X-rays and clinical appearance were similar. This time we cut him and he had a hairball blocking his bowel. Sometimes there is no way to be sure without surgery, but X-rays are the best way to try and distinguish the two.

Prevention

It is better to try and avoid acute bloat and blockage than to have to treat it. Have a good grass hay such as timothy available for your rabbit to eat at all times. Do not give rabbits

Table 3.1 Symptoms of selected digestive ailments.

	Acute bloat, total blockage	Severe GI hypomotility (stasis)
Pain	Rabbit exhibits signs of acute pain that came on suddenly	Rabbit may have been exhibiting signs of pain, but now pain is acute
Abdominal distension	Abdomen swells rapidly, feels tight and balloon-like (or doughy if rupture has occurred). Stomach sounds may be extremely loud.	Abdomen may have been larger than normal, but suddenly becomes very tight and distended
Fecal pellets	Fecal pellet production suddenly ceases	Fecal pellets may have been decreasing, and now cease abruptly
Food consumption	Rabbit stops eating suddenly, will not even accept favorite treats	Rabbit may not have had much appetite, but suddenly stops eating at all
Water consumption	Rabbit stops drinking suddenly	Rabbit may not have been drinking much, but suddenly stops drinking entirely
Body temperature	Usually low, 99°F or less	Usually low, 99°F or less
General demeanor	Extremely depressed, may sit hunched and/ or unmoving	Extremely depressed, may sit hunched and/ or unmoving
Other clinical signs that may be present	Rapid heart rate and rapid respiration rate, shock	Shock

Non-obstructive hypomotility (stasis)	Intestinal dysbiosis
Rabbit may at first show few signs of pain, as condition progresses more signs are apparent	Rabbit may show few signs of pain to severe abdominal pain
Distention of abdomen occurs gradually. May be from few to no stomach sounds.	May be some abdominal distension from gas
Fecal pellets decrease in size, and eventually cease	Watery or mucoid diarrhea often, but not always, present
Rabbit will at first continue to eat, preferring fresh greens and hay	Often ceases to eat normally
Rabbit may continue to drink normally at first, drink less as time passes, or in some cases may increase consumption	Variable
May be normal or below normal	May fall below normal
May be alert or depressed, somewhat active or inactive	Lethargic
No specific	Shock

Note: symptoms may overlap and vary in specific cases. This chart is provided only to give readers an idea of possible symptom differences.

food that includes whole dried corn, peas, or beans. (Frances Harcourt-Brown, in the *Textbook of Rabbit Medicine,* suggests that rabbits with dental problems may be at particular risk for blockage from these items as they may tend to swallow them whole.) Keep rabbits away from cat litter. Prevent your rabbits from eating plastic, carpet, and other indigestibles by thoroughly bunny-proofing your home and keeping an eye on their investigations. If you have a long-haired rabbit, keep it well-groomed. Be sure older rabbits get enough exercise to keep their digestive systems healthy. There is anecdotal evidence that gas could accumulate from rabbits eating vegetables such as cabbage and broccoli, so it would not hurt to avoid giving your rabbit such vegetables, as well as avoiding high-carb sugary treats. If you suspect your rabbit has pain from minor amounts of gas, give simethicone and monitor the rabbit very carefully for loss of appetite or signs of serious bloat.

It is also a good idea for any rabbit caretaker to purchase an inexpensive stethoscope and learn the normal sounds of their rabbit's digestive system. When a digestive disorder is suspected, you can listen for any changes (fewer noises or very loud noises) that could indicate a serious problem.

Gastric Ulcers

Gastric ulcers have been reported as postmortem findings in rabbits. Some veterinary practitioners suspect they may occur in association with digestive ailments, in rabbits with low-quality diets, and in cases of poisoning. There are no specific signs of gastric ulcers in rabbits other than abdominal pain.

Veterinarians are divided on the issue of treating rabbits for gastric ulcers. Some feel that gastric ulcers are rare in companion rabbits, and that treating a rabbit for them is generally unnecessary. Others prefer to treat for them as a precaution when dealing with digestive disorders, especially if the rabbit is being given NSAIDs. This is a decision you will need to make in conjunction with your veterinarian.

If ulcers are suspected, it is important to address the underlying factors. Reduce stress and improve the rabbit's diet. Be sure your rabbit's diet includes plenty of fiber in the form of timothy hay and that fresh water is always available.

Two kinds of medication are used to treat gastric ulcers in rabbits. One is omeprazole, which inhibits the mechanism that controls production of gastric acid. Prilosec® is an example of an omeprazole medication. The second type of medication used inhibits the secretion of gastric acid and reduces pepsin production. This includes cimetidine (Tagamet®), famotidine (Pepcid®), and ranitidine (Zantac®). The latter medications are used more often than omeprazole for rabbits. (Omeprazole has occasionally caused illness in other exotic species.)

Sucralfate (Carafate®) might also be recommended by some vets. It coats the stomach and heals ulcers without disrupting acid metabolism. It can be used with ranitidine, although it should not be taken in conjunction with cimetidine, tetracycline, phenytoin, or digoxin. If the rabbit is receiving Baytril® or Cipro®, administration of sucralfate should be at least a couple of hours after the former medications are given. Sucralfate requires stomach acid to make the protective gel that covers injured tissues, and should be given at least 30 minutes before any antacid is given to the rabbit. Sucralfate must be taken regularly to be effective—do not miss doses—and full protection may take a couple of weeks to achieve.

Disorders of the Cecum
Kathy Smith

As part of the digestive process, fiber is separated into large and small fiber particles. Smaller fiber particles (referred to as digestible or fermentable fiber) are sent to the cecum, where bacterial fermentation occurs. The cecotropes formed as a result of this fermentation contain essential nutrients, including volatile fatty acids, amino acids, and vitamins and are covered in a gelatinous coating that protects them from stomach acids when re-ingested.

Normally, your rabbit will eat his cecotropes directly from the anus. This process is referred to as cecotrophy and caregivers may be unaware this is happening. It is important that you and your family understand that this is a normal function and a necessary part of rabbit physiology and nutrition. Rabbits are creatures of habit, so if you interrupt or change their daily routine it may interfere with cecotrophy.

If your rabbit is overweight or has a condition such as arthritis that prevents him from easily harvesting his cecotropes, he may deposit them on the floor before eating them. Healthy cecotropes are soft, dark, shiny, have the appearance of a cluster of grapes, and have a very distinctive, pungent odor. Rabbits with overgrown or maloccluded incisors or other dental issues may also have difficulty harvesting their cecotropes.

Overproduction of Cecotropes

Excess production of cecotropes is usually caused by an improperly balanced diet. Unfortunately, the proper balance between hay, commercial (pelleted or extruded) food, and fresh produce (vegetables and fruit) varies from rabbit to rabbit and may change for an individual rabbit as a result of the aging process, illness, or physical injury/disability. In multi-rabbit homes, this may mean buying more than one kind of commercial food and/or hay and making "custom" salads for each individual or group.

If you begin noticing unconsumed cecotropes on the floor or in the litter box, try to encourage your rabbit to eat more hay. A diet too high in sugar, carbohydrates, or protein and/or one too low in fiber can cause over-production of cecotropes. If you have made any recent changes to your rabbit's diet, you may need to re-evaluate those changes. If changes were recommended by your veterinarian, be sure to discuss the problem with her.

If you have added new produce items, they may not be agreeing with your rabbit—or you may be giving too much variety for his digestive system to handle. When changing pellet brands or hay suppliers, it is a good idea to introduce the change gradually by mixing the old and new together. For rabbits with especially sensitive digestive systems, I even do this when starting a new bag of food or box of hay.

Excess production of cecotropes can lead to a messy bottom. This condition is uncomfortable for the rabbit and, in extreme cases, cecotropes can solidify and block the anal opening. A messy bottom also increases the risk of flystrike—even in indoor rabbits (remember, it only takes one fly to cause damage). Regular cleaning of the area is important until the underlying problem can be corrected. Your veterinarian may suggest shaving the area to make bathing easier, reduce irritation, and decrease the incidence of cecotropes adhering to the surrounding hair.

Cecal Dysbiosis

The production of healthy cecotropes depends on maintaining a delicate balance between bacteria and other microorganisms in the cecum. This balance changes with the time of day and cecal pH. Cecal dysbiosis can occur in conjunction with intestinal dysbiosis or it can be an independent problem.

Dysbiosis is most often caused by an unbalanced diet, antibiotics, or stress. As mentioned in the section on overproduction of cecotropes, there is no one diet that is right for all rabbits. (See section on Overweight/Under-weight later in this chapter for more information on diet.)

If your rabbit is (or has recently been) on antibiotics, verify that the antibiotic is actually safe for rabbits; oral forms of penicillin (amoxicillin, ampicillin, etc.), erythromycin,

Among his many physical problems, Murray's GI X-rays frequently showed an enlarged cecum.

and clindamycin can be fatal for rabbits. If your rabbit has taken any of these, seek immediate veterinary care—from a different vet than the one who dispensed the prescription! If the antibiotic is considered safe for rabbits, contact your veterinarian. She may want to discontinue antibiotic treatment, change medications, reduce the dose, and/or prescribe a probiotic such as Acid-Pak 4-Way, Equine Probios, or Bene-Bac to help restore the balance. Rabbits should not be fed yogurt as their GI system is not accustomed to digesting dairy products.

If antibiotics have not been given, consider whether stress could be the underlying cause of your rabbit's digestive problem. Keep in mind that because rabbits are prey animals, stress for them can be caused by simple changes in household routine, including new family members (human or animal), being moved (to a new home or a new space), household guests, or rearranging furniture.

Depending on the severity of symptoms, your veterinarian may prescribe any or all of the following:

- Fluids
- Pain medication
- Motility drugs (metoclopramide and/or cisapride)
- Syringe feeding
- Antibiotics
- Cholestyramine

There is some question among veterinarians as to whether motility drugs directly affect the cecum. However, many veterinarians do prescribe them for disorders of the cecum with the assumption that keeping the rest of the digestive tract functioning smoothly will ultimately benefit the cecum.

While many caregivers jump into syringe feeding at the first sign of any GI problem, I *personally* avoid it if the rabbit is eating some on his own—unless it is a rabbit who I know enjoys the extra handling and attention. For most rabbits, being restrained and "force fed" is stressful and there is always some risk of aspiration. It is actually easier and faster to syringe-feed than to spend hours waving favorite greens or hay under your rabbit's nose, hoping he will get tired of being pestered and will eat a bit just to get rid of you. I have also been known to sit and coax a rabbit to eat by hand-feeding an extruded food one pellet at a time. Veterinary texts by both Harcourt-Brown and Saunders and Davies suggest that extruded food is easier to digest than pelleted food and I have found most (but not all) rabbits enjoy it and tolerate it well. If you do need to syringe feed, extruded food softens quickly and easily in water and is not as likely as ground pellets to clog the syringe. *Note:* Some rabbits will eagerly take a pellet mush from a syringe (without being restrained) or will eat it willingly from a saucer.

If fecal analysis confirms the presence of clostridium or Giardia, your veterinarian may prescribe a short course of metronidazole. Sulfasalazine, a combination sulfa antibiotic and non-steroidal anti-inflammatory that has been used for inflammatory bowel disease in humans, has also been successfully used to treat dysbiosis by controlling pain, reducing intestinal inflammation, and helping control the population of harmful bacteria.

If clostridium is merely suspected, your veterinarian may choose to treat with cholestyramine, either with a single dose in the office or by prescribing it for you to give at home. Cholestyramine binds to the toxins produced by clostridium and eliminates them through the feces. Cholestyramine is not absorbed by the body, but it can dehydrate the intestines so it is crucial to give it exactly as prescribed, which should include giving generous amounts of water orally.

Cecal Impaction

Cecal impaction is a serious condition that requires aggressive and persistent care. It can result from other gastrointestinal ailments or can be an independent issue caused by inadequate water intake, ingesting clumping cat litter or other small fiber particles (including bulk laxatives) that absorb water, any type of pain, and/or stress. Owners may notice the absence of hard feces along with the presence of mucus but no diarrhea. In *Textbook of Rabbit Medicine*, Harcourt-Brown points out that "the onset of cecal impaction can be insidious." She goes on to say, "The condition may be mistaken for dental disease as the rabbits may

Solomon found a way to enjoy life at my house even while battling an impacted cecum.

pick at food, eat a little, and then drop it uneaten." Advanced cases will often show up on radiographs and/or abdominal palpation, where a "hard sausage-shaped structure" may be felt.

Cecal impactions are difficult to treat. Surgery is unlikely to be successful. Medical treatments include providing nutrition, managing pain, and maintaining GI motility while working to soften the contents of the cecum. Veterinary texts by both Harcourt-Brown and Saunders and Davies recommend liquid paraffin to help soften the contents of the cecum. For my rabbit Solomon, Dr. Noella Allan, my primary rabbit veterinarian, tried using KY lubrication gel for this purpose.

Cecal impaction is one condition where at least brief hospitalization may be required since, in addition to subcutaneous and oral fluids, IV fluids may also be necessary. Some veterinarians like to keep rabbits overnight, but one must weigh the stress caused by strange surroundings and separation anxiety against the benefits of hospital care. Unless the clinic is staffed 24/7, one alternative may be to provide one day of IV fluid therapy, then continue with sub-Q fluids and further intensive care in the home environment.

There is some controversy over the best method of pain management in cases of cecal impaction. NSAIDs such as Banamine® may be contraindicated because they interfere with prostaglandin production and prostaglandins help stimulate the emptying of the cecum. Harcourt-Brown suggests that carprofen, the active ingredient in Rimadyl®, has less effect on prostaglandin production than other NSAIDs. There is also a greater risk of gastric ulcers when NSAIDs are used on a rabbit who has not been eating normally. Many vets will prescribe preventative treatment with anti-ulcer medications such as ranitidine (Zantac®), famotidine (Pepcid®), omeprazole (Prilosec®), and/or sucralfate (Carafate®).

Some veterinarians prefer to use narcotic pain medication. The disadvantage is that these medications often cause drowsiness and/or may slow down the GI tract. A growing trend among veterinarians is to use NSAIDs and narcotics, using lower doses of each drug to still provide effective pain relief.

Siegfried lacks the normal dark side markings and may be a "Charlie" at risk for megacolon.

Prostaglandin therapy has been tried outside of the United States in a very small number of cases with some success reported. For more information see Harcourt-Brown's *Textbook of Rabbit Medicine.*

Congenital Agangliosis

Congenital agangliosis, also know as "megacolon" or "cow pile syndrome" (CPS) is a hereditary disorder of the gastrointestinal tract found in *some* rabbits with the "English Spot" or En En color gene. These rabbits are generally white with dark black or brown rings around their eyes and black or brown spots on their back. At this time there is no conclusive test for this disorder. The diagnosis is presumptive in rabbits whose color pattern is consistent with the syndrome and where other causes of the symptoms (parasites or a bacterial imbalance or overgrowth in the GI tract) have been ruled out by testing and/or unsuccessful treatment.

When I visited the Minnesota Companion Rabbit Society (MCRS) in November 2006, founder and president Joanna Campbell took me on a tour of area shelters and pointed out the "Charlies"—rabbits with the characteristic color pattern that is linked with the genetic predisposition for this disorder. These rabbits have fewer dark markings than normal because pigment is missing from some of the dark "spots" that are characteristic breed markings. It is thought that this particular defect impacts rapidly regenerating cells in the body, which include the lining of the digestive tract as well as hair. Joanna reminds us:

> Having the appearance does not mean they *will* develop issues. It's a risk factor, but not a certainty. Some rabbits are Charlies and don't ever have issues. Other rabbits are fine until they hit a major stressor (usually) and suddenly they have digestive issues. Once symptoms appear, there is no known way to revert to "normal" again.

It should also be noted that similar symptoms have been reported by both caregivers and veterinarians in rabbits who *do not have* the characteristic markings.

As the term "cow pile syndrome" implies, this condition consists of a number of clinical symptoms that are frequently seen together, but a specific underlying cause may not be known. Congenital agangliosis is believed to be caused by an improper development or malfunction of the colon and/or cecum. Rabbits with this disorder have trouble extracting essential nutrients from food, may not produce cecotropes, and frequently have difficulty maintaining weight. Although it is generally thought that rabbits with this syndrome have trouble absorbing and processing nutrients from food, each individual case is unique. Indeed, it is suspected that there may be a number of different disorders that are lumped into this category because of similar symptoms; this would explain why treatments that help one individual may actually worsen the condition for another.

The symptoms of this disorder include big, misshapen, soft fecal pellets, frequently covered with mucus, and a drippy bottom alternating with long, painful bouts of GI slowdown. During the spells of stasis, it may be possible to feel large masses of fecal material similar in consistency to ropes of play dough. This condition is nearly always episodic in nature, characterized by flare-ups followed by periods of relative improvement.

There is little agreement among veterinarians, experts, and caregivers about what diet or medications work best in these cases. Many caregivers have found that rabbits with this condition do not tolerate greens well; however, this may not be true for *your* rabbit—listen to what his body tells you. Because rabbits with this condition often need extra nutritional support, eliminating pellets may not be a good idea. Several caregivers have reported better tolerance for extruded food (such as Kaytee Exact Rainbow) than for either timothy or alfalfa pellets.

Opinions on medical treatment also vary. While several caregivers I know have nursed their megacolon rabbits through *many* episodes of severe GI slowdown, some veterinarians worry about the increased risk of the cecum rupturing with each episode. A veterinarian who has actually examined your rabbit should decide whether GI motility drugs are recommended or contraindicated—and this decision may vary from episode to episode. Some veterinarians will prescribe either a sulfa drug (such as Albon®) or metronidazole during flare-ups. In other cases, long-term use of these drugs may be recommended. Always check with your veterinarian before making changes to prescribed medications, but don't be afraid to speak up if you feel something isn't working. Just as you rely on your veterinarian's medical knowledge, she depends on you for feedback on how your rabbit is responding to treatment!

Most veterinarians and caregivers do agree on the following important points for rabbits with this condition:

- Encourage your rabbit to drink plenty of water.
- Stick to a routine. While most rabbits are "creatures of habit," daily routine is especially important with these rabbits.
- Once you find a diet that works, don't change it unless it stops working. Be consistent in what you feed and when you feed it.
- Encourage exercise. If your rabbit does not have a bonded companion, spend time each day encouraging her to play.
- Sanitation is critical. Be prepared to change the litter box and/or bedding several times a day. By keeping your rabbit's area spotless, you will help keep your rabbit clean, which will reduce the need for stressful butt-baths.
- Minimize stress. While this is important for all rabbits, it is especially important for ones with this chronic condition.
- Learn to recognize *your* rabbit's body language and begin treatment at the first sign that an attack is beginning. Work with your veterinarian to identify what symptoms can be managed with home care and when a vet visit is needed.

I first heard about CPS several years ago from Vineeta Anand. She shares her experience with her special lop girl, Raisa, who suffered from this condition:

It was apparent Raisa had health problems when I spotted her at the animal shelter. I knew if I didn't adopt her, she would be a certain candidate for euthanasia. She had a severe limp, and looked like she hadn't eaten in weeks. What I didn't know when I brought her home was just how severe her health problems were. And how she would become my special-needs rabbit who would play a key role in helping veterinarians and other caregivers diagnose and treat the gastrointestinal disease now commonly referred to as the "cow pile syndrome."

Raisa has battled cow pile syndrome for four years.

Raisa was always hungry, even though she was fed a large plate of mixed greens twice a day, along with unlimited hay. She stole my cat's dry food on more than one occasion. And she produced fecal pellets that looked like misshapen jelly beans rather than perfectly round "cocoa-puffs."

In the weeks leading up to her first attack of CPS, her fecals became so smelly and wet that I could no longer let her sleep on my bed. Her fecal tests were negative for parasites and overgrowth of bacteria. After puzzling over her worsening diarrhea-like fecals, frequently covered in mucus, my veterinarian advised taking her off greens and keeping her on a hay-only diet for a few weeks. She refused to eat the hay, and lost weight rapidly.

After two weeks, I sought a second opinion—a diagnosis of clostridium enteritis, which I later discovered was incorrect. But at the time, I didn't know better. She was prescribed metronidazole, and put on a diet of pureed infant food. Instead of improving, she entered into GI stasis, and nearly died after she aspirated the baby food and developed pneumonia. She was kept on oxygen for several days, and given antibiotics and subcutaneous fluids.

Her fecals gradually resumed a normal consistency, but continued to be misshapen. Within a year, she had a second major attack of CPS. Her symptoms began with constant dripping of watery brown fecal matter, along with incontinence, that led to urine burn. I had to wash her hind legs and bottom regularly for the rest of her life. The discharge gave way to severe and very painful GI stasis, which lasted for several days and in which it was possible to feel firm masses of fecal matter with the consistency of play dough in her belly when palpated.

Her weight and temperature fluctuated wildly. Although the normal temperature for rabbits is between 101°F and 103°F, her temperature swung as high as 105.7°F and as low as 96°F. For the rest of her life, Raisa cycled between periods of normalcy and severe GI stasis. During the bouts of stasis, she would be administered pain medications such as Banamine® and Torbugesic® and, later, when it became freely available, meloxicam.

She was also put on a maintenance regimen of subcutaneous fluids, getting anywhere from 50 or 60 cc once a day up to 240 cc when she went into bouts of severe stasis. Along with the fluids, she received motility drugs (both metoclopramide and cisapride) twice a day.

In developing a maintenance regimen, my veterinarian and I consulted actively with other veterinarians and rabbit rescuers who had experience treating rabbits with CPS. Among the various medicines and alternative supplements I tried but discarded were simethicone (for gas), sucralfate, omeprazole, chamomile tea with Acid 4-Pak, slippery elm and various other herbs, acupuncture, Chinese herbal medicines, and fresh alfalfa from a farm. None of them helped.

What did help, at least for a time, was administering Epsom salts, whose osmotic quality help to draw fluids into the GI tract, breaking down the fecal matter and, in combination with belly massages, helping to counteract bouts of stasis. I would make a solution of Epsom salts, dissolved in hot water with pharmaceutical raspberry flavoring, and administer that as needed. It is essential to keep the rabbit well hydrated when administering Epsom salts.

I learned to read Raisa: I could predict the onset of an attack when she began drinking a lot of water, sat hunched up, refused to eat, or ground her teeth in pain. I kept a stack of 1-cc syringes handy. In an attack, I would thaw frozen ice cubes of flavored Pedialyte®, and administer as much as 25 cc twice or more a day orally, followed by belly massages for as long as I could.

Raisa lived with the disease for four years and died in my arms on January 7, 2005.

Brenda and Jim Holden, volunteers with MCRS, agree with Vineeta on the importance of being "in tune" with subtle cues from their CPS rabbit. In September 2007, they lost their hearts (and their guest room) to Fawn, a brown-and-white Rex. During the previous four weeks, Fawn had been dumped at the shelter, placed on a strict diet (she lost two pounds during that time), spayed, and moved to Petco for adoption. Jim and Brenda found her at Petco with severe diarrhea. The MCRS vet gave her a "horrible prognosis" . . . and Jim and Brenda brought her to their home for hospice care. Apparently, no one explained that concept to Fawn!

When I spoke to Brenda on March 6, 2008, it was obvious that Fawn had taken over as queen of the household. Brenda described Fawn as a "vocal" bunny when she is upset, and knows she is embarrassed (as well as uncomfortable) when her bottom is wet and/ or messy. She is good about using the litter-box. The Holdens have found that Kaytee Soft-Sorbent litter/bedding absorbs the moisture, minimizing her "sitting in it" exposure—as does the fact that Jim (or Brenda) is there almost immediately to clean the box. Through trial and error, they have settled on a maintenance dose of metronidazole that produces decent-looking fecal pellets and minimizes butt leakage. Body language tells Jim and Brenda if Fawn needs pain medication or simethicone.

As Brenda talked about her, I could tell Fawn was a happy bunny—leaping, running, and even trying to climb the Christmas tree! Fawn has her humans trained to deliver her meals and offer treats at the same time every day. They let her nap undisturbed from 2:00 P.M. until 7:00 P.M. each day—after all, she has to rest up so she can shred cardboard boxes under the bed while the humans are trying to sleep!

Overweight/Underweight

Although it might appear to be a simple task, it can in fact be difficult to determine whether a rabbit is a healthy weight. Because of their build and their digestive systems, early signs of weight loss or gain may be missed. Unlike cats and dogs, a rabbit's gastrointestinal system operates at "full" all the time and this can mask a rabbit's true weight. Yet precisely because of their unique digestive system, rabbits are at high risk of serious complications if they are overly thin or overly fat. The weight of special-needs rabbits can be particularly difficult to keep steady. Some tend to gain extra weight from inactivity; others lose weight easily and must be given extra food.

Keeping a rabbit at an ideal weight can be difficult.

There is one general hint for checking a rabbit's weight—the backbone, ribs, and pelvis should be palpable but not too obvious. But the best way to watch your rabbit's weight is to weigh him or her at least once a month. Human infant scales can be used, or special scales can be purchased through rabbit supply businesses (Appendix III). If you have a larger rabbit, you can weigh him/her by first weighing yourself and then weighing again holding your rabbit and noting the difference.

Diet

No discussion on weight can avoid diet, and that continues to be a controversial subject among rabbit experts and care-takers. Although most agree that a good grass hay—timothy, orchard grass, meadow grass—should comprise the bulk of the diet, and that plenty of fresh water should always be available, of what the rest of a rabbit's diet should consist is still hotly debated. My personal opinion is that it depends upon the rabbit. What works best for one rabbit may not work for another. It may take a little experimentation to find out what diet is best for your particular rabbit.

Although a few rabbit experts still recommend a pel-let-less diet, most now acknowledge that a few measured pel-lets can help the rabbit receive adequate amounts of essential vitamins and other nutrients. It is theoretically possible to ensure a rabbit receives adequate nutrition via grass hay and fresh vegetables alone, but in reality it takes a lot of research to figure out precisely what combinations and amounts of vegetables the rabbit needs to ensure proper nutrition. (Not to mention the money it takes to buy them and the time to prepare them and coax the rabbit to eat all of them in the required amounts.)

It should also be remembered that not all rabbits have the same nutritional requirements. Some larger rabbits (e.g., Flemish Giants, English Lops) require higher protein for proper development, especially during their first two years. Long-haired rabbits such as fuzzy lops and angoras may require a higher protein and fiber content diet for their entire lives.

The amount of pellets recommended by various sources may be anything from one teaspoon to ¼ cup daily per five pounds of the rabbit's weight. The amount that works best is something that will vary according to the individual. I start at ¼ cup and then watch the rabbit's weight and cecotroph production closely. If the weight stays steady and there is no sign of excessive cecotrophs, I leave it at that amount. If the rabbit appears to be gaining weight or produces excessive cecotrophs, I reduce the amount of pellets (slowly!).

Whether to feed alfalfa or grass-based pellets is another controversial issue. Many experts recommend grass-based because, they claim, grass-based are lower in calcium and protein and higher in fiber. Well, maybe. It actually depends upon the individual pellet. Some good-quality alfalfa pellets are actually lower in protein and higher in fiber than some grass-based pellets. Read the labels. Also, not all rabbits will eat grass-based pellets, and a few rabbit caretakers have reported rabbits having a toxic reaction to grass-based pellets. Consider the individual case. If the rabbit has trouble with urine sludge, a grass-based pellet may in fact be desirable because of lower calcium levels. But for many rabbits, I believe a good-quality alfalfa pellet is fine, given in measured amounts.

Dr. Jason Sulliban, a veterinarian who often treats rabbits, recommends buying good-quality pellets in bags of five pounds or less. He explains that the smaller bags move faster, and warns there is no way to know how long larger bags of pellets have been sitting in warehouses and on the shelf. With the big bags, by the time a person gets to the bottom, active vitamins and minerals may be degrading. "If you purchase smaller bags," he advises, "you can be relatively sure the nutrient content of the pellets is nearly the same from the top of the bag to the bottom."

Extruded feeds, although they are not widely available in the United States at this time, are considered by some veterinarians and rabbit caretakers to be superior to regular pellets. Most pelleted foods are manufactured by compressing them at fairly low temperatures, theoretically allowing for the growth of bacterial and fungal populations. Extruded feeds are cooked and pasteurized mixes of precise nutritional content. They are more easily digested, and since each nugget or pellet of extruded feed contains nearly the same nutritional content, this prevents selective feeding. Although there are several extruded rabbit feeds produced in Europe (e.g., Burgess Supa Rabbit Excel®), I am only aware of one that is readily available in the United States: Kaytee® Exact Rainbow. One disadvantage is that these feeds are more expensive than regular pellets.

Vegetables are yet another topic on which all rabbit experts and caretakers do not agree. Although safe vegetables, especially dark leafy greens, are a valuable foodstuff, there are rabbits who appear unable to tolerate them in large amounts, if at all. Some veterinarians believe that getting a rabbit to tolerate greens is simply a matter of introducing them into the diet correctly, i.e., very slowly, one vegetable at a time, starting with very small amounts and slowly adding more as the rabbit's digestive flora alter to accommodate the new food. Other veterinarians believe that some rabbits have a genetic intolerance to fresh greens. My personal opinion: it depends on the rabbit. I believe some rabbits can come to tolerate greens by introducing them slowly into the diet and that others have a genetic intolerance. Rabbits are individuals.

Whether or not to give fruit and grains is also debated. Some experts feel the carbohydrate content of both is much too high. Others feel that fruit in particular is usually well-tolerated in small amounts and will not cause digestive upsets. There has even been some research done from which one could conclude that pectin, consumed in small amounts, may have a beneficial effect on digestion. I believe the key with both fruits and grains is the amount given to the rabbit. I do believe it is safest to give both these foods to rabbits only in small amounts, as a treat. I give my rabbits about a tablespoon of fruit per five pounds of rabbit each day. Occasionally, I will give about ½ teaspoon of oatmeal to a rabbit for a treat, or give it to an anorexic rabbit I cannot coax to eat anything else.

There are two last important points about diet. One is that *any* changes to a rabbit's diet, whether in kind or quantity, need to be made very slowly. The digestive systems of rabbits depend upon microflora that are specific for each foodstuff consumed. They need time to adjust. Changes that are made too rapidly can lead to serious imbalances (dysbiosis). The second point is that a rabbit's nutritional needs will change, depending upon age and health. You must keep watching your rabbit, and not think because a diet is successful now it can remain the same all of his or her life.

Probiotics

Probiotics are foods or medications containing live microorganisms (e.g., *Lactobacillus acidophilus)* that are expected to benefit the animal that consumes them. Usually these are microbes that are not normally present in a rabbit's digestive tract. Although it is widely accepted that rabbits can benefit from probiotics, there have been few studies done on the actual effects of these microbes, in rabbits or in other species.

It should be realized that the issue of probiotics is one that, at the time of this writing, is still not fully understood or adequately researched. Some veterinarians do recommend giving rabbits probiotics, particularly for various digestive ailments or when giving antibiotics, and caregivers and vets have reported what they interpreted as beneficial results. Although the introduced microbes are not normally found in the rabbit's digestive tract, it is thought that their presence helps produce the environment in which normal digestive flora can thrive, therefore benefiting the rabbit. Yet other veterinarians question whether the introduced microbes even survive passage through the rabbit's acid stomach.

In the one paper I was able to find that attempted to answer the question of whether there was benefit to rabbits from consuming a specific probiotic, the authors concluded that it was possible the probiotic might benefit rabbits under certain conditions. The authors of another paper pointed out that several factors, including the potential of the introduced microbes to become pathogenic, needed to be considered in determining the safety of a probiotic.

My veterinarian, Dr. William Kurmes, suggests that caretakers consider the use of probiotics carefully, especially in severely debilitated rabbits, at least until more studies are done. "It is possible that probiotics can cause infection in severely immunosuppressed humans, and probably in severely stressed or immunosuppressed rabbits as well," he cautions.

Overweight

If one of your rabbits is starting to look pleasingly plump, you might consider talking to your veterinarian about putting your rabbit on a weight-reduction diet. Obese rabbits are at risk for a host of serious diseases and conditions, including:
- Flystrike (from being unable to access cecotrophs)
- Atherosclerosis
- Hepatic lipidosis
- Bone fractures
- Heat stress/stroke
- Urine scald (from being unable to assume correct urination stance)

It is best if a weight-reduction diet is done under the auspices of a veterinarian because of the danger of hepatic lipidosis (Chapter 8). This is much more likely to occur in obese rabbits, and can be rapidly fatal if the process is not halted. Most likely, your veterinarian will have you stop giving treats and slowly reduce the amount of pellets in the rabbit's diet, making sure grass hay is always available. Selected fresh vegetables, especially leafy greens, may be recommended as a part of the diet. Exercise is also impor-

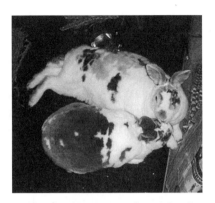

Obesity increases the risk of several serious conditions.

tant. An obese rabbit should be encouraged to move around. If the rabbit has no bonded partner, introducing a friend can help encourage exercise in some cases.

Underweight

A rabbit may lose weight for several reasons, including:
- Stress
- Illness
- Dental disease
- Inadequate nutrition

Stress and dental disease are perhaps the most common causes of weight loss. Severe stress, such as the death of a bonded partner, may be easy to figure out, but smaller stresses can also cause a rabbit to become anorexic (eat less or stop eating). Something as simple as having moved a rabbit's condo can cause enough stress that he or she loses weight. Diseases and other conditions—parasites, dental disease, metabolic issues, kidney disease, cancer—can also be a cause of reduced appetite and weight loss.

The biggest danger for a rabbit who stops eating as much or refuses to eat at all is the development of hepatic lipidosis (Chapter 8). If your rabbit stops eating it is important to contact your veterinarian *right away*.

Disease and stress are not the only causes of weight loss. While I was in the process of writing this book, several very sad cases of underweight rabbits were brought to my attention. These rabbits had turned into literal "bags of bones," and it was not even noticed until it was almost too late (and in a couple of instances the rabbit did in fact die). They were not suffering from a disease such as cancer; they had literally starved to death. Most of these rabbits had been put on a no-pellet diet, and the caretaker, believing they were doing the correct thing, did not realize the rabbit was getting *too* thin.

It is important to me to caution readers about this because I had my own experience with weight loss in my rabbits and realize firsthand how insidious it can be. It was after I had done a lot of reading and been spoken to by some rabbit experts who recommended no or very limited pellets be included in a rabbit's diet. I knew enough about nutrition that I felt some pellets were necessary, but I began to wonder—since I was hearing it from so many—if perhaps I should cut the amount down. So I began to slowly decrease the amount of pellets I gave my rabbits.

A couple of months later, I picked up one of my rabbits to put her in her condo, and noticed her backbone was a bit *too* palpable. I gave her a closer look, and realized she was getting much too thin although she was still eating lots of hay. Concerned, I checked all my other rabbits. Four more were becoming too thin. Out of my fourteen rabbits, only two had benefited from having the amount of pellets they received cut. Five had lost too much weight, and with the others there was no noticeable change.

I should have followed the oft-quoted advice of Kathy Smith regarding diet and rabbits: "If it's not broke, don't fix it." If your rabbit is doing well on a particular diet, don't change it.

Care
If one of your rabbits still has a good appetite but is

feeling a bit light when you lift him or her, and closer inspection shows he or she is losing weight, you might slowly increase the amount of pellets you give, and be sure plenty of good grass hay is always available. Offer a variety of safe fresh vegetables (introducing them slowly, one at a time), especially dark leafy greens. Remember: if the rabbit is getting noticeably thin, has a seriously reduced appetite, or has trouble regaining weight, consult with your veterinarian.

High-fat foods should *not* be given to underweight rabbits, because the rabbit's digestive system is not designed to cope with diets high in fat. Maria L. Perez, the manager of the Las Vegas chapter of the HRS, has had considerable experience with underweight rabbits. She suggests the following:

- Giving probiotics[2]
- Offering a variety of foods (e.g., greens, herbs, oatmeal, favorite treats)
- Mixing alfalfa hay with grass hay
- Hand-feeding
- Presenting food in different ways (e.g., chopped, pureed).

Maria sometimes makes "Punky pellet mush" to coax anorexic rabbits to eat. This is made by softening pellets in warm water and mixing them with canned pumpkin and a little banana. She may also offer "meatballs" made from Critter Be Better® or Critical Care® mixed with a little water. (Note: Rabbits may prefer the taste of one of these supplemental foods to another—if the rabbit won't eat one, try the other.)

Maria concluded her advice by repeating a comment from one of her veterinarians, "It is difficult to put weight on an herbivore," and emphasized that you need to do whatever it takes to coax an anorexic rabbit to eat. Weight loss is a very serious condition in rabbits because its effect on the digestive process can culminate in hepatic lipidosis (Chapter 8) and death if the process is not interrupted.

2 See above section on probiotics earlier in this chapter.

CHAPTER 4

INFECTIONS AND INFESTATIONS

Lucile C. Moore

Rabbits are susceptible to a variety of bacterial, viral, and parasitic infections. For some of these it will only be necessary to provide the rabbits special care for a limited time until they recover; others, such as encephalitozoonosis (EC), may require the rabbits be given special care for life.

Abscesses

Abscesses, localized collections of pus, are common in rabbits and difficult to treat successfully. Rabbit abscesses become encapsulated, and the pus tends to be very thick. Both these factors make the abscesses resistant to penetration by antibiotics. Rabbit abscesses are most often found on the head and limbs, but may also occur elsewhere, including on internal organs. They frequently extend to underlying tissues and bone, and if this happens the prognosis is more guarded. Signs of abscesses are variable. The rabbit may show no signs of pain and eat well, or may exhibit any combination of the following:

- Anorexia
- Observable swelling at site of abscess

• Loss of weight
• Lameness

Abscesses often develop in association with tooth problems (Chapter 7). They may also be associated with bite wounds, bone fractures, and foreign bodies in the mouth or nose, and they may also be a result of the spread of a bacterial infection through the blood to internal organs. Abscesses in

Roy recovered from a testicular abscess.

a joint will cause the joint to swell and the rabbit will probably develop a limp. Internal abscesses may occur around the heart, lungs, in the chest cavity, or on other organs. X-rays will be necessary to assess joint abscesses, and may help reveal the location of internal abscesses in some cases. Abscesses forming on the lungs may cause respiratory problems, but sometimes these internal abscesses will cause few problems until the rabbit is stressed or given anesthesia for another medical condition. Once abscesses spread through the bloodstream and become established in multiple locations, they are extremely difficult to treat. Whenever possible, culture and sensitivity tests should be done on abscesses, as a variety of bacteria may be present and will respond to different antibiotics.

Treatment

Many veterinarians report that lancing and draining abscesses is rarely an effective treatment in rabbits. Complete removal, taking large margins, packing with an antibiotic material, and following the surgery with a minimum of two weeks of antibiotic therapy (especially bicillin) is often the preferred protocol. If excision is not possible, as is common with foot and dental abscesses, both bone and soft tissue are thoroughly debrided, that is, as much of the pus and infected tissue, including bone, is removed as is possible. The area may then be packed with an antibiotic-impregnated material, providing a concentration of antibiotic at the site of the infection. Packing abscesses with antibiotic-impregnated polymethylmethacrylate (AIPMMA) beads is one method. The beads may be used alone or in conjunction with antibiotic therapy of two to six weeks. Amputation can be an effective treatment for abscesses in joints or limbs, if the infection has not spread.

Over the past several years, bicillin therapy has been increasingly prescribed following surgical removal of rabbit abscesses. Some veterinarians report the results are best when the bicillin is given for a period of eight to twelve weeks. Bicillin therapy alone has also been reported effective in treating cases of chronic abscesses and internal abscesses.

Retrobulbar abscesses, or abscesses behind the eye, are not uncommon in rabbits. Although they are most often associated with dental disease, this is not always the case. I found one of my own rabbits with his eyeball bulging partway out of the socket. The exophthalmos (bulging eye) turned out to be caused by an abscess behind the eye. There was no sign teeth were involved. I had two choices: to have the eye enucleated (removed) to make a more aggressive treatment of the abscess possible, or to try antibiotic therapy alone. Because teeth were not involved, I chose to try antibiotic therapy alone. He was put on bicillin and Baytril® for several weeks, the eye returned to a more normal position in the socket, and so far the abscess has not recurred.

Abscesses do tend to recur in rabbits, although if the abscess is well-encapsulated and the initial treatment is done before any spread has occurred, it is possible it will not recur. Abscesses that are not well-encapsulated increase the danger of the infection spreading. Some rabbits with chronic abscesses live fairly long lives without any obvious symptoms, although they may have subclinical infections of the lungs, kidneys, and heart and may need repeated surgeries and long-term antibiotic therapy. Very rarely, chronic abscesses may disappear. Also rarely, a rabbit may die suddenly from septicemia caused by the abscesses.

Respiratory Conditions

A host of different medical conditions may cause respiratory problems in rabbits, including obesity, EC, herpes, heat stroke, inhaled irritants, foreign bodies lodged in the nasal cavity, tumors, trauma, exposure to irritants, allergies, abscesses, bacteria, myxomatosis, and cardiomyopathy. Respiratory infections may occur in any rabbit, but older rabbits and permanently special needs rabbits will be more prone to them as they often have compromised immune systems and do not get the exercise that contributes to a healthy respiratory system. Symptoms of a respiratory problem can include:

- Nasal discharge
- Labored breathing
- Ocular discharge
- Anorexia
- Fatigue
- Sneezing
- Snoring
- Cyanosis

Open-mouth breathing is always a danger sign in rabbits (obligate nose breathers) and the rabbit may require oxygen or the immediate removal of an airway obstruction.

Infections can occur in the upper (nose) or lower (lungs) respiratory tract.

Upper Respiratory Infections (URIs, Snuffles, Rhinitis)

Bacteria multiply in the nose, causing a discharge that is at first runny and clear, then thicker and yellowish. The rabbit will often paw at his nose, wiping the discharge over his face and feet, where it will crust. If the infection is caught in the initial stages, it is easier to treat. In more advanced stages, the bacteria are not as responsive to antibiotic therapy and the infection may never be cured, although the symptoms may be controlled. Respiratory infections of the upper respiratory tract spread from the nose to the sinuses, the nasolacrimal duct, eyes, Eustachian tubes, middle ear, and finally to the lungs.

In the past, it was recommended that deep nasal swabs be done for culture and sensitivity. However, this technique is extremely stressful to the rabbit—many of whom resist the procedure and have to be sedated—and the usefulness of the technique is now being questioned by many veterinarians, one of whom states that deep nasal cultures rarely are of clinical significance. Although *Pasteurella multocida* is the most common bacteria found in respiratory disease, other bacteria, including *Staphylococcus aureus*, *Pseudomonas* spp., *Moraxella catarrhalis,* and *Bordetella bronchiseptica* may be found, as well as fungi, and it is likely that disease is caused by several organisms at the same time. For this reason, many rabbit vets now avoid doing deep nasal swabs and recommend using broad-spectrum antibiotics to treat upper respiratory infections in rabbits.

Chloramphenicol, some fluoroquinolones, azithromycin, penicillin, and sulfonamides (Tribrissen®) have been reported to treat various respiratory infections successfully. In printed veterinary conference notes, Dr. Jerry LaBonde suggests that antibiotics should be given for at least 21 days when treating URIs.

It is important to keep rabbits suffering from respiratory ailments clean. Rabbits with snuffles may have difficulty grooming themselves properly—if they can't breathe well they will have difficulty grooming because it will be hard for them to breathe and groom at same time. The exudates that tend to accumulate on the face and paws will need to be gently wiped off.

It is also important to keep the membranes in the nasal passages moist. This can be done by giving the rabbit more fluids, doing steam therapy, and by nebulizing medications. Rabbits with snuffles can often be helped with a simple home humidifier, or even by placing the rabbit in a steam-filled bathroom for a few minutes.

Pneumonia

Pneumonia is an infection within the thoracic cavity (lower respiratory tract). It frequently follows infections of the upper respiratory tract. In rabbits, abscesses may develop around the lungs or heart with pneumonia. Signs of pneumonia include anorexia, weight loss, depression, fatigue, and labored breathing (dyspnea). Although the bacteria most often found in cases of pneumonia in rabbits is *P. multocida*, the assumption cannot be made that it is the causal organism. Other bacteria that may cause pneumonia in rabbits are *Mycobacterium, Francisella, Yersinia, Moraxella catarrhalis*, and *Escherichia coli*.

The treatment protocol will often include fluid therapy, antibiotics, and nebulization or steam therapy. Nebulizers may be used as the most effective means of delivering the medication to the site of infection (Chapter 2).

Other Infectious Causes of Respiratory Disease

For myxomatosis and herpes, see viral disease section later in this chapter.

Additional Respiratory Ailments

Obesity. Excess weight is not an uncommon cause of respiratory problems. An obese rabbit's fat may literally squash the lungs, making it difficult for the rabbit to breathe. These rabbits may require nebulization to dilate their lungs and help them breathe better while they are put on a long-term weight-loss diet. Weight reduction in rabbits must be done very slowly to be safe (Chapter 3). Care is likely to focus on giving medications, and monitoring the rabbit's signs and food/water intake. Maria Perez, chapter manager of the Las Vegas HRS, has two rabbits she treats for respiratory ailments. One of the rabbits is obese, and the fat presses the lungs enough that she has to be given a bronchodilator and also be given oxygen two to three times a week.

Cancer. When cancers metastasize they may reach the lungs. As the tumors grow, it will become harder and harder for the rabbit to breathe. Antibiotics and bronchodilators

Chloe relaxes with a friend.

may help the rabbit temporarily. Maria Perez's other rabbit with a respiratory problem is Chloe, who has a slow-growing lung cancer. Maria nebulizes Chloe two or three times a day. See Chapter 2 for information on nebulizing rabbits, and Chapter 8 for more information on cancer in rabbits.

Trauma. A fairly common cause of trauma-caused respiratory problems in rabbits is from inhalant anesthesia (endotracheal intubation).

Another common trauma-caused respiratory injury is from foreign material (such as hay) getting stuck in the rabbit's nose or windpipe. A rabbit with something stuck in his nostril will paw at his nose constantly, trying to remove the obstruction. If you notice such pawing, and only one side of the rabbit's nose has lots of exudate, this may be a sign of a grass seed or similar obstruction in the nostril. If you cannot see it and remove it easily yourself, take the rabbit to a vet to have the obstruction removed.

Irritants and allergies. Rabbits are very sensitive to inhaled irritants, and the irritation from these may cause them to be susceptible to bacterial infections. Every effort should be made to avoid these irritants in your rabbit's space. Irritants to a rabbit's respiratory tract include but are not limited to:

- Air fresheners
- Ammonia (from litter boxes)
- Cigarette or wood smoke
- Disinfectants
- Dust from hay and/or bedding
- Paint fumes
- Perfume
- Petroleum-based products (varnishes, strippers, etc.)

True allergies are rare in rabbits, but do occur. Bacterial and other causes are usually ruled out before considering allergies as a cause of a respiratory problem. If an allergy is suspected, it is often treated with antihistamines or corticosteroids. Some vets feel the latter should not be used if the rabbit has chronic pasteurellosis or any other chronic infection, as corticosteroids may cause depression of the immune system.

Some experienced rabbit caregivers and veterinarians recommend giving a mild antihistamine such as Benadryl® to help alleviate the symptoms of environmental irritations and allergies. Discuss the possibility with your veterinarian.

Cardiovascular problems. Respiratory difficulties may occur in older rabbits from cardiomyopathy and arteriosclerosis (Chapter 9). Fluid will collect in the lungs, and it may be possible to hear a wheezing sound when your rabbit breathes. Collapse may occur. Your vet may take

Sweety had a thymoma, a tumor that can cause cardiovascular and respiratory problems as it grows.

X-rays to help confirm a diagnosis of cardiovascular disease.

Bacterial Infections

Pasteurellosis

By far the most common bacteria affecting rabbits, *Pasteurella multocida* can be spread through the air, on objects, or by direct contact with an infected rabbit. Most rabbits have the bacteria in their system, and normally their immune systems keep it in check, but if a rabbit is physically or emotionally stressed, this opportunistic bacteria may multiply out of control and serious infections could develop. Several other factors can predispose a rabbit to developing pasteurellosis, including infection by myxomatosis, corticosteroid use, inhaled irritants such as ammonia, cigarette or wood smoke, air fresheners, petroleum products, and many other stressors.

Multi-rabbit households, sanctuaries, and rabbit rescue centers will be at particularly high risk for the development of pasteurellosis in the rabbits. In these situations, keeping the environment at a steady moderate temperature and between 50%–60% humidity can help prevent its development. In all situations, good sanitation, especially frequent changing of litter, is helpful. Pasteurellosis may occur as:

- Rhinitis (snuffles)
- Dacryocystitis (infection of the nasolacrimal duct)
- Otitis media (infection in middle ear)
- Pneumonia
- Abscesses, including internal ones
- Conjunctivitis (inflammation of membranes of eye)
- Sinusitis (inflammation of sinuses)
- Pleuritis (infection of lining of thorax)
- Pericarditis (inflammation of sac enclosing heart)
- Septicemia (blood poisoning)

Treatment
Infection by *P. multocida* should never be assumed in any of the above cases. Culture and sensitivity tests are necessary for effective treatment. Nebulized antibiotics may be helpful with rhinitis and pneumonia, as this method delivers the antibiotic directly to the site of the problem. Antibiotic therapy may be prescribed from two weeks to three months.

Care
Care for rabbits with pasteurellosis will primarily be supportive; that is, monitoring foods and fluids, giving medications, and keeping the rabbit and his area clean.

Other Bacterial Infections
Staphylococcus aureus may be found in abscesses, rhinitis, ulcerative pododermatitis, and may cause fatal blood poisoning. When *S. aureus* is found in abscesses, it is more resistant to antibiotics. Chloramphenicol, enrofloxacin,and trimethoprim-sulfa have been effective against *S. aureus*. *Bordetella bronchiseptica* is often isolated from rabbits, and although it is not usually pathogenic, it can be, as can *Salmonella*. *B. bronchiseptica* infections in rabbits may be asymptomatic or cause diarrhea, emaciation, and death. *Escherichia coli* can cause serious enteritis in very young rabbits and can be a cause of urinary tract infections. *Moraxella catarrhalis* is an opportunist that may occasionally cause infections in a compromised rabbit, especially rhinitis and conjunctivitis. Your vet will discover if any

Avoid touching a rabbit's eyes to prevent introduction of bacteria and/or viruses.

of these organisms are present by doing culture and sensitivity tests and will then prescribe appropriate antibiotics and any other medications deemed necessary.

The ears are a common site of bacterial infection. Kathy Smith, author of *Rabbit Health in the 21st Century:*

> Some rabbits, especially lops, are prone to chronic ear infections. Lops may be more susceptible because the position of their ears creates a warm, moist environment that encourages growth of bacteria and yeast. Symptoms may include head shaking, ear shaking, sensitivity at the ear base, and/or anorexia (ear pain can become worse when chewing).
>
> It is important to know whether the pathogen is bacteria or yeast because antibiotic therapy is actually one of the *causes* of yeast overgrowth. Cytology (taking a sample from the ear, staining it, and examining under a microscope) may help your veterinarian to quickly determine whether bacteria, yeast, or both are present.
>
> For recurring bacterial infections, it is important to do a culture/sensitivity test since opportunistic bacteria like *Pseudomonas aeruginosa* frequently develop resistance to antibiotics. Baytril® Otic (enrofloxacin/silver sulfadiazine) is often prescribed along with systemic antibiotics. The silver sulfadiazine is effective against both yeast and many types of bacteria.
>
> Miconazole (Conofite®) is sometimes used topically for yeast-only infections. For severe yeast infections, some veterinarians prescribe systemic antifungal medications such as ketoconazole or nystatin.
>
> Some veterinarians have reported success increasing the time between flare-ups

with preventative ear cleanings. TrizEDTA® is an ear-cleaning solution that appears to inhibit the growth of some bacteria including *Pseudomonas*. Zymox® is an enzymatic ear-cleaning solution that also seems to inhibit the growth of both bacteria and yeast.

Viral Infections

Herpes

Between 60%–85% of the adult human population in the United States is infected with herpes simplex I virus, which causes "fever blisters" or "cold sores." Persons carrying this virus or other herpes viruses may not realize that herpes can be transmitted to rabbits, for whom it is a deadly disease. If an active lesion on a person's mouth or elsewhere is touched and the rabbit's face is then caressed, the rabbit may become infected through its nose or eyes. Herpes is rarely external in rabbits, but travels through the optic and olfactory nerves to the brain. It is eventually fatal. A definitive diagnosis of herpes cannot be made on a live rabbit, so a presumptive diagnosis would be made based on neurological symptoms and a history of exposure to a person carrying the virus.

The incidence of this disease in companion rabbits is not known, but since it is likely it is often misdiagnosed, some scientists and veterinarians believe it may be far more common than is realized, especially given the ease with which rabbits contract the virus experimentally. Symptoms of herpes in rabbits include:

- Restlessness
- Circling, spinning
- Sudden running
- Star-gazing (head slightly twisted, eyes staring upwards)
- Respiratory problems
- Seizures

• Coma

Acyclovir and famciclovir have been used to treat suspected infection in rabbits. As in humans, the virus may become latent and reactivate some time after the initial exposure. If you are infected with any kind of herpes virus, observe strict standards of cleanliness at all times, but particularly when you have active lesions. Always wash your hands before handling your rabbit, feeding or watering him, or cleaning his cage.

Myxomatosis

Myxomatosis is caused by a poxvirus that is transmitted through direct contact and by fleas, mosquitoes, fur mites, ticks, and biting flies. Outbreaks in areas where the disease is endemic correspond to times mosquitoes are breeding and active. In the United States, this disease is only endemic to the western coast in California and Oregon. Different strains of the virus have differing virulence. Symptoms include:
  • Swelling of lips, nose, eyelids, base of ears,
    genitals (sometimes with lesions)
  • Discharge from eyes and ears
  • Fever
  • Anorexia
  • Labored breathing
  • Rough coat
  • Lethargy
  • Seizures

Few affected rabbits survive, especially in the US where the endemic strain is more virulent than those strains found in some areas of Europe. However, a few rabbits do survive with intensive nursing care, and some rabbits appear to have a genetic resistance to the disease. The severity of the disease is greater with lower environmental temperatures, so if you have a rabbit with myxomatosis this is one time it is a good idea to increase the temperature of the rabbit's environment to between 80°F and 85°F (21°C–22°C). (Saunders and Davies, in *Notes on Rabbit Internal Medicine*, state that even higher temperatures will increase survival rates.)

Fluids should be given, along with nutritional support (syringe feeding may be necessary) and antibiotics to prevent secondary infections from developing (affected rabbits often develop secondary pasteurellosis). Affected rabbits are also at risk for developing GI hypomotility. Giving NSAIDs can help rabbits with myxomatosis, but corticosteroids should probably not be given because of their suppression of the immune system. The rabbit will need to have his eyes and nose cleaned frequently by the caretaker. If the rabbit recovers, he is likely to have partial or complete immunity to the disease.

Rabbit Calicivirus Disease
(RCD, also called Viral Hemorrhagic Disease, VHD)

RCD will not be discussed in depth in this text, because the virus is almost always fatal and extended care is not an issue. The virus, which has appeared in various locations across the United States, is easily spread through direct (mutual grooming) contact, insect vectors (blowflies that excrete the virus in feces, mosquitoes and fleas that transmit through blood), other mammals (after they eat infected carcasses and shed the virus in feces), and by fomites (objects) such as shoes, clothing, and dishes. The virus can live up to 105 days on cloth. It is inactivated by a 1% solution of sodium hydroxide or a 0.4% solution of formalin.

Rarely, early symptoms of depression, anorexia, and lethargy will be apparent in infected rabbits. More often the rabbit will die suddenly of acute symptoms.

Parasitic Infections

Many rabbits requiring permanent special care will be rabbits with parasitic infections, especially *Encephalitozoon cuniculi*, usually called simply "EC" by rabbit caretakers. Infections by the parasites *Baylisascaris* and *Toxoplasma* are less common, but will also require that intensive nursing care be given to affected rabbits. Ectoparasites, such as mites and maggots, will usually require special care for a short time, although untreated infestations of either—which are occasionally seen by rescue workers—can lead to permanent disability.

Ear Mites

Rabbits' ears may become infested with ear mites, *Psoroptes cuniculi*. Excessive head shaking/scratching and crusted exudates in the ears are usually the first signs noticed by the rabbit caretaker. Those affiliated with shelters or rescue centers may see cases come in where the infestation and crusting extends to the face, dewlap, neck, legs, perineal skin folds, and all the way to the feet. Sometimes bad infestations extend to the ear canal and lead to secondary bacterial infections that eventually cause otitis media, head tilt, and other signs of neurological disease. Infestations will be worse where the environmental conditions include low temperature and high humidity.

Treatment with antiparasitical drugs such as ivermectin or selamectin is usually prescribed. They are often given three times at intervals of two weeks because mites can survive up to three weeks off the host. It is not recommended that crusts be removed initially because this can leave the skin raw and bleeding and be very painful to the rabbit. Pain medications and/or antibiotics may also be prescribed if secondary bacterial infection is present or the rabbit shows signs of being in pain.

If you have other rabbits, you will need to observe very strict sanitation to try and prevent the spread. Some vets recommend treating all the rabbits in a household if one becomes infected.

Fur Mites

Several mites may cause dermatologic problems, especially in those rabbits who are stressed from illness or environmen-

tal factors. Symptoms of an infestation may include:
- Scratching
- Alopecia (fur loss)
- Sores and scabs (particularly on neck)
- Dermatitis and dandruff
- No symptoms (light infestations)

If you look with a magnifying glass, *Cheyletiella parasitovorax,* sometimes called "walking dandruff" may appear as a large, whitish, moving flake. *C. parasitovorax* can also affect humans, dogs, and cats. The true fur mite, *Leporacarus gibbus,* is brown. Eggs of both mites may be seen on hair shafts. Mites may not always be apparent in skin scrapings, however, and many vets will treat for them if clinical signs are present.

Sarcoptes scabiei and *Notoedres cati,* which cause scabies (mange), may also infest rabbits. Infestations by these mites will often result in a crusty dermatitis.

In the chapter "Dermatologic Diseases," from *Ferrets, Rabbits, and Rodents: Clinical Medicine and Surgery,* Hess notes that the mite *Demodex cuniculi,* normally found on rabbits, may cause clinical symptoms in rabbits stressed by illness or environmental factors.

Veterinarians often prescribe either ivermectin or selamectin for infestations of the above mites. Some experienced rabbit caretakers prefer selamectin (Revolution®) to ivermectin for treating the mites, finding it more effective in the long run.

Myiasis

Flystrike is a problem that is often ignored or underestimated by rabbit caretakers. Some simply do not realize the dangers; others think it will not happen if their rabbits are kept indoors. Several conditions predispose rabbits to infestation by fly maggots, including urine scald, obesity, and irritation of the perineal area. Special-needs rabbits are often at high risk of flystrike because of urinary incontinence and an inability to reach their cecotrophs.

Maggots of several different flies may parasitize rabbits. Larvae of three families of flies—the Muscidae (house flies), Calliphoridae (blow flies, including bluebottles and greenbottles), and Sarcophagidae (flesh flies) are responsible for most infestations. Although very rarely these flies may lay eggs on a healthy rabbit's fur, they are usually attracted by a wound or damp, soiled fur. A very diligent rabbit caretaker may notice eggs on the fur, but usually the first signs will be a loss of fur and reddened or infected skin at the perineal area.

Although some rabbits show few symptoms from flystrike, other rabbits may experience depression, pain, weakness, dehydration, and lameness. The greatest danger is that the rabbit may go into shock. Secondary bacterial infections may also occur. If the larvae enter any body opening, they can migrate through the central nervous system, causing neurological signs (head tilt, seizures, etc.).

The treatment for flystrike includes:
• Clipping the fur
• Removing the maggots
• Giving an antiparasitic
• Antibiotic therapy
• Pain medications

Some sources suggest blowing warm air on the rabbit's skin (using a hair dryer set on low) to draw maggots out for easier removal. After all the maggots are removed, the site should be cleaned every day and a cream (e.g., topical silver sulfadiazine) applied. Antiparasitics that may be prescribed by your veterinarian include ivermectin, selamectin, and nitenpyram. Fluid therapy, syringe feeding, and pain medication may be necessary. Some veterinarians have found carprofen to be an effective pain reliever for cases of flystrike.

A topical product to prevent flystrike in rabbits is available in the UK (Rearguard®), but an equivalent product is not yet available in the US. If you have a special-needs rabbit or are giving a rabbit temporary special care, inspect it *twice every day* during fly season and pay close attention to the anal area. Comb the fur with a flea comb to pick up any egg clusters. Control flies. Do not attempt to identify flies, but assume any fly found in an area where rabbits live is a danger and remove it. For those who live in areas with a serious fly problem, biological control such as Spalding Labs' Fly Predators™ (www.spalding-labs.com) may help.

Warbles

Warbles is caused by the larvae of bot flies. Bot flies are flies in four subfamilies of the family Oestridae. These large flies lay eggs near the host (which can also be a cat, dog, or even a person) and when the host passes by, the heat of the passing body stimulates the eggs to hatch and the larvae fall on the host. Each larva will cause a subcutaneous swelling from one to three centimeters across. There may be only one such swelling on the rabbit, or several may be present. If you look closely at one of these swellings, an air hole can be seen in the center, as can the larva itself when it comes up to breathe. Secondary bacterial infections can develop in these larval holes. *Never attempt to remove the larvae from these swellings yourself.* If the larva is crushed or damaged, it releases chemicals that will cause a life-threatening reaction in your rabbit. Symptoms may be few or many, and may include:

- Weakness
- Anorexia
- Dehydration
- Lameness
- Shock

After the veterinarian has removed the larvae, a course of antibiotics will probably be given, along with pain medication. As with the other fly larvae that can parasitize rabbits, these larvae can enter the nose or mouth and travel to the sinuses and through the central nervous system, causing neurological symptoms and death. Check your rabbit's body for swellings once a day during fly season.

Encephalitozoonosis

Encephalitozoon cuniculi is an intracellular protozoan parasite spread primarily through spores in the urine of affected animals. Spores remain infective four weeks, and may be inhaled or ingested. (Mites and fleas can act as vectors, also transmitting the parasite.) The contents of the spores are injected into cells of the host, which eventually rupture, releasing other spores. The body of the rabbit responds to the infection by the creation of antibodies, and lesions called granulomas develop. Granulomas are localized areas of inflammation where the infection is being fought, and are most common in the brain, kidneys, heart, and spinal cord. It is the presence of these granulomas that actually cause most of the symptoms of this illness. If the parasite travels to the middle ear, the accumulating pus and fluid from the granulomas cause the rabbit to twist its head, resulting in the classic EC symptom of head tilt.

Sometimes symptoms of EC may never show, because the immune system of healthy rabbits keeps the infection under control. In other rabbits, symptoms may develop when the rabbit becomes physically or emotionally stressed. Symptoms that may occur include:

- Head tilt
- Rolling
- Head nodding
- Stargazing (head slightly twisted up, eyes staring upwards)
- Nystagmus (uncontrolled movement of eyes)
- Cataracts
- Paralysis/paresis, especially of the hind legs
- Incontinence
- Ataxia (incoordination, weakness)
- Behavioral changes, especially mental impairment

Perry has head tilt.

- Kidney disease
- Seizures
- Tremors

Any combination of these symptoms may occur. A few rabbits with EC may improve without treatment, but most will require medical intervention to limit the spread of the parasite and the damaging granulomas in the body of the rabbit. Without treatment, some rabbits showing symptoms may die or become so ill they need to be euthanized.

If EC is suspected, an antibody titer will likely be done, usually twice, at a two-week interval. A positive titer simply indicates that the rabbit has, at some times in his life, been exposed to the parasite. It does not necessarily mean that neurological symptoms presenting in the rabbit are the result of EC—many healthy rabbits also test seropositive, although two negative titers are usually assumed to mean that any neurological symptoms currently present in the rabbit are *not* caused by EC.

"Serology can be helpful but is far from diagnostic," Frances Harcourt-Brown states in a paper titled *"Encephalitozoon cuniculi* in Pet Rabbits." She further notes that a definitive diagnosis of *E. cuniculi* as the cause of disease is difficult in a live rabbit, and comments on the lack of laboratory studies monitoring antibody titers over the natural lifespan of rabbits, and the question of whether rabbits eventually become seronegative even though they may have residual lesions from the rabbit's immune response to the parasite.

Still, the titers are usually considered the most useful tool for a presumptive diagnosis of EC that is available at the time of this writing. (A test to detect live protozoa is under development and may be available by the time this book is published.) Lacking a better method for determining whether EC is responsible for symptoms, many vets choose to go ahead and treat for EC if the titers show high amounts of EC antibodies.

Some veterinarians feel that EC is probably over-diagnosed in rabbits at this time. Other vets disagree. It is possible that incidence of the disease varies according to geographical region, although in several studies in both the UK and US, around 50% of companion rabbits test positive for antibodies to the parasite.

If EC is suspected, the vet may attempt to rule out other causes of neurological symptoms (Chapter 8) before deciding to treat for EC. Sometimes this can be simple, but unfortunately, some of the other diseases that cause neurological symptoms are also difficult to diagnose with certainty in a live rabbit.

Treatment

The treatment protocol usually consists of giving antiparasitical drugs to eradicate the parasite itself and to give anti-inflammatories to control granulomas caused by the microsporidian. Granulomous lesions may be found in the eyes, kidneys, liver, heart, brain, and elsewhere. It should be noted that killing the parasite does not repair the damage that has already been done by the parasites.

At the time of this writing, the most common treatment for EC is to prescribe a benzimidazole (albendazole, fenbendazole, oxibendazole, thiabendazole, cambendazole). These drugs suppress the rabbit's immune system, so caretakers will need to be on guard for the development of bacterial infections if their veterinarian prescribes one of them. Some vets prescribe an antibiotic such as Baytril® or trimethoprim-sulfa to be taken in conjunction with a benzimidazole. Overall, albendazole has been used more frequently than other benzimidazoles in the US; fenbendazole in the UK (a medication containing fenbendazole that was formulated specifically for rabbits, Lapizole, is marketed by the UK company Genitrix).

A geographical difference may exist in the frequency of benzimidazole use in the US: Kathy Smith, author of *Rabbit Health in the 21st Century,* comments that in her experience, albendazole is prescribed more often in the western US, oxibendazole in the Midwest, and fenbendazole in the East. Ivermectin, anti-dizziness medications such as meclizine, antibiotics (oxytetracycline in particular), and other medications may be prescribed in addition to the benzimidazoles.

There are other medications that are being used to treat EC, although some veterinarians may consider these experimental and resist trying them. One is lufenuron (a chitin inhibitor), which many caretakers of EC rabbits prefer both because they see improvement after the rabbit has been treated with it and because it is given only once or twice a month and is therefore less stressful on the rabbit. Artemisinin (from sweet wormwood) and pyrimethamine, both used to treat malaria in humans, have been used to treat EC in rabbits with reported success. A medication some have claimed has caused "fast and dramatic improvement" in their EC rabbits is ponazuril (Marquis®), commonly used as an antiparasitical for horses.

If your rabbit has EC and is not responding to treatment with benzimidazoles and you wish your vet to consider treatments with one of these lesser-used medications, it might be a good idea to research them on the Internet, print out any trustworthy reports you find, and take them in to your vet. If you can find a vet elsewhere in the US who has successfully used these treatments, see if he/she is available for a phone consultation with your vet.

Care

Rabbits with EC may require anything from a little extra to intensive nursing over a long period of time, depending upon the damage done by the granulomas. Sometimes, the care that is required is for mental incapacity. Donna Jensen, who has cared for special-needs rabbits for over 15 years, has one rabbit, Charlotte, who suffered mental impairment as a result of EC. Donna says Charlotte is similar to a person suffering from Alzheimer's.

Charlotte's greatest pleasure is staring at the garden, so every year Donna plants a garden especially for Charlotte. For many years, Charlotte enjoyed her work as an "educational bunny," joining Donna at nursing homes and schools for informative presentations on rabbits.

Charlotte

Alternative methods of healing (Part II) may be effective for alleviating various EC symptoms. Donna cared for another EC bunny who rolled from head tilt. Acupuncture sessions once every six weeks for balance stopped the bun's rolling.

For a story detailing the care of a presumptive EC rabbit with paralysis, see Kim Clevenger's story at the end of Chapter 6. Patti Henningsen's rabbit, Rebecca, was apparently successfully treated after being given a presumptive diagnosis of EC. Patti tells her unusual story:

> Rebecca is a very special rabbit. She exemplifies the power of positive thinking and not ever giving up. Rebecca is what they call a "Dutch mismark," and she was a stray rabbit living in the backyard of the house we had just bought, our first house. "How appropriate," we thought, as

we had been rescuing rabbits for several years. And we had caught strays in the past. But this was a house in the boonies and there were many places to hide. And Rebecca, or "Blackie" as we then called her, was a stray by choice. She had escaped the negligent care of our neighbors and their two unfriendly dogs. Rebecca is a smart old girl, and she figured out how to

Rebecca, safe and clean in her new home.

live up and down the street and escape capture by us the whole time. We built traps, we tried everything. She was one foxy rabbit. Everyone put out food for her but she would not be caught.

After nearly two years of trying, and the very worst winter and summer on record—with three feet of snow one winter and 104-degree days for weeks on end one summer—she was still a stray. We would sit inside and think "I wonder how Blackie is doing. Is she OK?" and worry. I used to tell her, "Blackie, if you ever need anything, you come and see us."

Then the 9th of November 2004, I left in the morning to do a leg of rescue transport and there she was lying under the crab apple tree. In a hurry, I noted it and left. She had been so close so many times before, sitting just on the other side of the fence in the neighbor's yard while my pointer/collie mix bayed at her like a rabid coonhound. But when I returned many, many hours later, she still lay there. I ran inside and told my husband, "Blackie's lying under the crab apple tree and she's sick!" We seized the moment, surrounded her by an exercise pen and brought her inside. Once there, I hydrated her and fed her and began to spoil her like she had never known. Early veterinary assessment showed she was anorexic, or "cachexic" as they said. She just could not gain weight. Finally, after almost a year, she worsened and became paralyzed in her hind legs.

At that point I took her to Dr. Lisa Carr (then of Kentlands Veterinary Hospital, now of Stahl's Exotic Animal Veterinary Services— SEAVS—in Vienna, Virginia), who sent for an *E. cuniculi* titer. It came back very high, and Dr. Carr told me of a new treatment for EC shown to be very promising, a 30-day treatment with fenbendazole (not albendazole or oxibendazole). She also put her on Baytril® for the 30 days, and I told Dr. Carr that I wanted to add to this an anti-protozoan herbal tincture from a woman who treated animals allopathically.

Concurrently though, we did buy Rebecca (Blackie was not a lady's name, and actually we morphed both into the nickname "Bleckie") a wheelchair. She hated nothing more in the world than that wheelchair. But I put her in it while I gave her the regimen of fenbendazole, Baytril®, and EC tincture. I also did a sort of physical therapy on her (massage is counter-indicated with this type of infection). I would lay her on the bed on her side and put my palm against her hind foot and

In the hated "wheelchair."

push it in towards her body as if she were getting ready to thump. At first she had no reaction, but after a week or more into the therapy, there started to be some resistance. After nearly four weeks of all of this—wheelchair, medicines, and PT, there was a marked resistance in her hind feet. And then ever so slowly, by the end of the whole treatment, she started to make the effort to hop. It was pathetic to watch at first, but this gal, our little "hobo" as we would call her, had a will-to-be and a will-to-hop like I had never seen.

Of course, we were extremely close during this period. We would watch long "chick flicks" together. She especially liked ones where couples would argue, during which she would turn to me and try to thump; she would just give me the most expressive head turn a rabbit ever did. And all the while, I'd be pushing my palm on her hind feet. I believe the combination of all of this, our very close relationship, the time and love, the medicine and tincture, the hate of the wheelchair, and the appreciation, on her part, of being a house rabbit as opposed to a "street" rabbit, gave her the sheer willpower to tell that insidious protozoan to scram and it did.

A month or so after treatment had begun, Rebecca was hobbling around on all fours. Within two months, as very well documented by Dr. Carr and the entire staff at the hospital, she could walk again. And by about two to three months later, she was hopping on the bed (may I mention that it

Rebecca hops onto the bed.

is a double-pillow-top and very high bed?) and chewing my sheets (see picture of her sitting on the bed after hopping up there on her own for the first time). I try to tell everyone who has an EC bunny about all the things involved with her success, but mostly it falls on deaf ears. This is one case that cannot be denied, however. Rebecca triumphed, and a vet from one of the most respected veterinary clinics in the country can attest to it. So there! The little stray from Sherman Avenue turned out to be a Sherman tank and to this day, she continues to inspire me and be one of my very best friends in the universe.

Raccoon Roundworm (Cerebral larval migrans)
More threatening to a rabbit's life than EC is an infection by the intestinal nematode *Baylisascaris procyonis*, or the raccoon roundworm. (Nematodes affecting skunks and weasels will also parasitize rabbits in a similar fashion and with the same prognosis.) If raccoon feces should somehow contaminate the feed, hay, or bedding of your rabbit and

subsequently be ingested, your rabbit can be parasitized by this nematode. This is more likely to occur if you live where there is a population of raccoons, although imported feed or bedding contaminated with raccoon feces could potentially be infective—the eggs remain viable up to a year or even longer. Persons involved with rabbit rescue may see cases of roundworm, because rabbits that have been dumped in the country where raccoons live are especially at risk.

Once they have been ingested by a rabbit, the eggs hatch and the larvae migrate through the body, eventually reaching the brain. Symptoms of *B. procyonis* infection include:

- Head tilt
- Circling
- Rolling and falling
- Incoordination
- Tremors
- Nystagmus (uncontrolled movement of eyes)
- Paralysis
- Seizures

The damage caused by the nematode is permanent, even if the parasite is killed. It is theoretically possible for the rabbit to survive if the parasite is killed before the disease has progressed very far, but any damage that has already occurred will remain. Treatment with oxibendazole has been reported to be successful in slowing the progression of presumptive *B. procyonis* infection in some cases, but for severely affected rabbits the most humane choice may be euthanization.

Toxoplasmosis

This may occur in households with cats. It is more likely to be a problem in a chronically ill rabbit, and is included for that reason. The parasite *Toxoplasma gondii* is a protozoan. Rabbits could potentially contract this parasite should they consume hay, feed, or bedding contaminated with infected cat feces or should they step into cat feces and then clean their feet. Cat feces must be at least two days old to be infective.

Infection in rabbits is usually subclinical; that is, symptoms will not be seen. Younger rabbits or rabbits with compromised immune systems from other diseases may become clinical, or exhibit symptoms. These symptoms may include:

- Anorexia
- Incoordination
- Fever
- Lethargy
- Muscle tremors
- Seizures
- Posterior paresis (weakness) or paraplegia
- Quadriplegia

Treatment

If toxoplasmosis is suspected, a blood test will be done to determine if the rabbit has been exposed to the organism. According to most sources, this parasitic infection appears to respond best to potentiated sulfonamides such as trimethoprim-sulfa, pyrimethamine, and doxycycline.

CHAPTER 5

SPRAINS, DISLOCATIONS, FRACTURES, AND PODODERMATITIS

Lucile C. Moore

After the ears, a rabbit's legs are probably his most distinguishing physical feature, with the huge, powerful hindquarters and smaller, even delicate-looking, forelimbs. But the combination of a relatively light skeleton with powerful muscles predisposes rabbits to both fractures and dislocations. Most people who share their lives with rabbits will at one time or another encounter a problem with some form of limb injury.

Sprains and Strains

A sprain is the tearing or stretching of a ligament or tendon near a joint. Sometimes the term "sprain" is used specifically for injuries to a ligament, and injuries to a tendon are called "strains." Possible symptoms of such an injury in your rabbit would be a limp and signs of pain. Should you observe these signs in your rabbit you cannot assume it is a sprain or strain, however, as rabbits with fractures or dislocations may also limp. It will be necessary to take the rabbit to your vet and have X-rays (radiographs) done. If it does turn out the injury is a sprain or strain, cage rest and medication for pain is usually all the treatment that is necessary. The rabbit would also need to be monitored for any signs of intestinal slowdown as a result of the injury (Chapter 3).

Occasionally, a caretaker may be puzzled and concerned to find a rabbit's toe sticking straight up. According to Dr. Bill Guerrera:

> [This is] most likely damage to the flexor tendon or collateral ligament. These seldom heal because of poor blood supply to ligaments and tendons. If they are not painful and do not cause locomotion problems I leave them alone and call it "character."

Dislocations (Luxations)

Rabbits are prone to dislocations, or luxations, as your veterinarian may call them. Technically, these are injuries to the connective tissue that actually holds a joint in place. Rarely, a vertebral luxation or subluxation (partial dislocation, misalignment) may occur in the spine, causing paralysis of the hindquarters (Chapter 6). More common in rabbits are dislocations of the hip and "knee." These may occur as the result of trauma or from a rabbit struggling while being held improperly without support to the hindquarters. Dislocations have also occurred from a child pulling on a rabbit's leg. Symptoms of leg joint luxations include:

- Limping
- Swollen joint
- Pain

An X-ray is usually necessary for diagnosis. The goal in treating a luxation is to reduce (restore to normal position) the joint and keep it stabilized while scar tissue forms and helps hold the joint in place. A reduced luxation can often be held in place by a bandage, lightweight leg splint, or a rod. Occasionally, they must be held in place by a pin inserted through the joint before the limb is splinted. Pins are normally removed after about three weeks; the splint after an additional two or three weeks.

At times, a dislocation can heal without pinning or splinting. In one case, a rabbit with a dislocated leg was placed in a small pen and allowed only very restricted exercise for several months. Slowly, the rabbit healed and regained normal mobility.

Unfortunately, dislocations in rabbits have a tendency to recur. Arthroplasty can be one solution to a hip dislocation that recurs. This is where the head of the femur (leg bone) is removed so there is no longer a "ball and socket" joint, and the muscle is stitched to hold the hip in place. The leg may need to be manipulated to prevent the muscles remaining in a contracted position. Pain medications and a course of antibiotics will also likely be prescribed.

Care
Care of rabbits with joint luxations will vary, but may include:

- Administration of antibiotics and/or analgesics
- Monitoring food and water intake
- Watching for signs of gastrointestinal disturbances
- Limiting activity
- Massage
- Keeping the perineal area clean and dry if incontinence is present

It can be a good idea to limit the rabbit's space as well as his activity to prevent the limb from becoming re-injured. If the floor is smooth, adding a straw mat or another type of nonslip surface will also help. See Chapters 1 and 2 for more care hints.

Fractures
Rabbit bones are relatively brittle, and fractures (breaks or cracks) are not uncommon. Possible causes are legion: a rab-

bit's leg or foot may get caught in cage wire and the bone snap when the rabbit struggles to get free, the rabbit may be accidentally stepped on or shut in a door, an object might fall on the rabbit, or the rabbit may kick hard enough while being held improperly to break the spine. Old age, a lack of calcium in

Solomon came through successful surgery for a broken jaw.

the diet (unusual except in rabbits receiving no commercial pellets in their diet), and not enough exercise will make a rabbit even more susceptible to fractures. The good news is that rabbit bones heal quickly, often within three weeks (method of treatment may extend this healing time).

A rabbit who has a limb fracture will favor that limb. If the rabbit favors the leg and limps, but can still take some weight on it, it may be fractured, dislocated, or sprained. It may dangle, in which case it is most likely broken. A broken toe is less obvious and may go unnoticed. A rabbit with a broken spine may be able to move his legs slightly, but will more than likely be unable to move his hind legs and will drag himself by the front limbs or be reluctant to move at all (Chapter 6). Signs of pain will usually be present. A fracture requires emergency care if:

- There is bleeding.
- The rabbit is in shock.
- Spinal damage is suspected.
- The rabbit is in respiratory distress.

Although the sight of a rabbit's leg dangling uselessly is very distressing, most limb fractures that have not broken the skin do not require immediate emergency care (although the sooner a fracture is stabilized the better the prognosis).

If your rabbit does not display any of the above symptoms suggesting he needs emergency care, and you suspect he has broken a bone:

- Keep the rabbit as immobile as possible by confining him to a small cage or padded box.
- Determine if the fracture is open (the skin is broken) or closed (no visible outside wound).
- Arrange for the rabbit to see a veterinarian as soon as possible.
- Monitor the rabbit for signs of shock and respiratory distress. If these occur, obtain emergency care immediately.
- Do not attempt to set a bone yourself or try to push a protruding piece of bone back under the skin.

Fractures are classified in several different ways in order to determine the best course of treatment. A *closed* fracture is one in which the skin is not broken. In an *open* (compound) fracture the skin is broken, exposing the wound to the environment and increasing the danger of infection. Fractures occurring beneath the elbow are more likely to be open fractures because there is little soft tissue over the bones. (LaBonde, in conference notes titled "Rabbit Medicine and Surgery," recommends that vets wait 72 hours before doing surgery on fractures beneath the elbow, because of the risk of bone death due to poor blood supply that is a possibility in such fractures.) A *comminuted* fracture is one in which the bone is splintered, or has more than two broken pieces. Because rabbit bones tend to shatter easily, many fractures are both comminuted and contaminated. These are very prone to osteomyelitis, or infection of the bone, and require the administration of antibiotics.

Open fractures are further classified into grades. In a grade I fracture the bone has penetrated the skin but there is little soft-tissue damage. A grade II fracture has external damage to the soft tissues, and a grade III fracture is one in which there is considerable soft-tissue destruction and bone contamination.

The goal in treating a fractured limb is to:
- Remove any foreign material and dead tissue (debride)
- Restore alignment (reduce)
- Immobilize the bone until healing can take place (stabilize)
- Treat or prevent bacterial infections
- Provide pain relief

The veterinarian will manipulate the bones to restore alignment and then hold them in place by a splint, pins through the bone, or plates. Most often, pinning is the method of choice. Rarely, and usually for larger rabbits, the bones are held in place by plates.

Splints, Casts, and Slings

Rabbits are difficult to splint because of the shape of their limbs, their active nature, and their tendency to chew on casts, so pinning a fracture is probably the most common treatment. However, in cases where the fracture is closed or a grade I open fracture, reduction and splinting can be a less invasive and less costly alternative if you have the time to nurse the rabbit. In some cases, the location of a fracture or the size of the rabbit—fractures in smaller rabbits can be more difficult to treat—may prevent use of a splint, and a sling may be used instead. The

Ruby's broken leg was stabilized with a sling over her hip.

splint and cast should be made of hard material the rabbit will not chew. An E-collar placed around the neck can help keep a rabbit from chewing on a cast, but many rabbits become so stressed by the presence of the collar that they have to be removed. If the fracture is above the elbow, a splint should go over the shoulder or hip, and this is difficult in rabbits.

Suzanne Pani, who has rescued many rabbits, has had three rabbits with broken toes. She took them to three different vets, and all three set the foot differently. However, in each case little splints covering the back of the foot were devised for the rabbits. Suzanne reports that when the splints were removed after about a month, the rabbits were fine.

Because rabbit bones heal so quickly, the length of time a cast or sling is left is critical. If left on too long, scar tissue may develop clear to the bone and cause permanent lameness. Four to six weeks are usually adequate for a stabilized fracture to heal enough to take weight, depending on the age and health of the rabbit.

The caretaker will need to watch for any swelling caused by a too-tight cast, soiling, and/or pressure sores. The rabbit should be confined to a small area, and not allowed to be too active while healing is taking place. Pain medications and/or antibiotics may need to be administered.

No Stabilization

Occasionally, a veterinarian will recommend doing nothing for a fracture except keeping the rabbit quiet, relatively immobile, and pain free, allowing the break to heal on its own. This might be suggested in cases where the fracture is a hairline fracture, involves a bone that is supported by another bone, or in cases where the break is in a location that is difficult to immobilize. A person's financial situation may also affect whether this suggestion is made. Although some method of stabilization is generally preferred, allowing a break to heal on its own can be successful under some circumstances.

Dr. Jason Sulliban had one case of a fractured femur in a rabbit where the client's situation did not allow her to consider other, more expensive or care-intensive treatments:

> The fracture was already three to four days old when I saw the rabbit. We put him in a very small cat carrier to minimize the use of the leg. It didn't heal ideally, but it healed.

Dr. Jamie Sulliban commented that she has chosen the option of doing "nothing" at times for toe fractures or for other minor fractures. "Sometimes it is an option, but it is not ideal," the doctors concurred.

Pinning

Most likely, a veterinarian will recommend pinning a limb fracture, and in grade II or III fractures, external fixation by pins or plates may be necessary for the best chance of healing. In this method pins are placed through the bone to hold pieces in a position for maximum healing potential. Pins have an advantage over other methods of stabilization because they share the load with the bone so the bone does not take all the rabbit's weight. Because of the small size of rabbit bones, very small, smooth intramedullary pins (threaded or partially threaded pins may cause damage) are used. For very small rabbits, a hypodermic needle may be used to pin a fracture. According to Kapatkin, in the chapter on orthopedics in *Ferrets, Rabbits, and Rodents: Clinical Medicine and Surgery*, three pins should be placed per segment if possible, angling them to prevent pullout, and inserted at low rotational speed. (A single pin may not be sufficient to hold the bone in place, and manual insertion of pins may cause wobble, leading to pin loosening.)

The pins are usually held in place with external fixators placed about one centimeter from the skin. (Kapatkin suggests that external fixator clamps and bars should not be used, and comments that bone cement and acrylics made into bars works better because they resist chewing.) The external fixators are normally removed after four to six weeks, although the age and health of the rabbit, among other factors, may affect the timing. However, if the fixators are left in too long (12+ weeks), the strength of the bone will be less than if they are removed earlier. Pinned fractures will need to be checked about every two weeks for pin loosening.

Although pins are often the method of choice at this time, many rabbit caretakers have reported problems with them. Some of these problems may occur from the method of placement (manual insertion not being recommended), and from using too few pins—three per segment, spread evenly over the fractured segment, is usually recommended, when possible. Dr. Bill Guerrera explains:

> [Using a single pin] is never ideal because it only stabilizes bending forces, and does not control rotational forces. However, if this was a young (bone regeneration is faster in younger animals), otherwise healthy rabbit with an oblique fracture—minimizes rotation—it would most likely heal normally if a splint was also used. In general, any stabilization would help control pain and increase the likelihood of healing.

Plating

Bone plating is rarely done for rabbits because of the small size of their bones. However, according to Redrobe, in the chapter "Surgical Procedures and Dental Disorders" in the first edition of the *Manual of Rabbit Medicine and Surgery*, plates made for human fingers can be utilized.

With fractures in larger rabbits and open breaks of the humerus or femur, plates can be used to stabilize the fracture. Care must be taken in screwing the plates in, because of the brittleness of a rabbit's bones. (Plates also prevent load sharing, may delay healing, and may contribute toward nonunion.) They are normally removed after six to eight weeks.

Excision Arthroplasty

Arthroplasty may be done for fractures as well as dislocations. In an online article appearing on the Rabbit Charity website, Bailey describes doing an excision arthroplasty as for a cat on a rabbit. The decision to try the procedure was made because immobilization of the fracture site was likely to be difficult, as was limiting the rabbit's activity. The arthroplasty was reported to be successful.

Medications

It is important that a rabbit with a fracture be given pain medication, especially for the first week. A stronger pain medication such as an opioid may be needed the first few days; NSAIDs are usually sufficient afterwards. Pain medication can be reduced after this time, but continue to monitor the rabbit for signs of pain and resume pain meds if he appears to be suffering.

With open fractures, a course of antibiotics will be prescribed to minimize the risk of infections developing. Rabbits with open fractures are at high risk of developing abscesses and osteomyelitis, or infection of the bone. The prognosis for both of these conditions is poor, so keeping the rabbit on the full course of antibiotics prescribed is critical.

Complications

There are several complications that may develop with fractures:

- *Delayed union*—healing takes longer than expected. Determine cause.
- *Nonunion*—no bridging of fracture. Additional surgery is called for, possibly including bone grafts.
- *Malunion*—bone heals in abnormal position. This is usually caused by improper alignment or a shift out of alignment. It is not always necessary to correct a malunion.
- *Abscesses*—it is not uncommon for abscesses

to develop where facture occurred.

- *Posttraumatic osteomyelitis*—infection of the bone, often with *Pseudomonas*. Open fractures are at especially high risk. Treatment is difficult and amputation may eventually be necessary.

Care

Care for rabbits with fractures will vary depending on the method used to fix the fracture. In general:

- Give the complete course of antibiotics, especially in cases of open fracture.
- Keep rabbit confined and quiet.
- Control pain, especially the first week.
- Although not all experts agree on the necessity, caretakers may choose to collect and feed the rabbit his cecotrophs if he can't reach them himself.
- Watch for soiling if the rabbit can't clean his hindquarters himself.
- Monitor food and fluids and watch for signs of stasis developing.
- Watch for complications of the fracture, including swelling, pin loosening, abscesses, malunion (not in correct position), and bandage chewing.

Manipulating and exercising limbs healing from fracture may not be a good idea, so do not do this unless it is recommended by your veterinarian. The authors of one study concluded that

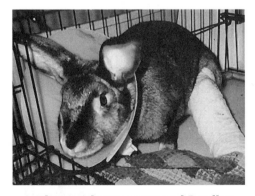

Anthony tolerates cast and E-collar.

exercised joints were stiffer than those left alone, and that passive exercise additionally traumatized the healing tissues around fractures.

Once the cast is removed, you will need to watch the bottom of your rabbit's feet for hairless, reddened spots and fur wear. Sometimes these will occur if the bone was not aligned perfectly or came slightly out of alignment during treatment and healing. To prevent such spots from developing into open ulcers, a piece of moleskin can be placed on the worn spot, or New-Skin® brush-on liquid bandage can be applied.

Amputations

Rabbits adapt fairly well to amputations, especially if they have three legs remaining and the amputated limb is a rear limb. Amputations are usually performed as a last resort to save the life of the rabbit in the cases of severe ulcerative pododermatitis, osteomyelitis, tumors, complex fractures, and septic arthritis. Bone cancer in a limb, because it is slow to metastasize, may often be treated successfully by amputation, although one veterinarian recommends radiographs be done first to be sure the cancer has not metastasized to the lungs. Amputations may also be an alternative in cases where a person is unable to afford expensive surgeries even if they are likely to save the limb. Missy Ott, an educator with the HRS, has found that the younger the rabbit the better he will adjust to an amputation. In her experience, rabbits one year and under will adapt quickly and well to amputations while those over a year old take considerably more time.

However, there may be alternatives to amputation in some cases. When it was discovered that Joe Marcom's foster rabbit, Sugarplum, had osteomyelitis in her right ankle, amputation at the hip was recommended. Joe was unable to accept this.

Instead, we went with long-term antibiotic therapy: Chloramphenicol sub-Q every 12

Sugarplum

hours, and Pen-G sub-Q every other day for six months.

One week after ending the treatment, she had a follow-up exam, which showed no pain and swelling. Although the foot is pointed outward, she has full use of the leg, which she had kept drawn up tight against her body before treatment began.

Procedure

Muscles are removed from the farther limb by cutting through the tendons. The bone is then cut with a high-speed saw (rabbit bones shatter easily and cutters can't be used). The end of the bone is plugged with bone wax, and a cushion of muscles is made for the stump. Forelimb amputations are usually done at the shoulder. If the scapula is removed, the rabbit looks more pleasing, but some veterinarians prefer to leave the scapula to provide some protection to the chest area. Hind limb amputations are usually done mid-thigh rather than at the hip joint. The stump is left to protect the perineal area and genitalia.

Tail amputations are occasionally done in older rabbits, excessively obese rabbits, or disabled rabbits who develop severe urine scald due to their inability to adopt normal stance to urinate.

Possible Complications

If the rabbit is a very active one, the bone could penetrate through the skin if an amputation was done through a limb rather than by disarticulating a joint.

Sore hocks (pododermatitis) can develop due to changes in how weight is born on remaining limbs. See following section.

Ulcerative Pododermatitis

Pododermatitis, frequently called sore hocks (although the hocks are not involved), is common in rabbits who have had a broken or dislocated limb. Essentially, ulcerative pododermatitis is pressure sores on the bottom of the feet, almost always the hind feet. The condition can range in severity from a mild inflammation to severe osteomyelitis, or infection of the bone. Rabbits are prone to develop this condition because they have no footpads. There are several factors that predispose rabbits to pododermatitis:

- Obesity
- Large size
- Lack of fur on feet
- Nervous thumping
- Incontinence
- Long nails, especially of hind feet
- Housing with wire floors or hard surfaces
- Extended periods of time spent in confined spaces
- Injuries or conditions that affect weight distribution

Pressure sores must be taken seriously because affected rabbits can develop anorexia, gastrointestinal problems, and, in severe cases, even die from septicemia (blood poisoning). Special-needs rabbits should be checked daily for any signs of pododermatitis, and healthy rabbits at least monthly. The first indication will be a hairless area of reddened skin, then an ulcer may develop (bleeding is possible at this stage), become infected with bacteria (pus may be exuded), and be covered by a thick black-looking scab. From this last stage, the infection may spread to underlying bone and eventually result in septicemia. Pay special attention to your rabbit's heels, as this is where these sores usually develop, although they can develop other places on the foot as well.

Reddened areas can be kept from getting worse by protecting them with moleskin or brush-on New-Skin®, and

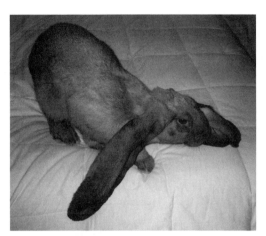

**Large rabbits are more prone
to develop pododermatitis.**

by keeping bedding clean and dry. I have used both moleskin and New-Skin®, and have found that which is more effective depends upon the rabbit. With my little Polish rabbit, who has a weight-distribution problem from a previously broken leg, I am able to prevent lesions from developing by keeping the bottom of one of her feet covered with moleskin. She leaves the moleskin alone, and when it eventually starts to come loose, I simply replace it with a new patch. My English lop is more of a problem. Her worn spots come from her large size and my wood floors. She pulls moleskin off, so I have been trying the brush-on New-Skin® liquid bandage. It seems to be more effective, but it is necessary to hold the rabbit for about 10 minutes while the liquid dries (and it has a sharp scent unpleasing to rabbits), which can be difficult! It also needs to be replaced when it wears off.

If the reddened areas progress to lesions, take the rabbit to a veterinarian to determine the extent of the infection. Lesions may be cleaned with an antiseptic solution such as Dermisol® Solution, ChlorhexiDerm™ Flush, or Betadine®; treated with a cream; and bandaged with a lightweight dressing such as Tegaderm™. If the lesions are infected with bacteria (usually *Pasteurella multocida* or *Staphylococcus aureus*), the veterinarian may prescribe antibiotics. Infected lesions are almost never cut out because there is so little soft tissue on the feet of rabbits. If severe abscesses develop, they may be packed with antibiotic-impregnated material. Pain medication is usually necessary for advanced cases, as this condition is very painful to the rabbit. Infection can cause the foot tendon that allows the rabbit to spring up and make fast getaways to become displaced, in which case the rabbit will be permanently disabled. Should the pododermatitis involve the bone, and not respond to medications, amputation may be necessary to save the rabbit's life.

Ointments for Treating Pododermatitis

If pressure sores are caught at the early stage, it is often possible to treat them with ointments and bandages, which is why daily checking is so critical for at-risk rabbits. Remember, unless the rabbit is unable to reach his foot because of other problems, he is going to lick some of the medication off. For this reason, you should never use anything that could harm your rabbit if consumed in small quantities. Creams with corticosteroids should be avoided for this reason. Creams with antibiotics and those with zinc oxide could potentially affect the rabbit negatively if enough is consumed (although they are often used without problems and many veterinarians recommend these creams). If one cream does not appear effective, or you suspect a negative reaction, try another.

Correct the underlying causes of the pododermatitis—keep the rabbit's claws trimmed, provide a softer surface for the rabbit that will allow his claws to sink in, increase hay and reduce pellets if he is overweight (Chapter 3), and if his weight distribution is affected from an injured leg or amputation, try to keep sores from developing by cushioning any hairless spots.

The following creams and ointments have been recommended for ulcerative pododermatitis by veterinarians in practice or in veterinary texts:
- Aloe vera gel
- Bactoderm® (mupirocin) topical ointment
- Bactroban Cream®
- Calendula gel
- Dermisol® Cream (care should be taken that

the rabbit does not consume any of this cream, since it contains acids. It may be prescribed in cases where removal of dead tissue is desired. Bandage foot thoroughly and watch to be sure the rabbit does not remove the dressings and ingest the cream)

- Neosporin® (not Neosporin Plus)
- Oxyfresh pet gel (aloe vera with oxygene®)
- Silvadene® Cream (silver sulfadiazine, available as Flamazine® in Canada)
- Triple antibiotic cream (this has the potential to cause dysbiosis if consumed in large enough quantities)
- Zymox® topical cream *without* hydrocortisone

Bandaging Feet

Sometimes a rabbit can be prevented from licking medications off the feet by bandaging the feet. Cover the lesion with the prescribed ointment, overlay this with a lightweight dressing such as Tegaderm™, and hold the dressing in place with a stretchy self-adhesive bandage such as PowerFlex or 3M™'s Vetrap™. A few rabbits will immediately sit down and devote their energies to removing your carefully done bandaging, but others will tolerate it.

CHAPTER 6

COPING WITH PARESIS AND PARALYSIS IN YOUR RABBIT

Lucile C. Moore

Paralysis and paresis (muscle weakness) in rabbits are probably the most common conditions of permanently special needs rabbits, although both can be temporary conditions.

Paralysis, or plegia, is the total loss of use of an area of the body. Paresis is weakness in an area of the body. Both are caused by damage to the spinal cord or motor areas of the brain, and the signs are:

- Difficulty in moving or a reluctance to move
- Dragging the body by use of forelimbs
- Urinary and fecal incontinence

Paralysis and paresis are further differentiated:

- *Hemiparesis/hemiplegia*—weakness/paralysis of one side of the body. This is rare in rabbits, but may occur as a result of a stroke or type of spinal disease.
- *Paraparesis/paraplegia*—affects the lower half of the body and involves two legs. This is usually caused by trauma, although a congenital spinal abnormality, disease such as *E. cuniculi*, toxoplasmosis, spinal tumor, spinal abscess, poisoning, or degenerative disc

disease such as spondylosis may also cause paraparesis or paraplegia.

- *Quadriparesis/quadriplegia*—affects all four limbs. This can be caused by a spinal fracture or dislocation, concussion, cancer, congenital spinal abnormality, diseases such as toxoplasmosis and *E. cuniculi*, abscesses, poisoning, and degenerative disc disease such as spondylosis.

The prognosis will vary, depending on what is causing the paresis/paralysis and to what extent it has developed. Whether the condition is permanent or temporary, rabbits with paresis or paralysis will require a great deal of care. They will need extra grooming; possibly require expression of the bladder; need to be fed cecotrophs; given medications; and be constantly monitored for gastrointestinal trouble, pressure sores, flystrike, and urine burn. Yet despite all these issues, paralyzed rabbits can still have good-quality lives. Stephen F. Guida, a volunteer for Brambley Hedge Rabbit Rescue, comments:

> Inside every special-needs rabbit is a normal rabbit constantly trying to be like every other rabbit. They are not burdened by self-pity or the possibilities of what might have been. They do not consume endless hours of wondering "Why did this happen to me?" Their complete and total acceptance of their condition paves the way for them to have as high a quality of life that they can, given their situation.

However, not everyone will share this view. One issue that may arise when caring for a paralyzed rabbit is the reaction of others, including veterinarians. There are those who feel the "humane" thing to do is to euthanize a paralyzed rabbit, no matter how healthy the rabbit is otherwise. (It has even occurred that persons who have cared for severely disabled animals have been turned in for animal cruelty.) If your veterinarian's opinion differs strongly from yours on this issue, you may need to think about finding another veterinarian whose views are more compatible with yours.

Floppy Rabbit

"Floppy rabbit syndrome" is a term used in the United Kingdom for cases of sudden-onset muscle weakness or paralysis that affect the limbs and neck and have no obvious cause. The rabbit may not be able to raise its head or move its limbs, yet body temperature, heart rate, and respiration are usually within normal ranges, and the rabbits are able to eat and drink if the food and water are placed right next to them. Most rabbits affected with sudden and unexplainable paralysis recover fully, usually within a few days, although some do die, often from respiratory failure.

Several causes have been suggested for such cases, including plant poisoning, hypercalcemia (excessive calcium), hypokalemia (potassium deficiency), hepatic lipidosis, myasthenia gravis, encephalitozoonosis, and reaction to medications. Most likely, the condition is caused by several of these factors, and as rabbit medicine progresses they will be differentiated.

Currently, treatment of rabbits with floppy rabbit syndrome consists of fluid therapy and supportive care. If the rabbit is able to eat and drink, hold the dishes directly in front of him so that he can. Clean the rabbit of any urine and feces, and collect and feed cecotrophs. Be sure the area he is kept in is quiet and stress-free, and the ambient temperature even. See Chapters 1 and 2 for basic care information.

Splayleg

"Splayleg" is an imprecise term that is commonly used to describe any condition that affects a rabbit's limbs so he is unable to bring his legs together under his body in a normal fashion. Splay-leg usually affects the hind limbs, but does occasionally affect the forelimbs. The condition may not appear to hinder the rabbit's movement much at all, or it may be so severe it causes paralysis.

You may sometimes see the term "breeder-caused splayleg," referring to splayleg occurring in very young rabbits who are

Peanut's splayed legs show at a young age.

overweight and are being raised on a slippery surface. It is arguable whether this splayleg is acquired or whether these are genetic splayleg situations that are exacerbated by the described conditions. Providing a surface on which the rabbits can get traction may improve these cases. Other possible causes of splayleg are fractures and hip dysplasia (abnormal growth and/or development) from non-genetic causes.

Genetic splayleg is an inherited autosomal recessive gene. These rabbits have one or more skeletal deformities, usually in the leg bone, but deformities in the hip (twisted hip or femoral shaft) and forelegs may also occur. Sometimes an effort is made to correct the splayleg by hobbling the legs with a soft fabric tie, sometimes with a stiffer brace between, but this can be stressful to the rabbit, and the effectiveness variable. Dr. Bill Guerrera:

> If you are trying to correct the problem in an older rabbit, there is no success with this procedure. If you are trying to allow better ambulation by pulling a leg out of the way, then it may be beneficial.

Many rabbits are only lightly affected with splayleg and are able to get around quite well without hobbling and can have a good quality of life. It should be noted that rabbits with genetic splayleg may have other congenital problems, and caretakers should be aware of this potential. It is also not unusual for rabbits with splayleg to improve slightly during their early adulthood, although this positive trend may reverse as they grow older. Rabbits more severely affected with splayleg may require the same kind of nursing and care that is given to rabbits with damaged spines.

If a rabbit with splayleg is able to get around on his own, the best care is supportive. Be sure the rabbit has a good-quality diet and always has water available. If the rabbit is partially or completely incontinent, keep the fur on the hindquarters cleaned. Allow the rabbit to exercise as much as he is able, but check the bottoms of the feet for pressure sores from abnormal weight distribution. If fur wear is seen, brush-on New-Skin® liquid bandage or a piece of moleskin can be placed over the area and replaced as necessary.

Theresa Romaldini's rabbit, Peanut, a lionhead rabbit, showed splayed legs from the early age of two weeks. Theresa adopted him at eight weeks, and at two years old he is happy, curious, and gets around well despite his splayed legs. Peanut has had some other (apparently) congenital problems as well, including cataracts and kidney problems. The hardest issues Theresa has had in caring for Peanut are his tendency to develop urine scald and the difficulty of treating the sores that develop on his front legs and feet due to his abnormal locomotion.

Spinal Fracture, Luxation (Dislocation), and Subluxation (Partial Dislocation)

A "broken back" in a rabbit is caused by a fracture or dislocation of the lumbar vertebrae that compresses or severs the spinal cord. Vertebral fractures and dislocations are the most common cause of paraplegia in rabbits. Lack of exercise, old age, and/or a diet low in calcium (unlikely except in cases where rabbit receives no commercial pellets) predispose rabbits to fractures.

The signs of a spinal fracture or dislocation will vary depending on the actual site and severity of the injury, but will often include:

- Inability to move, abnormal movement, reluctance to move
- Loss of feeling in the skin
- Difficulty in grooming the anal area
- Gastrointestinal stasis
- Incontinence
- Failure to urinate
- Ataxia (incoordination and weakness)

An X-ray (radiograph) will be utilized to confirm the presence of a dislocation or fracture, although many spinal luxations may actually be back in place by the time the rabbit is seen by the vet. For these latter cases, treatment of cage rest and an anti-inflammatory steroid may suffice. The rabbit may regain use of his legs over a three- to five-day period as the swelling around the spinal cord goes down. A glucocorticosteroid such as dexamethasone may be given to help prevent damage to the cord from the swelling.

Fixation of limb fractures is common, but spinal fractures are rarely fixed, although they can be. Fixation of a lumbar fracture is pictured in Chapter 7 of the first edition of *BSAVA Manual of Rabbit Medicine and*

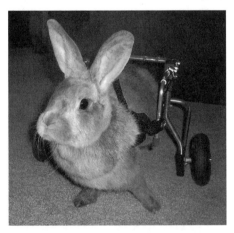

Karla is suspected of having caudal lumbar spinal luxation and spinal cord injury.

Surgery. In notes from a 2006 veterinary conference, Johnston comments that fixation of lumbar fractures in rabbits is "probably underutilized." It is likely this technique will become more common in the future, brightening the prognosis for rabbits with fractured spines.

If you suspect a spinal injury in your rabbit, do not delay treatment. Urine retention, which sometimes accompanies spinal injuries, could cause fatal complications, and occasionally immediate surgery can prevent permanent paralysis. Do not let the rabbit drag itself around by his front legs at first. This could prohibit healing. If the spinal cord is not transected, the rabbit may respond to extended cage rest (one person had two rabbits who recovered fully from spinal fractures and who initially had rear leg paralysis). If the cord has been transected, the rabbit will require extensive care for the rest of his life. With such care, however, many of these rabbits can still have quality lives.

Other Causes of Paresis/Paralysis

There are many other causes of paralysis and muscle weakness in rabbits, including degenerative disc disease such as spondylosis (Chapter 9), a bone tumor or abscess causing spinal compression, trauma to or tumor in the brain, poisoning, a parasitic disease such as encephalitozoonosis or toxoplasmosis (Chapter 4), or bacterial infections.

Care of Paralyzed Rabbits

Whatever the cause of your rabbit's paralysis, many of the care issues will be the same: keeping the perineal area clean and dry, providing access to food and water, giving medications, and keeping the rabbit interested in his environment and interacting with others. Dr. Susan Keeney, a veterinarian with extensive experience treating rabbits, considers keeping the rabbit clean to avoid urine burn to be the single most important care issue with disabled rabbits. See Chapters 1 and 2 for care hints.

When it is okayed by your veterinarian, physical therapy can be helpful to rabbits with muscle weakness or paralysis. Shannon Cail took her rabbit, Bailey, to physical therapy sessions. She describes his sessions:

> For the next five weeks we traveled to Sterling Impression Animal Rehabilitation Center of New England in Walpole for his physical therapy sessions. His physical therapist, Cathy, would gently work with Bailey each week for about 30 minutes. Specific exercises and massages were performed that focused on atrophied areas and joints. After each session we left with exercises to work on at home. At the end of five weeks, Bailey was discharged; with orders to come back if need be, but to continue his therapy regimen at home. Cathy said that of all her patients, Bailey was her most difficult yet. She couldn't believe a four-pound bun had that much [feistiness] and determination. I believe that's what kept him going through it all.[1]

One positive step a caregiver can take to improve the quality of a disabled bun's life is to add massage to the paralyzed rabbit's daily routine. Jodi McLaughlin, Certified Massage Therapist, describes a basic massage routine for your disabled rabbit.

Nurturing Massage for the Disabled Bunny
by Jodi McLaughlin, CMT, Animal Massage Provider

Massage is simply purposeful touch. Caregivers of dis-

---

1 Cail, Shannon. 2006. An Extraordinary Journey: A Rabbit's Fight for Survival Against the Odds. *Rabbit Tracks* 3.

abled bunnies massage their bunnies every time they groom or pet with healing intent. Grooming in the animal kingdom is perhaps the earliest form of massage, and most disabled bunnies not only require, but desire, frequent grooming for quality of life.

Diego waits on the massage table *après bain*.

The demands on a disabled rabbit caregiver are far greater than the care of a healthy bunny. Not only does the disabled bunny need a gentle nurturing environment, so does the often-stressed caregiver. Massage offers enhanced relaxation and circulation, but is most importantly a form of meditation for both giver and receiver.

Daily bathing and medication time creates the perfect opportunity to slow down, nourish, and celebrate the unique human-disabled animal bond. Approach each touch session with heightened healing intent. A disabled rabbit may not be able to scratch or properly groom many areas of its body. The caregiver can employ simple techniques, such as stroking with a soft-bristled baby brush, or using finger circles, to gently stimulate the superficial skin layers of the face, focusing on the jaw and base of the ears. Many physically challenged bunnies enjoy light tapping or finger fluttering along the compromised feet for a mini reflexology session. Finger nibbles along the tail and the loose skin at its base pleases many disabled buns.

Often a less mobile bunny can lie on just one

side. The muscles along this "down side" may become weakened and stretched. This is an impossible area for bunny to groom. Lightly raking the fingers from belly to spine, or light skin rolling here, can create one contented tooth-purring lagomorph. Sharing these moments of bliss is uplifting to the most weary bunny caregiver.

Creating a regular routine and special grooming/massage space is not only crucial for bunny's comfort, but allows opportunity for impromptu one-on-one time. Consider the entire environment, making sure it is quiet, temperate, and supportive for both of you. Assess your own posture and be certain the surface is safe for bunny. A sheltered and padded grooming table is my personal favorite for massage time. Have rolled towels and small pillows available to support bunny's body, perhaps placed under the "down hip," or cradling a hardworking "support" arm and shoulder. Place a smooth rock under bun's feet for a sense of grounding, mold a rice-filled sock along bunny's body, or use your free hand and arm to stabilize and gently lift bunny's "downside." Conscious deep breathing and laying on of hands can often release a quivering muscle while offering a sense of security for our most vulnerable bunny companions. The body must feel supported to relax fully. Calm physical contact is very restorative and nurturing and helps to slow the breath. Each moment of the grooming/massage session must be focused on gentle support of the disabled rabbit's body-mind-spirit.

Caution: Never use deep pressure, traction, or stretching. Deep vein thrombosis, or blood clotting, is a high risk for any physically challenged being. The use of deep or aggressive strokes or techniques is never appropriate for small rabbits and is especially dangerous for a fragile disabled bunny. Instead, encourage bunny's legs to move, if ever so slightly, by light brushing of the compromised feet. Always check with your rabbit-savvy veterinarian before doing any bunny massage. Let your vet know you appreciate the value of massage for small animals, especially house rabbits.

Every day is a gift. Slow down, breathe mindfully, and take time to nurture your disabled bunny with the power of touch. See with clear eyes. Feel with fresh fingers. Each day's needs are unique. Be gentle, be supportive, and be present. Nurture without challenge. You and your precious disabled bunny will both be nourished.

Problems to Watch For in Paralyzed Rabbits

Pressure sores will have a tendency to develop in rabbits with paralysis. It can help to create a layered bedding (Chapter 1) and to move the rabbit's position. Place a layer of egg-crate foam or bubble wrap under a soft top layer of bedding to help prevent their occurrence.

The digestive system functions much better in rabbits who are able to exercise. Rabbits with paralysis/paresis will need to be watched extra carefully for signs of *gastrointestinal hypomotility* (Chapter 3). Try to coax your paralyzed rabbit to eat hay by offering it in handfuls.

Volvulus, although rare in rabbits, can occur in paralyzed rabbits and older rabbits. The intestine, which does not have the tone of a normal intestine, twists upon itself and creates a blockage. This is extremely painful for the rabbit, and will be fatal if there is no immediate intervention, although the surgery to correct volvulus is itself extremely high risk.

Rabbits with mobility issues will be at risk of *respiratory problems* because their chests may not expand and contract fully, failing to expel pathogens. Be on the watch for any discharge from the nose and eyes, and contact your veterinarian promptly if you notice any.

Urinary *incontinence* and resulting urine burn can be helped by trimming fur, applying spray-on protective bandages, expressing the bladder, and the use of diapers. See Chapters 1 and 2 for detailed information.

With time, unused muscles will *atrophy* as they lose the nerve sensation necessary to "fire" the leg muscles. The legs of a paralyzed rabbit may at first dangle and be flaccid, and later draw up or stiffen. According to Dr. Susan Keeney, flexing and extending the legs can keep the blood flowing better and help with muscle mass. However, you should never perform any physical therapy on your rabbit without first receiving an OK from your vet. Depending upon your rabbit's specific case, physical therapy might be contraindicated.

Self-mutilation can occur in rabbits with paresis/paralysis. It is possible this occurs when there is some sensation—such as a tingling—that causes the rabbit to bite and chew on the spot in an effort to stop the unusual feelings. There is no simple answer to this problem if it develops. In some cases, an E-collar can prevent self-mutilation, but not all rabbits are able to tolerate the collars. If your rabbit is one of the latter, you will have to use your ingenuity to come up with a solution. One person whose rabbit chewed on his genitals was able to solve the problem simply by diapering (Chapter 1) the rabbit.

Blood clots (deep vein thrombosis) are a danger for every paralyzed rabbit. Blood in the limbs of inactive rabbits (it is not necessary for the rabbit to be paralyzed) pools and thickens. If a piece of a clot breaks loose, it will cause a life-threatening pulmonary embolism when it reaches the lungs. Physical therapy may help prevent blood clots, but never provide physical therapy without first discussing it with your vet.

Two Paralyzed Rabbits

Diego

Jodi McLaughlin's rabbit, Diego, is an example of a paralyzed rabbit who has achieved a high-quality life through the use of both traditional and non-traditional treatments:

As a baby, Diego was rescued, along with 400 other rabbits, in a 2002 SPCA raid on a Mar Vista, California, animal hoarder's home. May 5 of 2003 he mysteriously injured his back while living at a no-kill L.A. rabbit shelter. Although X-rays of his spine showed no obvious injury, his back legs were paralyzed.

Poster bunny Diego, the picture of health.

I was studying holistic animal massage therapy in September of 2003 when I visited the sanctuary where Diego was living. Once I spotted "D" languishing in a pen and connected with his sparkling chocolate eyes, I could not forget him. Diego came home to live with me the following week. He proved to be a true California rabbit. Our opinionated "Vitamin D" bunny loved the sunshine, fresh ocean air, and organic herbs my beach cottage offered. Massage, Tellington Touch©, acupuncture, and acupressure treatments gave him improved mobility, but over time complications from his injury caused incontinence and frustration.

We ordered a custom-made Doggon' Wheels cart in September '04. After a short adjustment period, he has continued to understand the benefits of the cart and lies patiently on the grooming-massage table while I hook him into his "chariot." He takes off running as soon as his powerful front legs hit the floor. Diego's most recent nickname, "Ben-Hare," says it all about his chariot-racing abilities, amazing personality, and stamina. At 5+ years old, Diego continues to thrive with daily baths, bodywork, regular bladder expression, and fresh cranberries and herbs for his urinary and immune systems. When we moved to the Amish countryside of Pennsylvania, Diego bonded with our blind bunny tabby and friend Berry. "D" is truly a poster bunny for the quality of life that is possible for a disabled bunny.

Cart Tips from Diego, aka Ben-Hare
by Jodi McLaughlin

OK, first plan on at least a 2–3-week adjustment period! That funny thing freaked me out for a while.

Check to be sure the cart is fitted properly. We bunnies must have adequate room from harness to saddle. My cart had to be sent back and lengthened cuz I was all squished in. I also needed a tummy strap added to support my belly since I had chewed my chest strap. Oh yeah, and I needed little stirrups added to hold my feet up off the ground.

So once everything seems OK, start off with your sweetie bun using just the saddle. Let your bun build up arm and chest strength for about a week. Give daily saddle/strap time so he can drag himself around and get used to the feel of the darn thing. My mom put me outside in the grass and on carpeting for more traction. Be sure the leg holes are big enough, too. My leg holes were too tight at first, ouch!

After your bunster is used to the saddle, put on

"Ben-Hare" investigates a pansy during an outing.

just the harness for a few minutes each day, oh say maybe 2–3 days. Your bun may be like me and chew the chest strap. Mom decided to get rid of that nasty thing. Didn't need it, and eventually everything else kept me in the whole get-up. But I got used to the harness cuz Mom gave me lots of distractions while I was in it. She keeps the harness pretty tight, just under my arms. She puts one finger under the harness to be sure it fits just right.

Next she put me in both those contraptions, saddle and harness, and let me run around. This all took a week or more, but I settled down. The snacks were yummy and I had some new toys, alright!

Finally Mom put me in the whole kit 'n kaboodle, I mean cart. I was not happy. I was buckin' and pushing myself backwards for a few minutes. Then Mom put me down on the carpet and braced my back end from going backwards. Took me awhile, I am very stubborn, but I figured out I could go forward . . .cool! And then I learned how to take the corners real wide, and that I could lie down and rest, but I can't get under anything that is too low, like my favorite furniture.

Grooming friend Stuffy

Most days now I am in the cart for an hour or two. But never ever unattended and always with my water and hay at the edge of the track. So just take this whole cartin' thing slow, and you will love it! Heck, I've been using my chariot for three years now. It keeps me frisky and gives me a great workout. I'm one crazy bunny in the cart, it's just so darn fun. I can really roll, baby.

This is bunny cart gospel according to me, Diego Rivera.

Tiffy

Kim and Terry Clevenger learned firsthand what caring for a paralyzed bun entails when they made the decision to provide the care necessary to enable their rabbit Tiffy to continue to share their lives despite her EC. They have generously consented to share their story here in the hope others may benefit from what they learned. "Paresis/Paralysis" by Kim Clevenger, member of the Kansas City, Missouri, chapter of the HRS, and "Tribute to Tiffy" by Terry Clevenger, first appeared on www.rabbit.org, and are used with the authors' permission.

Paresis/Paralysis
by Kim Clevenger

Tiffy came into our home after being in three other homes the first year of her life. She was a very social bunny and a favorite with all who met her. She had an attitude and a strong personality which would benefit her greatly during the challenging last months of her life, enabling her to get through her back leg paralysis with courage and spirit. This information on how to care for a bunny that has lost back leg usage is dedicated to my husband Terry who amazed me with his nurturing and sacrificial care of our beloved bunny Tiffy. He was rewarded with devotion and many, many kisses from Tiffy as well as appreciation and admiration from me.

Puff and Tiffy

General Thoughts

1) Herbs are extremely helpful in any medical situation and I found them to extend Tiffy's life and quality of life by two years after her symptoms of unbalance first appeared. Acupuncture and chiropractic care can also greatly improve a bunny's condition and quality of life. It is important to be in contact with a professional veterinarian who is knowledgeable in these areas if you plan to participate in them. In the Kansas City area at this time, the House Rabbit Society recommends Dr. Pam Truman at Metcalf South Animal Hospital for acupuncture and herb care.

2) Do not change medications or herbs unless the bunny's situation worsens. If your current regime is working well and the bunny is stable, don't change.

3) Do not underestimate the emotional part of care—a bunny receiving daily attention and nurturing will be in better physical condition than one that does not.

4) Realize that you and other family members will need to modify your lifestyle to provide extra physical and emotional care. During her paralysis time, Tiffy was checked on at least five times

per day. My husband or I or a friend or neighbor would come during the day to check on her, exercise her, put out a fresh diaper, and give her fresh veggies/hay/feed.

5) Realize that a bunny's deteriorating condition will affect his or her animal companions as well as the human family members. You may see behavior in them that you did not expect, even aggression, and it may be necessary to separate them for a period of time. If so, keep them in an area where they can still see each other.

Creating an Environment for a Bunny without Back Leg Usage

Creating a Bedding Area

In creating areas for Tiffy that I called nests I used materials that were soft, absorbent, and flexible. These materials included foam rubber (which can be obtained at a fabric store in different heights and then cut to any size you desire), rubber-backed 100% cotton rugs, flannel sheets/shirts, towels and material used for babies (baby blankets, etc.). I also used disposable diapers to avoid her being wet. I used the size of diaper that matched her weight—newborn size because Tiffy weighed three pounds. I found the Huggies® brand or type not to work well because I wanted them to lay flat. These materials could be arranged so Tiffy was sitting up or lying down.

For the sitting up nest which I used during the day, first place a thin piece of foam rubber (1–2 inches high) large enough to make a bedding area—for Tiffy this was one by two feet. Then place an all-cotton rubber-backed rug. Place a diaper folded out flat where bunny's bottom will be. Then place a higher piece of foam rubber (several inches high and the length of the bedding area) on the edge of the rug to serve as a support. Place a flannel sheet/shirt, towel, or baby material bunched up and arranged in a U shape against the piece of foam rubber sup-

Eating stand setup

port. Then place veggies/feed/hay elevated to a position where bunny can reach them—for Tiffy I used a Tupperware container turned upside down with a plate on top if it.

Tiffy at eating stand.

Place bunny so that the front portion of the U shape serves to support the front half of the body and elevates it to the height where bunny can reach the veggies as desired. Place the front feet on top of/over the edge of the U shape. Then form the other part of the U shape around the body on the side and around the back area supporting both against the piece of foam rubber support. This will en-

Maggie visits Tiffy in her laying-down nest.

able bunny to eat or rest as he or she desires.

For the laying-down nest that I used overnight, still place a thin piece of foam rubber, an all-cotton rubber-backed rug, and a diaper folded out flat. Then take multiple pieces of flannel sheets/shirts/towels/baby material and wrap around to make a back support not as tall or firm as the higher piece of foam rubber. Also wrap it around the side and make a gradual slope in front and place veggies and hay where bunny can reach them. It is good to cover bunny with the material to keep him or her warm overnight.

I found it helpful to spread the sheet/shirt/towel/baby material in a larger area around Tiffy so that her companions Puff and Maggie could lay with her to share her veggies and enjoy the softness of her bedding.

Creating an Eating Stand

To enable Tiffy to be in different positions during the day and also to eat sitting up when she first received her veggies, I created what I call an eating stand. I made it out of common house shoes purchased at Wal-Mart and duct tape. I used 5 house shoes total (that was the right height for Tiffy) laying them on top of each other and inserting the heel part of one into the toe part of the nest one and then securing with duct tape wrapped around the whole thing. I put small pieces of foam rubber in the toe portion of the top pair to create side supports.

For the veggie holder I used Glad food containers—I turned one upside down and a second duct

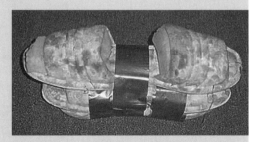

House shoes form the base of the eating stand.

taped to it right side up with a portion cut out of one side for eating. I found the Glad food containers easier to cut than regular Rubbermaid or Tupperware plastic. I tried various sizes until I found the right size for Tiffy.

Vegetable holder

After the eating stand and veggie holder are ready, place veggies in the holder with the side cut out toward the eating stand. Then place bunny in the stand no more than 10–15 minutes. At times Tiffy would get restless and work her way out ending up on her side on the floor with no support. For

Tiffy eating at her stand.

eating time, this is a wonderful way to give bunny an upright position that closely resembles the normal eating position. You may need to supplement side support with a towel bunched up on one or both sides.

Creating Exercise Time
It was important to get Tiffy up on a regu-

Kim supports Tiffy's stomach.

lar basis and exercise her. In the beginning of her losing use of her back legs we were able to utilize a cart, which is equivalent to a wheelchair for a person. We used one that a talented friend made for us using Tiffy's measurements and also one loaned to us from someone who had ordered it from Doggon' Wheels

Tiffy kissing Kim.

(Appendix III) custom-made for their bunny. After a period of time the carts did not work as Tiffy's front leg usage came and went. At that point we would hold her stomach and allow her to move around as she desired. Exercise time for a back leg paralysis bunny is better done in short periods of time (10–15 minutes) several times a day instead of 1 or 2 lengthy sessions per day. Be sure to stop and allow them to rest when they want to do so. Tiffy was exercised at least 5 times per day. Usually exercise time involved eating at some point. We would support her for this by holding her up by her stomach.

Caring for a paralyzed bunny requires dedication and work. It involves time and energy and money. Most importantly it involves love—both from human to bunny and bunny to human. I was ready to euthanize Tiffy before my husband Terry was. He chose to extend her life and care in her paralysis. She knew the sacrifice we were making to create a quality life for her. After her paralysis, she began kissing us and became more affectionate than she had been. She left us when she was ready. She stopped eating one day and died the next day in Terry's arms. I hope this information will be helpful to you if your journey of love with a bunny takes you down this road. I know for our family it was well worth it.

Tribute to Tiffy
by Terry Clevenger

Rabbits have always been my wife's thing, and al though I help with their maintenance, and certainly feel bad when we lose one, I've never considered myself an integral part of their care. However, there's an exception to everything, and Tiffy turned out to be that one exception.

My wife had warned me for over a year that, with Tiffy's *E. cuniculi*, we should be prepared to see her go downhill rather quickly. I managed to evade reality until after Kim got back from a trip to see her folks this past January. There had been no signs whatsoever that Tiffy was ailing, but shortly after Kim's return, she lost the use of her back legs. The sight of her trying to maneuver around with just her front legs was both alarming for us, but also encouraging, as Tiffy seemed to be unaware of her handicap, and gallantly tried to live a normal life.

However, I once again had to face reality when Kim told me that, with me going back to school after Christmas break, and with her at work all day, there would no longer be anyone around to provide the increased care Tiffy was requiring, and the humane thing would be to put her down.

Well, the day came to take her to the vet for the procedure. I sat on the bed with Tiff and Kim, and confessed my great reluctance to go through with it. My argument with Kim was I still saw a lot of spirit and life left in our little white mass of fur, and it just didn't seem the right thing to do, at that point, any way. Kim emphasized that without someone available during the day to dry her off from wetting herself, and getting her fresh food and exercising her legs, it just wasn't good to let her go all day. I (fairly immediately, acting out of emotion and not logic) piped up that I would come home from school every day and take care of her.

Terry and Tiffy

School consisted of an internship at a nearby community college, and my schedule there was such that I could plan a slightly long lunch period to dash home, get Tiffy re-situated and fed, and run back. This I did for the next three or four months. It was terrible, grueling, sacrificial work, especially when I had to see that little head pop up from her nesting area when I came in her room, and start moving around rather excitedly, knowing some extreme TLC was at hand. I also really hated having to pick her up and snuggle with her, petting her, and, later, having to endure the misery of her "bunny kisses"; she knew what we were doing for her, and she generously let her appreciation be known!

Over those months Kim and I devised all sorts of little inventions to help Tiffy's condition. One contraption—and that's indeed what they were—was a variation on the idea of a chariot-like device that she could get into and, with the use of her front paws, maneuver herself around our den, with a rear wheel assembly taking the place of her useless legs. Although rather humorous for us, it never really worked that well for her, and we gradually abandoned this little experiment (however, we owe great gratitude to Bob for his tireless engineering and tinkering with this idea!)

Kim also became quite talented at figuring out

ways to prop Tiffy up against small blankets and pillowcases, so she had support against her back to be able to eat and drink, plus enjoy her surroundings. Although Kim's different configurations cannot be detailed here, it was important to give her the ability to have access to food.

Caring for Tiffy during this time was never a chore or burden. Her spirit and spunk was such that Kim and I seemed to dote heavily on her, something the other rabbits did not fail to notice! We seemed to compete for who would hold her in the evening while we watched TV, and, since somebody had to clean up the bunny rooms (Kim), I usually won that honor.

Besides her tremendous spirit, something else that was very evident about Tiff was her incredible appetite. Anytime we brought her food, she would devour it with the zeal of someone lost in the desert for a week! We could never figure out where she was putting it, as she remained rather thin. However, Kim revealed that it was the disease that was eating up the calories, only giving the illusion of our heroic bunny holding off its terminal effects.

I remember spending a very fun Sunday afternoon parked in front of the television, with Tiffy parked contentedly in my lap, waking every several minutes, just long enough to nibble on some veggies or wrap a front paw around my thumb and lick my hand at some length. The phrase "wrapped around her finger (paw)" was never better illustrated!

A few days later I had to go out of town for an overnight trip. When I got back in the evening, Kim reported that Tiffy had not eaten for 24 hours or so, and she was quite worried about her. Indeed, when I knelt down on the floor to pet her and love on her, she did not respond as usual. Nor would she give in to my attempts to feed her. Kim spent a restless night with Tiffy, trying to get her to eat something, anything, and watching to see that her bathroom habits were continuing. The next morning she brought Tiff into our bed, waking me with the announcement we needed to get her in to the vet. Our ailing bunny lay next to me while Kim tended to the other rabbits, and then headed to take a shower, after which we would take her in. Tiff seemed to need to hold her head up, almost like she needed air. I got up and was holding her upright to help her breathe better, but something told me she wasn't right. I urged Kim to get dressed, as we didn't have time for her shower—we needed to leave NOW! I dashed out to the car, and just as I opened up the driver's door I could feel Tiffy go limp. Kim came up and took her so I could drive. I backed out of the driveway, and as I shoved the car in first and took off down the street, looked over at her in Kimmie's arms; "She's gone," I told my wife. Kim tried to keep Tiff alive by talking to her, but she just slumped in Kim's arms. We decided to make the trip anyway, just in case there was still a heartbeat. We were in the vet's office a few minutes later, and he put a stethoscope on Tiffy's chest. A few minutes later he took the tips out of his ears and shook his head at us, then kindly left us alone for our good-bye.

Kim and I are glad she went the way she did—on her terms, Kim likes to say—quick and painless. We did not relish the prospect of taking her in, seemingly healthy and alert, and putting her to sleep. I'm also extremely glad I was so adamant about not having her euthanized early on. "What if" would always have been a haunting thought for me. I've never had such an experience with one of our bunnies. I hope, in some ways, I never have another. But this was a very, very special few months with "just an animal."

Tiffy was six years old or so when she died. I

know in rabbit years that's retirement age, but it just seems so short. Tiffy never was very big or fat; she always had the look of a young bunny. I think that's what made her, even in advanced years and with her illness, always look so cute. She was just a big fluff of fur; you could hardly tell if you were looking at her head or rear. And then after her legs gave out, she really laid it on thick with bunny kisses as we gave her all the special care we could. Her incredible spunk her last few months was the icing on the cake for all the reasons we came to love her so much.

CHAPTER 7

DENTAL DISORDERS

Lucile C. Moore

Rabbit teeth grow continuously throughout a rabbit's life, the incisors at about 2 mm a week and molars at a slightly slower rate. Rabbit teeth don't have a true root—the roots are actually elongated crowns and are not attached as securely as are the teeth in carnivores like cats. Rabbits' teeth must wear constantly and keep their alignment to remain healthy. If the diets of rabbits kept in the home do not include enough fiber and/or calcium, the rabbits are at particularly high risk of developing serious dental problems. Some breeds—dwarf breeds and lop rabbits—that were bred for cuteness of face may have dental disorders caused by the shape of their jaws. Dental disease in any rabbit can lead to other medical conditions, such as moist dermatitis, watery eyes, dacryocystitis (inflammation of the nasolacrimal duct), gastrointestinal disorders, abscesses, and osteomyelitis (infection of bone). Signs of dental disorders will vary, but will often include:

- Drooling
- Bad breath
- Discharge from eyes
- Pain
- Failure to groom

- Anorexia
- Weight loss

Home care of rabbits with dental disease will be likely to include:
- Supplemental feeding by syringe if the rabbit is unable to consume his usual foods
- Feeding the rabbit his cecotrophs if he is unable to collect them himself
- Pain control
- Keeping the fur around the mouth and neck clean and dry

There are many different dental problems that can arise with rabbits. Some may be caused by diet, some result from trauma, others are genetic. One term that will come up in any reading on rabbit dentistry is acquired dental disease, or ADD. Harcourt-Brown, author of *Textbook of Rabbit Medicine*, describes the stages of this syndrome: deterioration of tooth quality, acquired malocclusion, the elongation of tooth roots, and the possible development of periapical abscesses. Various causes of ADD have been suggested, including a lack of tooth wear, improper wear, and genetic jaw shapes (more likely in dwarf and lop breeds).

Zsa Zsa, healthy after problems with maloccluded teeth and jaw abscesses.

Harcourt-Brown herself suggests metabolic bone disease (MBD) as a cause of ADD. In MBD, the deposition of minerals in the teeth is affected by a lack of calcium, phosphate, and vitamin D in the rabbit's diet. This leads to other problems that eventually result in acquired malocclusion or other ADD.

The average rabbit caretaker needs only to understand that ADD is very likely to affect their rabbit at some time in its life, and that perhaps they can slow its appearance by feeding their rabbit a proper diet. It is necessary that rabbits have adequate calcium in their food, as well as other minerals and vitamins. There is disagreement among veterinarians and other rabbit professionals regarding the effect of commercial rabbit pellets on rabbits' teeth. Some feel pellets do not wear the teeth properly. Others point out that according to the results of some recent studies, the lack of minerals rather than improper wear may be the primary cause of ADD, and commercial pellets provide needed minerals.

For companion rabbits a compromise diet may work well: a diet including a small amount of high-quality alfalfa or timothy pellets each day could help ensure proper nutrition, and a good-quality grass hay could comprise the bulk of the rabbit's diet. It should be recognized that various grass hays will contain differing amounts of fiber and minerals and may encourage different chewing motions. Fiber and mineral content of commercial pellets will also vary.

In the past, it has often been suggested that rabbits be given chew sticks or blocks of wood to help wear down the teeth. Many veterinary professionals no longer believe this is a good idea, and that it can, in fact, be a cause of fracture and acquired malocclusion. Dr. Mark Burgess, who has an exotic animal practice, explains:

> Rabbit teeth grow constantly. The front teeth (incisors) grow faster than the cheek teeth (molars and premolars). The cheek teeth are worn by chewing food, especially grass hay with its abrasive fiber.
>
> The incisors, however, are not worn by eating; these teeth aren't used for chewing but only for biting. It has been commonly recom-

mended that wood blocks or other hard objects be provided to wear the incisors down. However, no gnawing is needed to wear the incisors. The main thing that wears an incisor is the opposing tooth hitting it. Rabbits and rodents grind these teeth against each other when *not* eating or gnawing, and that is what keeps them short and honed sharp. Pets without anything hard to gnaw on will still have healthy incisors year after year.

Ironically, chewing on wood or metal may actually damage the incisors and lead to tooth overgrowth! This is because most rabbit and rodent incisors are long and delicate and not intended for biting anything harder than grasses and food. (An exception is the beaver, which has short stout incisors built for gnawing wood.) When a rabbit bites down on wood, the pressure from the hard unyielding material may twist and damage the tooth roots, eventually leading to crooked tooth growth (malocclusion). Once the teeth become misaligned they *will* overgrow, and no amount of gnawing will keep them short. The only resort then is to trim the incisors every 3 or 4 weeks, or occasionally to extract all the overgrown teeth.

My advice is this: let the incisors wear themselves as they are designed to. If you want to provide chew toys to minimize boredom (or to prevent cage bar biting) then you can provide your rabbit cardboard toys. Non-inked cardboard such as toilet paper rolls are fun toys and won't harm teeth. If swallowed, cardboard is simply plant pulp and won't hurt the gut either.

Malocclusion

One of the most common dental problems in rabbits is malocclusion, both of incisors and molars. Incisor malocclusion may be inherited as an autosomal recessive trait, most often in lops and dwarf breeds. This type of malocclusion will be noticeable from an early age. Malocclusion may also be acquired from trauma (as when a rabbit pulls on cage wire with his teeth), tumors, abscesses, favoring an infected tooth, and from metabolic bone disease (unlikely except in cases where no formulated pellet food is provided). This last can often be seen in the horizontal ridges that may develop across the teeth. If caught early, it can be corrected by making amendments to the diet.

Incisor malocclusions are more noticeable in rabbits than molar malocclusions, as the lower incisors may sometimes be seen curving tusklike out of the rabbit's mouth. Upper incisors may curl up and back, eventually piercing the palate. Surprisingly, most rabbits learn to take in food despite maloccluded incisors, although not all are able to do so, and a preference for soft foods

Lauren, before her incisors were removed.

could be an early sign of tooth problems. I have had two rabbits with maloccluded incisors. One was unable to eat when his incisors got too long, the other, who was a rescue with untrimmed teeth when I obtained him, was eating well despite the extremely long incisors protruding from his mouth. He used his lips and tongue to manipulate the food and pull it in around his "tusks."

Overgrown incisors may also cause problems with the

tear ducts, because the tear ducts are very close to the roots of the incisors. Sometimes the overgrown incisor root causes a blockage in the tear duct. If this happens, tears and pus may run down the rabbit's face. The veterinarian may treat this by prescribing an antibiotic ointment or by flushing the duct. (If antibiotic ointments are prescribed, watch that excessive amounts of the ointment are not groomed off and ingested, as this might cause intestinal dysbiosis.)

Clipping to reduce the length of the teeth risks fractures, and filing or burring can cause injury to soft tissue. Extracting maloccluded incisors is often the best long-term solution (see section on extracting teeth later in this chapter). Most rabbits are able to eat hay and greens after incisor removal if they are presented in bite-sized pieces. Jen Hendricks, whose rabbit companion, Thumbelina, had maloccluded incisors removed, suggests chopping enough salad into bite-sized pieces to fill a gallon-sized sealable storage bag, thus reducing the caregiver's daily workload.

However, there are cases where extraction of the incisors is not possible or is too risky. The rabbit may be medically compromised from other conditions (as was my first rabbit with maloccluded teeth) that may cause you to decide it is too high risk for the rabbit to undergo anesthesia and extraction. If this is the decision you reach after consultation with your vet and, if possible, a specialist, you will need to have the incisors trimmed every four to six weeks. Waiting longer than this will risk fracture of the teeth by accident and possible injury to the mouth of the rabbit.

Maloccluded molars present a different set of problems. Maloccluded molars may also be an acquired or an inherited condition, although inherited molar malocclusion is rare. Acquired molar malocclusion is often the end result of a diet poor in fiber and minerals, but tumors and periapical abscesses can also cause molars to grow out of alignment, as can the rabbit favoring an infected or painful tooth. Acquired malocclusion of molars will be most noticeable in older rabbits. The misaligned molars develop sharp spurs—

Capello, one of the authors of *Rabbit and Rodent Dentistry Handbook*, describes them as "sharp as a scalpel blade"—that lacerate the rabbit's tongue and cheek. According to Frances Harcourt-Brown, upper (maxillary) molars tend to flare sideways, cutting the cheeks, and lower jaw (mandibular) molars tend to flare toward the tongue, cutting it. These lacerations are extremely painful, and the rabbit may stop eating and drinking, show signs of severe pain, and possibly develop abscesses. Signs of maloccluded molars include:

- Drooling
- Refusing to drink
- Pain
- Gastrointestinal hypomotility
- Anorexia

The veterinarian may be able to tell if there are any spurs that have developed by feeling the side of the cheeks and looking at the molars with an otoscope. If any problems are found, or the veterinarian feels a more thorough exam is needed, the vet may recommend an examination of the teeth while the rabbit is under anesthesia. X-rays can be taken at the same time to check the tooth roots for periapical abscesses.

In contrast to maloccluded incisors, extracting maloccluded molars is usually *not* recommended by most vets unless an abscess is involved. Instead, maloccluded molars are often clipped, burred, or filed while the rabbit is under general anesthesia. There are special molar clippers made just for this procedure. If the molars are burred or filed, extreme care must be taken not to damage soft tissues of the mouth. Burring down to the gums is not recommended by most rabbit dentistry experts, as this will prevent rabbits from eating the fibrous food necessary for optimal digestive health. Molars usually do not need to be trimmed quite as often as the incisors, but will still need to be done about every six to eight weeks, although this can vary with individual rabbits and be as little as once or twice a year or as often as every two to three weeks. Different vets have more expertise with one method than another, and this may affect the trimming method your veterinarian recommends.

Fractures

Rabbit teeth fracture easily, and the teeth of rabbits with diets low in calcium (again, unlikely except in cases where no commercial pelleted foods are given) will be especially prone to fracture. Incisors may fracture when a rabbit pulls on cage wires with his teeth, or from the trauma of the jaws snapping shut if the rabbit is dropped or jumps and strikes the floor with force. Although fractures usually go down the tooth, Dr. Capello describes first premolars with ADD fracturing across the tooth when rabbits chew hard things like nuts or seeds.

Tooth fractures are dangerous, as periapical abscesses often develop from fractures. If tooth pulp is exposed by a fracture, it is likely to be painful to the rabbit, and he should be given analgesics. Exposed pulp may also become infected and lead to apical abscesses. In the chapter "Small Mammal Dentistry," in *Ferrets, Rabbits, and Rodents: Clinical Medicine and Surgery*, Crossley recommends capping these fractures with a calcium hydroxide cement (normal tooth-filling materials prevent proper tooth wear). Always have a vet check a tooth fracture to determine the extent of the damage and the best course of treatment.

Facial Abscesses

Facial abscesses are usually, although not always, a consequence of acquired dental disease, tooth fractures, or metabolic bone disease. They may be due to tooth root penetration, or they may develop in cheek tissues at ulcers caused by spur lacerations. Periapical abscesses often involve both soft tissues and bone and are very difficult to treat successfully. Most involve lower (mandibular) teeth, although sometimes abscesses are associated with teeth in the upper jaw (maxillary teeth). Those that develop in maxillary teeth often involve the nasolacrimal duct and may result in a retrobulbar abscess, or abscess behind the eyeball. This type of abscess can cause the eye to bulge from its socket as it develops. Because of the location, these abscesses are extremely difficult to treat successfully, and enucleation (removal) of the eye may sometimes be advisable.

Tasha developed repeated jaw abscesses.

Enucleation is not always necessary for successful treatment of these abscesses, however. The authors of an article in the March 2007 volume of the *Journal of the American Veterinary Medical Association* describe treating such an abscess without removing the eye. The treatment described included trimming of the teeth, tooth removal, debridement of the abscess, flushing the abscess cavity with antimicrobials, and antibiotic therapy based on culture and sensitivity tests. Two months after the surgery, the rabbit was doing well and the bulging of the rabbit's eye was minimal.

Abscesses that develop from lacerations caused by molar spurs have a fairly good prognosis since the cause (the spur) can be removed. The protocol is to remove the abnormal tooth growth by clipping or burring the spur, debriding the area, and treating with antibiotics. Sometimes, these abscesses can affect the alignment of teeth, so caretakers will need to be on the watch for any developing malocclusion.

Abscesses due to tooth root penetration are more difficult and have a less hopeful prognosis, particularly as they tend to develop "fingers" that extend outward and may involve the bone. Usually they will not respond well to antibiotic therapy alone. The treatment protocol for these abscesses usually includes debriding the area thoroughly, packing the wound with some kind of antibiotic-containing material (beads, sterile gauze), followed by antibiotic therapy for two to six weeks. The rabbit may be reluctant to eat while recovering and must be encouraged to eat with special foods he particularly likes or to be syringe-fed. Fluid therapy may also be given. The veterinarian may also decide the diseased molars need to be extracted and the root socket flushed out.

When possible, culture and sensitivity testing should be done because bacteria in facial abscesses vary. The infection could be pure *Pasteurella multocida* or *Staphylococcus aureus*, but mixed infections are also possible, and anaerobic bacteria are not uncommon in facial abscesses. Capello, in the *Rabbit and Rodent Dentistry Handbook,* warns that the material at the center of the abscess is usually sterile, and that the sample should be taken from the capsule wall.

Enrofloxacin is a commonly used antibiotic in treating facial abscesses, but the anaerobic bacteria often present in facial abscesses are not sensitive to enrofloxacin. When a sensitivity and culture test is not possible or not available, Capello recommends using enrofloxacin or marbofloxacin plus bicillin antibiotic therapy for two to six weeks. He further notes that repeated flushing and debridement after the initial surgical treatment of a facial abscess are often necessary.

Tooth Extraction

Having a rabbit's teeth extracted may be recommended by your veterinarian for several reasons, including malocclusion, abscesses, fractures, and loose teeth. Tooth extraction will usually require that the rabbit be put under general anesthesia, and recovery time from the operation can be fairly long in some cases. In general, removing the incisors is a simpler operation than removing molars.

Incisor Extraction

Your veterinarian may ask you to consider having a rabbit's incisors removed because of any of the following:
- Malocclusion
- Fractures
- Loose tooth
- Loss of an opposing tooth
- Dental disease

Extraction is often considered the best solution for congenital malocclusion of incisors by many vets, especially for younger rabbits. It will remove the stressful monthly sessions with the veterinarian to have the teeth trimmed, and is unlikely to affect the rabbit's ability to eat.

Extraction of incisors because of acquired malocclusion is not always neces-sary. Sometimes repeated trimming of the tooth opposing the one with acquired malocclusion al-lows occlusion to return to normal, provided there was no damage to the tooth apex. If the apex is damaged, extraction may be advised, although ex-tractions of incisors with acquired malocclusion have been reported to be less successful than extrac-

Elvis (lionhead) had his incisors extracted.

tions of incisors with congenital malocclusion. Incisor ex-tractions that are done on older rabbits may also present problems. The teeth of older rabbits are more brittle and therefore more likely to fracture, the tooth roots may be elongated, and abscesses are more likely to develop at the extraction site afterwards.

If you and your veterinarian decide incisor extraction is advisable, the rabbit will most likely be put under general anesthesia for the tooth removal. The usual procedure is to remove the tooth, curette the space, debride (remove infected tissue) thoroughly, and flush the cavity with an antimicrobial solution. If no infection is present, the cavity is often sutured. If infection is present, the space may be left unsutured to allow repeated flushing. This prevents food becoming impacted in the space.

Extracted maloccluded incisors.

If all the germinal tissue is removed during the extraction, the incisor will not grow back. However, if any of it remains—even the tiniest bit—the tooth will grow back. Any time you have an incisor removed you should watch the rabbit's mouth closely during the time from 4–8 weeks after the removal. If you notice a tooth growing back, contact your vet. It is usually a simple matter to remove the new tooth, although very rarely a tooth may grow back in an abnormal direction, causing serious problems.

You should ask your veterinarian about pain medication for the rabbit whenever a tooth is removed. The mouth can be quite painful afterwards, and the rabbit may require analgesics to promote recovery and encourage him or her to eat. The loss of the incisors will be unlikely to affect the ability to eat in the long term, as the rabbit will pull food into the mouth with the lips. However, since the rabbit will no longer be able to slice through food, you will need to cut harder food (e.g., carrots) into small pieces.

Molar Extraction

The most common reasons for extraction of premolars and molars, called cheek teeth, are loose teeth and abscesses.

Loose cheek teeth are often removed easily, but extracting molars with infection present can be difficult, both because more than one tooth is often involved (requiring removal of all involved teeth), and because the bone may be infected (osteomyelitis).

Usually the procedure begins with exposing the abscess pocket and removing all the pus from the cavity. The cavity is flushed, the roots of the teeth identified, all involved teeth removed through the abscess pocket, and infected bony tissue debrided. Veterinarians differ on whether the cavity should be packed with antibiotic-impregnated material and closed or left open to flush. Some vets prefer to pack the space with antibiotic material such as AIPMMA beads and suture it closed. Other vets prefer to suture the abscess cavity open (marsupialization) and flush it repeatedly. (Rabbits tend to wall off abscesses, eventually leading to their recurrence. It is possible this may be avoided by the latter method.)

After the surgery, pain medication and a course of antibiotics are likely to be prescribed for the rabbit. Since both anaerobic and aerobic bacteria are likely to be present, some veterinarians suggest that bicillin (effective against anaerobes) along with a broad-spectrum antibiotic such as marbofloxacin is an effective combination after molar extraction.

There is disagreement among professionals as to whether the opposing molar or molars should also be extracted. Although some vets feel opposing molars should be removed or the rabbit will not be able to eat correctly, others point out that this does not help because each cheek tooth opposes two others. Remaining teeth tend to curve in toward the empty space, and since dental disease was already present the rabbit is likely to require continuing dental care (e.g., spur reduction) in any case.

Care
Most likely, a rabbit who has had a tooth extracted will be

alert and eating again within a couple of hours after the surgery. However, some are slower to recover than others, and many need a great deal of coaxing to eat after mouth surgery. Maria L. Perez, manager of the Las Vegas chapter of the HRS, has cared for several rabbits after tooth extractions. "You have to keep them comfortable and keep them eating," Maria advises. She has had success with the following aftercare regime:

- Fluids administered twice a day
- Prokinetics given for 3–4 days
- Pain medication (Metacam® or Buprenex®) for 3 days, given in conjunction with a gastric protectant such as famotidine
- Administration of simethicone if intestinal gas is suspected
- Feeding a supplemental pellet such as Critter Be Better® pellets
- Syringe feeding with a supplemental food or canned pumpkin if the rabbit won't eat on his/her own

When the rabbit is feeling better, Maria suggests weaning him/her off syringe feeding by offering "meatballs" made of Critical Care® or Critter Be Better® mixed with a little water. She also suggests giving microgreens or vegetables that have been chopped into tiny pieces.

Because rabbits normally remove bits of loose hair with their incisors, rabbits who have had incisors removed may need help grooming. Brushing the rabbit daily should help remove any loose hair.

CHAPTER 8

OTHER ILLNESSES AND CONDITIONS REQUIRING SPECIAL CARE

Lucile C. Moore

Neurologic Disease

Diseases affecting the neurological system are fairly common in rabbits. Two often-encountered symptoms of neurologic disease are head tilt (wryneck, torticollis) and seizures. Determining the actual cause of the symptoms can be difficult, even for veterinarians. Dr. William Kurmes explains:

> The symptoms of neurologic disease are often very similar despite many different underlying causes. This is because the symptoms are more related to the location affected, rather than the specific cause. Sometimes the specific symptoms can be used to determine the location of a localized lesion, while other, more generalized symptoms can be caused by many different or more diffuse diseases. Veterinarians and doctors use a list of possible causes called a "differential diagnosis." A veterinarian will use the history (age, sex, onset and duration of symptoms, housing, diet, etc.) to help determine which problems are the most likely cause of the disease and which tests are most likely to help determine a specific cause. Once a spe-

cific cause is determined, the correct treatment is more likely to be used. Sometimes, a specific diagnosis is difficult or impossible to determine, but a good differential diagnosis will help to determine which problems are more likely than others—then it may be worthwhile to try the treatment the rabbit is most likely to benefit from.

The following outline demonstrates some of the possible causes of neurologic disease in rabbits:

Infections
- Bacterial—*Pasteurella multocida,* many other bacteria
- Viral—rabies, herpes
- Protozoal (single-celled parasites)—*Encephalitozoon cuniculi, Toxoplasma*
- Parasitic—*Baylisascaris*

Physical
- Trauma—brain, spinal
- Stroke (not well documented, but suspected in older rabbits)
- Heat stroke
- Spondylosis (arthritic degeneration of spinal joints)
- Neoplasia (cancer)

Toxic
- Metal poisoning (lead)
- Plant toxins (milkweed)
- Strychnine
- Drug toxicity

Metabolic
- Pregnancy toxemia

- Liver and/or kidney disease

Nutritional
- Vitamin deficiencies—vitamin A, E
- Mineral deficiencies—calcium, magnesium, potassium

Developmental
- Syringomyelia [progressive disease of spinal cord]
- Achondroplasia [abnormal development of cartilage]

Care

Care of rabbits with neurologic disease will vary depending upon the cause of the neurological symptoms. Head tilt is the most common symptom of neurologic disease a rabbit caregiver is likely to encounter. The actual cause of head tilt is a change in the sense of balance in the inner/middle ear or brain. One care issue that appears to be constant for head-tilt rabbits, whatever the cause of the symptom, is that

Charlie has head tilt, but in this photo she looks simply inquisitive.

the more active the rabbit is, the better he will learn to compensate. Caregivers may have a tendency to limit a head-tilt rabbit's activities—don't. Encourage a head-tilt rabbit to move around so that he learns to adapt and compensate.

Seizures

Seizures can be even more frightening to the rabbit caregiver than head tilt. A rabbit having a seizure may at first appear disoriented or restless. This may be followed by muscle tremors, chewing, salivation, uncontrollable leg spasms, eyes rolling back in the head, urination and defecation, and unconsciousness.

If you are alone with your rabbit when he has seizures, speak quietly to the rabbit during the episode, which will normally last from one to two minutes. Clear the area to minimize the chances of the rabbit hurting himself. Then wrap the rabbit in cool wet towels and take him to a veterinarian. If the seizures do not stop after two minutes, place the rabbit in a box padded with pillows or soft towels, and take him to a vet. A veterinarian will likely administer fluids and give drugs to control the seizures (if they have continued) and stabilize the rabbit. Diagnostic tests (blood, urine) may then be done to attempt to determine the cause of the seizures, if unknown. In EC rabbits, seizures may occur unexpectedly and the rabbit may recover completely or be left blind or comatose.

Jennifer Heaton, a shelter volunteer, took a young rabbit experiencing seizures under her wing. The rabbit, Bianca, suffered violent seizures, during which she would at times run headlong into walls and doors. These seizures would occur about every two days. At other times, the rabbit appeared healthy and happy. Jennifer modified Bianca's living area, padding it so Bianca would not harm herself during seizures. Two of the drugs her vet prescribed to control the seizures were phenobarbital and an injectible, fast-acting valium. The cause of these seizures was not determined.

Epilepsy, although very rare in rabbits, does occur occasionally, usually (not always) in blue-eyed, white rabbits. Rachel Marek's rabbit, Bugger, was diagnosed with epilepsy. When his seizures became more frequent, Rachel made the decision to have him put on medication to control them. Bugger now receives a twice-daily dose of phenobarbital. His vet schedules checks on Bugger's liver function, which could be affected by the drug.

Hearing Loss

Deafness can be inherited, the result of trauma, a middle ear infection, a severe infestation of ear mites, or a disease such as EC. Hearing loss can occur at any age, but is more common in older rabbits. Lop rabbits, who may have difficulty cleaning their ears, can have buildups of wax and exudates in the external ear canal that will affect their hearing. A significant number of rabbits have hearing loss. In one study, about one-third of adult rabbits were found to have otitis media (infection with accumulation of pus, debris, and wax in the ear canal), which is assumed to cause some hearing loss. Common bacterial genera associated with otitis media are *Pasteurella, Bordetella, Escherichia, Proteus, Staphylococcus,* and *Pseudomonas.* If an infection of the middle ear extends to the inner ear, head tilt may occur.

Although hearing loss in rabbits is not uncommon, it can be difficult to assess. A person may in fact have a partially or totally deaf rabbit and never realize it because the rabbit will pick up on cues from their caretaker, other animals, and vibrations. Kathy Smith, author of *Rabbit Health in the 21st Century*, notes that a deaf rabbit often won't startle at loud noises with no excessive vibration, but will startle at those loud noises that produce a vibration.

If you suspect your rabbit has some hearing loss, try to get him where he cannot see you or any other animals, and then test him by making a loud noise (but not so loud it would have strong vibrations) and watch for any response. Notice whether he is ever surprised by your approach when you come from a direction where you can't be seen.

Care

Hearing can rarely be restored, but deaf rabbits function quite well, and the other senses compensate for the loss of hearing to a great extent. Stephen F. Guida, who is a volunteer with Brambley Hedge Rabbit Rescue, comments:

> I have found [deaf rabbits] can startle easily because they cannot hear us coming up to them. Moving slowly into their field of view and gently touching them first before picking them up—almost like "asking permission" to handle them, which I think is a good idea for any rabbit, disabled or not, will usually help avoid a panicked, startled reaction to our activities.

Flashing lights on and off before entering a room will signal to a deaf rabbit that you are coming. If the rabbit is housed on a wooden floor rather than cement, he may be able to pick up vibrations and know when he is being approached. Deaf rabbits can sometimes learn to communicate by hand signals, claps, or even stamping feet on a wooden floor. Companion rabbits sometimes work well with deaf rabbits—the deaf rabbit soon learns to take his cues from his bunny buddy. This is not always successful, however. Joanne Wilcox was unable to socialize her deaf bunny because he was frightened by what appeared to him as the other rabbits sneaking up on him. Each rabbit is different; figure out what works best for your particular bun.

Loss of Sight

Rabbits may be born blind (more prevalent in certain breeds), or lose their sight from an injury, cataracts, diabetes, glaucoma, or a disease such as *E. cuniculi* (the lens ruptures and the rabbits develop cataracts, although they may not completely lose their eyesight). An inherited glaucoma (an autosomal recessive) sometimes occurs in white New Zealand rabbits.

Blind rabbits, like deaf ones, generally adapt quite well to their handicap. Kathy Smith, author of *Rabbit Health in the 21st Century,* has experience with blind rabbits, and offers the following article of care tips:

Caring for a Blind Bunny
Kathy Smith

Rabbits have a more balanced dependence on their five senses than we humans do. Blindness will probably upset you more than it upsets your bunny. Minimize environmental dangers, stimulate the remaining four senses, and watch your blind bunny blossom!

Minimize Danger

If your blind bunny is bonded with another animal, carefully observe interactions with his friend. In rare cases, a rambunctious companion can inadvertently injure a blind bunny. Usually, however, a bonded mate will adjust to his companion's needs, often becoming a "seeing eye rabbit."

Keep your blind bunny's space as consistent as possible, especially if he does not have a bonded companion to help him navigate around obstacles. Avoid moving furniture around and keep litter box, food, and water in the same place.

Kathy's first blind bunny, Choca Paws.

Think before you move your blind bunny to different living quarters. Weigh the risks in his current area against the stress of moving and learning his way around a new space. Take cues from your bunny. If he seems content where he is, make every effort to adapt his current space to his new needs: reduce clutter, re-route human traffic, and provide protection from sharp furniture corners.

If you do have to move your blind bunny, start with a small area and preserve the layout of his key furnishings (litter box, food, water, bed, even toys). Resist the urge to launder or replace rugs, towels, or bedding as part of the move. It is important for your blind bunny to have things with his scent to help him feel at home in a new space.

Carefully supervise whenever a blind bunny explores a new area. Note how he moves, often nose to the ground. Be ready to step in if he begins to panic, but resist the urge to jump to the rescue because *you* think he is in trouble. Understand that he will occasionally run into things or appear to be trapped. Admire how resourceful he is at learning his way around and working things out for himself.

Remind children to be especially calm around your blind bunny. Quick movements and sudden loud noises—both normal parts of childhood play—are more likely to frighten an animal who cannot see. If startled, a blind rabbit can easily become disoriented and hurt himself. Warn *all* humans who visit to move carefully around your blind bunny. Point out that a startled rabbit may dart from a safe spot to an unsafe one, such as directly under their feet. Repeat these cautions as often as necessary, until you are sure they are second nature to the other humans in your rabbit's life.

Take extra precautions to protect your blind bunny from other household pets. A cat or dog who has always been safe around your rabbit may not realize that his playful antics can frighten or hurt a blind bunny. It is important to closely supervise your rabbit's interactions with other animals.

A rabbit who has begun to lose his sight may still be able to see changes in light and shadow, which can be frightening to him. Shadows often equate to danger for a prey animal. Consider the impact sudden changes in the room's lighting or wispy curtains blowing in the wind have on a room's shadows and change décor to minimize impact.

Stimulate the Other Four Senses
Always speak as you approach a blind bunny. Keep your voice soft and maintain a consistent tone. This is a good practice with sighted bunnies as well.

Spend time talking to your bunny, especially if he does not have an animal companion. Whether you believe he understands or not, the sound of your voice speaking loving words will help him know he is safe.

Spend extra time sitting on the floor next to your blind bunny, petting him. Touch lets him know you are near and that you love him. Spending time on his level will help alert you to potential hazards.

Try not to pick a blind bunny up any more than necessary unless you are certain he enjoys it. Being lifted off the ground is fright-

Oliver, an older blind rabbit.

ening to most bunnies and can be even more frightening to one who cannot see.

Your blind bunny may enjoy the feel of a soft, fluffy bed; towels; or baby-safe soft toy. Watch carefully to ensure he doesn't try to chew fabrics. Stuffed balls with bells inside (designed for infants) are relatively chew-proof and have been a favorite toy with many of my bunnies.

If your rabbit is old enough for greens and tolerates them well, offer fragrant treats. Parsley, cilantro, dill, and other bunny-safe herbs can stimulate your bunny's senses of smell and taste. If you have not fed these before, introduce them one at a time and stop if you notice changes in fecal output (size, consistency, or amount) or tummy noises, or signs of GI pain.

Scent will become an important way for your bunny to recognize you. Resist the urge to experiment with fragrances: stick to one brand/scent of shampoo, conditioner, and other cosmetic items. Also use caution when changing cleaning and laundry products. Using gentle, natural, and unscented products is safest for all rabbits.

Animals are surprisingly sensitive to human emotions. Your blind rabbit will continue to feel like a normal rabbit unless you make him think otherwise. Animals are very resilient to changes in their abilities, and their success in adapting to change can be a real inspiration.

Behavioral Issues

Sometimes, a rabbit may develop physical problems as a result of behavioral issues. Ms. J. Medawar, who has had experience with such rabbits, offers the following observations:

Often rabbits that have experienced past abuse, neglect, physical or psychological trauma may display nervous and/or aggressive behaviors. It is important to understand that, providing pain has been ruled out as the cause of the behavior, the aggressive rabbit and the nervous rabbit are two sides of he same psychological issue: fear. The nervous rabbit is overly cautious, apparently fearful of everything, and lacking in confidence. The aggressive rabbit may seem to be full of rage, temperamental and overly confident, when in fact he is every bit as fearful and insecure as his anxious counterpart.

While these behaviors are easily observed, what is sometimes less obvious is the correlation between the behavior and more serious medical conditions. Barbering, anorexia, and ileus are all conditions which may affect a rabbit with an anxiety issue. Barbering, a psychological issue often associated with neglect or a lack of environmental stimuli, can progress from over-grooming or trimming of the rabbit's own fur, or that of a partner, to a medical issue if the rabbit causes physical injury to itself or the partner. Repetitive bouts of anorexia and ileus may be common in the anxious rabbit. The stress the rabbit feels due to his lack of confidence with another animal or caregiver (or new situations such as a move or routine vet visit) may trigger a reluctance to eat for several hours, GI slowdown, or full GI stasis.

Often there is no readily perceived trigger to an episode, leaving his caregiver frustrated as to cause and effect. Regular, supervised, safe, out-of-cage exercise, appropriate diet, new stimuli (such as a variety of toys), and positive, confidence-building experiences are important, and useful in managing frequent barbering, anorexia, or ileus in those rabbits. Some rabbits may shrug off the experiences of their past easily, while others may take years to make progress in conquering their fears.

Adopting or fostering a rabbit with an anxiety issue will require a high level of commitment from the new caregiver.

Kidney and Bladder Disease

Rabbits are prone to several kidney-related problems, especially as they age. Some can be partially controlled by diet; others may require medical treatment and/or surgery.

Sludgy Urine (Hypercalciuria)

Because of their unique calcium metabolism, rabbit urine normally has some calcium particles. In a healthy rabbit who gets enough water and exercise, the particles are excreted. But in older rabbits, obese rabbits, rabbits who are not able to get adequate exercise, rabbits who cannot adopt the correct urination posture, and rabbits who do not drink enough water, the particles are not adequately excreted and begin to accumulate. As the condition progresses, the rabbit urinates off the top layer, leaving the particles. This is bladder sludge. The bladder may become weak and distended, and the rabbit may develop urine scald and incontinence. Eventually, the excessive particles may irritate the bladder lining, blood may appear in the urine, infection set in, and a dark, foul-smelling discharge be excreted. Rarely, the sludge may cause an obstruction. Radiographs are necessary for diagnosis.

Rabbits absorb all the calcium they take in, excreting the excess in their urine. In the past, it was thought sludgy urine was probably caused by excessive calcium in the diet; now it is believed to be caused by a combination of factors. If caught early, sludgy urine can sometimes be treated by increasing the rabbit's water intake, encouraging activity, possibly reducing calcium in the diet (many vets still recommend this), and expressing the rabbit's bladder. If the rabbit is reluctant to drink, some veterinarians recommend flavoring the water with a bit of fruit juice (that has no added sugar) to encourage fluid intake. Where infection has set in, antibiotics will be prescribed, and fluids and syringe feeding may be necessary.

Laura and Peter Franco's older rabbit, Elaine, has problems with bladder sludge:

> She usually shows symptoms by becoming lethargic, with less interest in food. By the next day we will notice her straining to urinate by lifting her butt way up in the air. She also begins to pee smaller amounts outside her litter box with a white chalky consistency to the urine. She has responded well to subcutaneous fluids; 100 cc for the first day, 50 cc after the initial hydration for a few more days and a course of Baytril® for 10–14 days. She is on a lower calcium diet.

Urolithiasis

Uroliths are crystals, usually calcium carbonate or calcium phosphate, that precipitate out of a rabbit's urine when the pH is higher than normal (8.5–9.5; normal urine is 8.2). These crystals may be found in the ureters, renal pelvis, bladder, or urethra, and will be visible in radiographs. Excessive amounts are more common in male rabbits and older rabbits, although they can occur in any rabbit. Lack of exercise, nutritional imbalances, age, low water intake, drinking well water, and obesity may predispose rabbits to the condition, and a genetic factor may exist as well. The occurrence of calcium oxalate uroliths may be related to the consumption of oxalates (high in alfalfa and spinach). Some veterinarians believe uroliths develop in response to an obstruction in the urinary tract: excessive sludge, tumor, adhesion, or abscess. Symptoms of urolithiasis include:

- Failure to use litter box for urination
- Inability to urinate (if actual obstruction present)
- Straining to urinate with hind leg and tail tremors

- Urine burn
- Excessive licking of perineal area
- Anorexia
- Pain (grinding teeth, hunching)
- Weight loss

If a rabbit is unable to urinate at all, immediate veterinary treatment is necessary to save the rabbit's life. In this case, something will actually be obstructing the urinary tract, and without prompt intervention the rabbit will die.

Diagnostics that may be performed by the vet may include radiographs, urinalysis, ultrasound, and bloodwork. Treatment will depend upon the location and size of stones. (In some cases where stones do not cause problems, no treatment may be necessary.) If the crystals are smaller and not completely obstructing the urinary tract, non-surgical treatment is preferred. Smaller uroliths can sometimes be eliminated by increasing the water in the rabbit's diet, possibly by subcutaneous fluids. Most vets do not believe the crystals will dissolve with diet change, but reducing the amount of calcium and protein is usually still recommended. Sometimes flushing or expressing the bladder will be necessary to remove smaller crystals not being excreted from the bladder by the rabbit's normal urination. Do not attempt to express your rabbit's bladder without instruction from a veterinarian—if a urolith is actually obstructing the urinary tract, manual expression of the bladder could rupture it. Depending upon the location of larger stones, urethral flushing or surgery may be recommended. The surgery carries fairly high risks.

Urinary Tract Infections (UTIs)

The presence of sludgy urine and uroliths will predispose rabbits to UTIs, although they may also occur in rabbits without those conditions. Abnormal-smelling urine, dark-colored discharge, and loss of litter box habits are signs of a possible UTI, but these infections are often asymptomatic, and therefore very dangerous. According to Harvey, in the article "Rabbits: Geriatrics and Chronic Disease," older rabbits and those who are debilitated from another condition carry a relatively high risk of developing septicemia (blood poisoning) from UTIs.

Urine culture may be more effective than urinalysis in confirming the existence of a UTI. However, taking a urine sample with a needle (cystocentesis) may be risky unless the veterinarian is very experienced treating rabbits. The procedure carries the risk of puncturing the cecum unless it is done correctly, when the bladder is full and the rabbit positioned properly. Samples for culture and sensitivity can be taken other ways, e.g., catch from bladder expression. Although alternative methods do risk contamination, cystocentesis also carries a small risk of contamination from intestinal fluid. Fluids and antibiotics are commonly prescribed for UTIs. In response to my question about which drugs (in general) are good for treating UTIs, Dr. Bill Guerrera wrote:

> Usually the sulfa drugs (TMS) have good penetration into the urinary system. The fluoroquinolones are great because they cover a broad spectrum. Again, selection should ideally be based on culture and sensitivity. Injectable antibiotics are given if there is a problem with absorption or you want to give an antibiotic that is harmful if given orally (penicillins), but are not always more effective.

Acute Kidney Failure

Acute kidney failure can often be treated if it is recognized in time. It may be brought on by:
- Hypothermia
- Hyperthermia
- Extreme stress, including fright
- Severe GI disease
- Plant toxins/mycotoxins/nephrotoxins
- Muscle damage (especially from predator attack)
- Severe dehydration

Symptoms of acute kidney failure include:
- Excessive urination
- Excessive drinking
- Failing to urinate
- Urine scald
- Anorexia
- Lethargy
- Dehydration
- Bad breath

Treatment for acute kidney failure is likely to include the administration of fluids, anabolic steroids (as an appetite stimulant), and antibiotics to prevent bacterial infections. Some veterinarians caution that sulfonamides and aminoglycosides should be avoided. Acute kidney failure can cause stomach ulcers, which may need to be treated with a medication such as sucralfate.

Chronic Kidney Failure

Chronic kidney failure is often seen in older rabbits, obese rabbits, and rabbits with EC, anorexia, cancer, cysts, and urinary tract infections. A blood test (blood urea nitrogen and creatinine) will verify suspected renal problems. Symptoms of chronic failure include:
- Urine burn
- Hypercalcemia (high calcium)
- Hypocalcemia (low calcium)
- Hypokalemia (low potassium)
- Lethargy
- Anemia
- Anorexia
- Dehydration
- GI hypomotility

Chronic kidney failure can be managed by giving fluids and electrolytes, minimizing calcium intake (if calcium is high), increasing potassium intake (if the rabbit is hypokalemic), and restricting phosphate intake (carrots, bananas, and tomatoes are high in phosphate). Anabolic steroids may be prescribed as an appetite stimulant, to increase the retention of electrolytes, and to reduce urea and the breakdown of proteins. Other drugs may be prescribed as well. When Shannon Cail's rabbit, Bailey, went into renal failure, one of the medications he was given was an experimental drug, mirtazapine, to help reduce nausea caused by the kidney failure.

Courageous Bailey

Hypothermia and Hyperthermia

Hypothermia

Hypothermia, loss of heat, is a sign of a very serious condition needing prompt attention to avoid the rabbit's death. If the rabbit is hypothermic, the rectal temperature will be below 100°F (37.7°C). This may be encountered in rabbits recovering from anesthesia, rabbits suffering any pain, rabbits that have acute bloat, GI hypomotility, mycotoxicosis, or are in shock.

To help prevent hypothermia in a rabbit who has had an operation and has had fur shaved off, it may be enough to turn the heat up a little or cover the rabbit with a light baby blanket.

When treating rabbits with gastrointestinal hypomotility, taking the rabbit's temperature frequently can help catch any drops in body temperature. (See Chapter 2 for information on taking your rabbit's temperature.) If the rabbit's temperature starts to fall, you will need to act promptly to bring it up. Corded devices such as electric heating pads are not recommended because of the risk of getting the rabbit too hot, and also because of rabbits' tendency to chew cords. Many rabbit caretakers use a microwaveable SnuggleSafe® disc to keep their rabbits warm. I like to use a corn-filled pillow heated in the microwave. It holds heat for a long time, and conforms to rabbit's body. Whatever method you use to bring up your rabbit's temperature, be sure not to get the rabbit *too* hot. Once it is up to the normal range (101°F–103°F), reduce the amount of added heat. Ensure bunny is able to maintain body temperature once he reaches normal range by follow-up temperature taking.

Hyperthermia

Hyperthermia, or heat stress, is as deadly as hypothermia. Rabbits do not sweat and cannot pant in the fashion of a dog or cat to lower their temperature, and in general do better at lower environmental temperatures than high ones. Heat stroke can occur to a rabbit in your home if the weather becomes unexpectedly hot or if a rabbit is confined in a cage near a window or heat source he cannot move away from. Watch for these signs of heat stress:

- Labored breathing (dyspnoea)
- Disorientation
- Weakness
- Seizures
- Prostration
- Anorexia
- Fluid in lungs
- Rectal temperature over 105°F (40.5°C)
- Cyanosis
- Unconsciousness

If your rabbit has heat stroke, you must take action immediately to save your rabbit's life. Cool him *gradually* with cool wet towels, wet the ears with cool water, and give fluids to reduce the danger of renal failure. Take the rabbit to the vet as soon as possible. The prognosis for heat stroke is not good, and even if the rabbit recovers he will need to be monitored for kidney (renal) failure for several days afterward.

Remember that any temperature over 85°F (29°C) is potentially dangerous to your rabbit, especially if it is also humid. If the ambient temperature rises this high, you must take steps to cool the rabbit. Provide lots of cool water—try placing ice cubes in a dish of water. Frozen water-filled juice cartons can be wrapped in towels and placed next to the rabbit. Fans with damp towels hung in front of them can help cool the air and relieve the rabbit's stress if it is not too humid. A too-hot environment can also cause alopecia (loss of hair).

Shock

Although some of the signs of hypothermia and hyperthermia are present when a rabbit goes into shock, technically they are different conditions. Shock occurs when there are changes in the circulatory system. There are three kinds of shock: hypovolemic, cardiogenic, and distributive. (Usually when shock is discussed it is hypovolemic shock, or a drop in blood flow, that is meant.) Unless the progression of shock is stopped, the rabbit (or any other mammal in shock) will die.

Signs of shock in a rabbit include:
- Grayish or bright pink mucous membranes (easiest to observe in gums and eyes)
- Low body temperature
- Weak pulse
- Loss of consciousness

To prevent shock from progressing to death, it is necessary to raise the body temperature and give fluids. Your vet may also administer drugs to help return the circulatory system to normal.

Cancer (Neoplastic Disease)

The growth of tumors (neoplasms) is not uncommon in rabbits, although abscesses are a more likely cause of un-identified masses in a companion rabbit. Neoplasms may be benign or malignant and may occur in rabbits of any age, although older rabbits have a higher incidence.

The medical terminology for the various types of tumors can be very confusing to the caretaker with little medical background. In general, the term for a particular neoplasm reflects the area of the body in which it is found and the type of tissue in which it arose. For example, sarcoma is the term used to designate neoplasms that arise in mes-enchymal (connective) tissue. Therefore, a lymphosarcoma is a malignant neoplasm in lymph tissue, a liposarcoma is such a neoplasm in fatty tissue. Carcinomas are tumors that develop in epithelial tissue. An adenocarcinoma would be a malignant tumor that originated in the epithelium of a gland or glandular tissue.

Although uterine cancer is extremely common in intact adult female rabbits, it is not a danger to spayed fe-male companion rabbits. (Cancer of the mammary glands frequently occurs in conjunction with uterine cancer, but is rare in spayed rabbits, although it may occur if a spay was incomplete or done when the rabbit was older.) Two types of cancer some veterinarians and caretakers have reported seeing in companion rabbits with some frequency are lym-phoma and thymoma. Lymphomas are neoplasms of lymph tissue. They may occur in any organ, such as the eye, spleen, liver, and kidneys. Rarely, cutaneous lymphoma (neoplasms in the skin) may occur, appearing as swellings over the shoul-ders. Lymphoma is usually multicentric, or occurring in sev-eral different areas. This makes it particularly difficult to treat. Symptoms are often general. The rabbit may be lethargic; have diarrhea, respiratory difficulties, and limb paresis (weak-ness); lose his appetite; and eventually become emaciated. At other times there may be no observable sign of anything wrong until an affected organ fails.

Missy Ott, an experienced House Rabbit Society educator in Florida, had a rabbit who suddenly appeared unwell. She immediately took the rabbit to a veterinary hospital where the rabbit died two days later. A necropsy showed cancer that had spread throughout the body cavity, although the rabbit had shown no sign that anything was wrong until the end. This is not an unusual occurrence in rabbits with cancer.

Thymomas are neoplasms of mixed cellular origin (lymphoid and epithelial) in the thymus (a gland in the chest). Thymic lymphosarcomas are tumors originating in the lymph tissue of the thymus. The latter type of neoplasms usually affects other organs as well. There may be no observable signs of thymomas until the tumor grows large enough to disrupt the function of other organs, at which time the rabbit may show respiratory or cardiac distress. If the neoplasm puts pressure on the esophagus, the rabbit may regurgitate food. The eyes may bulge (exophthalmos) if the tumor presses on the jugular vein. Although excision (if possible) appears to give the most hope for a cure, radiation therapy has been reported being successful on some rabbits with thymoma.

At 10½ years of age, Fidgit developed a thymoma.

Rabbits may also be affected by benign skin tumors caused by viruses. The oral papillomavirus is the most common. Oral papillomas occur on the tongue and elsewhere in the mouth and are observed as numerous small whitish growths. Eventually they disappear, leaving the rabbit immune. Shope papilloma is endemic to cottontails, and only rarely affects domestic rabbits in the US. The Shope papillomavirus causes the growth of horny warts that most often appear on the eyelids and ears. These warts are usually scratched off and heal with no complications, but, infrequently, squamous cell carcinoma may develop from one. Shope fibroma virus causes benign skin tumors that usually appear as swellings on the legs, feet, and ears. The tumors may remain several months, after which they regress. Skin tumors that are not associated with these viruses may also occur in rabbits, although rarely, including cutaneous lymphoma and metastases from other cancers.

Anal papillomas may also occur in rabbits. These wart-like growths are benign neoplasms that are not related to the above-mentioned papillomas. They bleed easily, and the sight of them growing out of the anus may frighten a caretaker. Often they cause no problems and are left untreated until they regress. In other cases, a veterinarian may recommend excision.

There are many other cancers that can affect rabbits, including various neoplasms of the liver, kidneys, testes, and gastrointestinal tract. A variety of diagnostic tests may be ordered by your vet if cancer is suspected, including radiographs, ultrasound, and a CBC (complete blood count). A chemistry profile may be run to help the vet determine organ involvement. Fine needle aspiration may be done to determine whether a questionable mass is cancer, abscess, or cyst. If cancer is present, your vet may do a full-body X-ray to look for any metastases. A biopsy or excision will be necessary for a definitive diagnosis of the specific cancer, but the rabbit may be treated without one on a presumptive diagnosis.

Treatment

In general, cancer is very difficult to treat in rabbits, both because it is often multifocal and because the rabbit may show no sign of the disease until it is well-developed. Chemotherapy and radiation may be tried, but at the time of this writing limited success has been reported with these methods in rabbits. Some vets report that their most successful treatment is often excision, but this is not a viable option unless the tumor is located where it is operable and has not metastasized.

Sometimes a cancer may be growing slowly enough that a quality life can be extended for several months to several years. Maria Perez, manager of the Las Vegas HRS chapter, has a rabbit with a slow-growing lung cancer. By providing Chloe with supportive care (including nebulization), Maria has been able to give her a near-normal life for some time.

If your rabbit is given a diagnosis of cancer, you will have difficult decisions to make. You will need to weigh your rabbit's condition, the progression of the disease, the rabbit's desire to fight, and your own financial and personal situation. You may decide euthanasia is the most humane option, you may choose to try an aggressive treatment program including chemotherapy or radiation, or you may opt to extend the rabbit's life with supportive care as long as the rabbit retains quality of life and shows a desire to live. It is necessary to listen to what the rabbit's behavior is telling you and then follow your instincts.

Kathy Smith, author of *Rabbit Health in the 21st Century*, has chosen different paths with different rabbits:

> When my beloved Smokey was diagnosed with cancer ten years ago, he made it clear he would do *anything* to spend more time with me. It was hard for me to choose surgery and chemotherapy for him, knowing that was not what I would want for myself. Looking back, I understand he came into my life to teach me the lessons I learned during our five-month battle together. I am grateful for his courage— and for a husband who supported my decisions both emotionally and financially. Before deciding to try the second chemotherapy drug, I remember asking Smokey's vet (Dr. Teresa Bradley), "What would you do if he were your bunny?" I will always be grateful for her

response: "If he were my bunny, I would have to stop because I would be out of money."

Since Smokey's death I have learned about a variety of alternative treatments, and I consider these options for my own health care as well as veterinary care. I am more likely to choose an alternative approach for conditions like cancer where traditional treatments (surgery, radiation, and chemotherapy) are harsh, more often causing side effects that destroy quality of life than actually curing the disease. When traditional treatments are both expensive and offer little hope, as they did with my second rabbit diagnosed with cancer, Ebony, a few months ago, trying a holistic herbal preparation gave me the peace that comes with "trying something" without subjecting him to uncomfortable procedures and unwanted handling.

Since Ebony's death, my Dante has taken me a step further in the education process. I now understand that the right answer for some patients (regardless of species) is to make the difficult *choice* to do nothing to either speed up or slow down the dying process. I now try to let my rabbit's reaction to treatments/medications—even those given for pain—be the guide that lets me know if my help is welcomed or if I am interfering with a natural process.

As Kathy Smith points out, cancer is a disease for which non-traditional treatments can be of great benefit, especially when used in conjunction with traditional protocols. See Part II for detailed information.

Cardiovascular Disease
Kathy Smith

There has not been a lot written about cardiovascular disease in rabbits, perhaps because symptoms often come on slowly and are subtle enough to be missed by even the most observant caregiver. A wide variety of cardiovascular ailments that affect humans can also affect rabbits including (but not limited to):

- *Cardiomyopathy.* Any disease that affects the myocardium (muscle of the heart wall), usually resulting in an enlarged and less efficient heart.
- *Pulmonary congestion.* Accumulation of fluid in the lungs.
- *Congestive heart failure (CHF).* Abnormal condition that reflects impaired cardiac pumping caused by valve damage, reduced blood flow to the heart muscle (due to coronary artery disease), or cardiomyopathy. Symptoms may include pulmonary congestion or peripheral edema (swelling).
- *Arrhythmia.* Irregular heartbeat.
- *Heart murmur.* An extra or unusual sound heard when listening to the heartbeat with a stethoscope. Heart murmurs may be caused by congenital heart defects or by heart valve problems caused by infection, disease, or the aging process. While heart murmurs in rabbits bear further investigation, they do not always require immediate treatment.

While researching this section I e-mailed Dr. James K. Morrisey at the College of Veterinary Medicine, Cornell University, and asked what types of heart disease he was seeing most often in pet rabbits. Dr. Morrisey replied:

> We see mostly dilated cardiomyopathy in rabbits. This means the heart muscles get weak causing the heart chambers to enlarge and the muscles can't pump blood out of the heart as well. This causes blood to "back up" in the vessels and fluid to leak out into tissues, such as the lungs, abdomen or around the heart. I've also seen a few cases in which the larger vessels and one case in which the heart valves became calcified but I haven't seen problems with this. This calcification could predispose them to heart disease because it would make their hearts have to work harder.

My primary rabbit veterinarian, Dr. Noella Allan, has treated several cases of heart disease in rabbits. She explains the difficulty veterinarians face in detecting heart problems during routine office visits:

> When I began performing physical examinations on house rabbits, I found it much harder to differentiate their heart sounds and rhythms because the hearts beat so much faster than in cats and dogs (especially during office visits, which may be stressful). I'd pick up irregularities in the rhythm, abnormal sounds, and more muffled sounds, making it necessary to perform additional diagnostics.

Murray was a "heart bun" in all senses of the word. We developed a deep bond over the years as we dealt with chronic ear, teeth, bladder, and gastrointestinal issues.

Dr. Allan noticed his enlarged heart in June of 2002, when he was X-rayed during one of his many bouts of GI slowdown. She ordered diagnostic tests and consulted with a cardiologist to determine the best treatment protocol. Dr. Allan explains:

Murray guarded the refrigerator, demanding cranberries just one month before he was diagnosed with an enlarged heart.

> I do the initial work-up and, depending on the need, obtain additional information from electrocardiography (ECG, read by a cardiologist to help analyze abnormal sounds or rhythms), echocardiograms (ultrasounds, performed by a radiologist or cardiologist to help evaluate structural and functional abnormalities), or thoracic radiographs. The latter test helps determine the size and shape of the heart, lung concerns, or the presence of a tumor of the thymus (thymoma) that may present with clinical signs similar to heart disease.
>
> Since the radiologist who performed the cardiac ultrasound (echo) was not as familiar with normal rabbit heart measurements, we supplied healthy rabbits of equal size to supply normal baseline readings for this and future ultrasound studies.

After reviewing the results of Murray's ECG and echocardiogram with the cardiologist, Dr. Allan started Murray on a low dose—one she had used before on rabbits with no problems—of enalapril (an ACE inhibitor). Within a couple of hours of his first dose, Murray (who had shown sensitivity to other medications, specifically opiates) was extremely lethargic and "zoned out." Rather than discontinue the treatment, we cut the dose in half and, over time, were able to slowly increase it back to the original dose.

Three months after his diagnosis, a more sedate Murray still enjoyed his cranberries.

In the months that followed, Murray still required frequent (every five to eight weeks) filing of molar spurs under anesthesia. Dr. Allan and I held our breath each time, but Murray did surprisingly well. During this time, Dr. Allan began putting Murray on pure oxygen as he was coming out of anesthesia, a practice she continues to use on my rabbits whenever she does a dental procedure.

After several months, Dr. Allan discovered another heart problem during one of Murray's exams—an arrhythmia (irregular heartbeat). She ordered another ECG and echocardiogram, consulted with the cardiologist, and placed him on atenolol, a selective beta blocker. Because of Murray's sensitivity to medications, Dr. Allan decided on a twice-daily dose, which he tolerated well.

Two months before his death, Murray's declining health was visible in his rough coat.

Murray lived 10 months after his initial diagnosis of heart disease. He died peacefully while I was at work—in fact, he looked so comfortable on his blue bunny rug that I actually took pictures before I realized he wasn't breathing. Dr. Allan and I suspect that Murray's heart problems were caused, at least in part, by infection. He spent most of his life battling ear infections caused by a resistant strain of *Pseudomonas* bacteria. Dr. Allan noticed that his arrhythmia seemed to worsen whenever we took him off antibiotics and improved again when we restarted antibiotic therapy.

From my experience with Murray I know how expensive cardiovascular diagnostics can be. Since some caregivers may not be able to afford *all* recommended tests, one of the questions I asked Dr. Morrisey was what diagnostics he had found most useful in rabbits. He responded:

> I think that an echocardiogram is the most helpful tool to really assess cardiac function. ECGs aren't as helpful in my experience because the rabbits rarely have electrical abnormalities, although we always do them to make sure we're not missing something. Radiographs are also useful screening tools to see if the heart is enlarged.

Of course, whenever financially possible it is best to perform all recommended diagnostics to get the most complete and accurate medical assessment.

Heart disease can be congenital, resulting from improper development before birth. Suzanne Trayhan, founder of House Rabbit Network (HRN), a rescue group in the Boston area, has dealt with several cases of cardiovascular disease. In her article "Rabbit Heart Disease—Two Case Studies," Suzanne discusses the first two cases she encountered with family members Hazy and Sasha.

Her article begins with the story of Hazy, who she noticed was becoming less active and less social the summer she turned five. Suzanne describes her experience with Hazy:

> An ultrasound revealed that she had two structural defects in her heart. The most severe was the pulmonic stenosis. The second was a small VSD [ventricular septal defect], 3–4 mm. The first ultrasound didn't show much damage to her heart. Over the next three years, her health steadily declined. She didn't require any medication and for the most part functioned normally. The changes were subtle ones in her behavior. Two years later she was responding poorly in the summer heat. While the other rabbits seemed fine, she would be laying in her cage panting, breathing hard. Another ultrasound showed that the defects were damaging her heart. The right ventricle wall was thickened. The aorta was enlarged, resulting in a large difference in pressure on each side of the valve. In Hazy, what I noticed was an intolerance to any form of heat and dizziness. When fall arrived, she seemed to be doing much better. The following summer was not a good one. In August Hazy suddenly refused food and appeared to be out of it. Respiratory rate appeared to be high. She was placed on Lasix® and enalapril. Hazy responded well to the medication and started reverting to her old self. A mere ten days later, she seemed overly stressed from receiving her medication, but settled down within 15 minutes. When I woke up the next morning, she had passed away.

Sasha's arrhythmia was discovered during a follow-up visit for a completely unrelated problem. In the same article, Suzanne describes her experience with Sasha:

> She was six years old and didn't display any symptoms at all. I may not have found it until it was too late, if it weren't for that appointment. We scheduled an ultrasound and echocardiogram, which showed that the left atrium and ventricle were enlarged. Her heart rate was 360 beats per minute and irregular. Systolic function was mildly decreased. The assessment was atrial fibrillation, volume overload and mildly decreased left ventricular systolic function. The cause of these changes was not evident. At that time we couldn't find any other cases of rabbits with this condition, so we tried enalapril and followed the dosage for cats. Her heart started beating normally again. For the next eighteen months she functioned as a normal rabbit who just needed medicine every day.

Dr. Allan notes that "cardiovascular disease often ends in pulmonary edema, which is associated with congestive heart failure." Indeed, this is what finally happened with Sasha. The signs were very subtle. Suzanne noticed she seemed slightly slower in her routine and that sometimes she stuck her nose up in the air. Suzanne emphasizes that if a bun holds his nose up in the air to breathe *or* has trouble breathing when flipped on his back these may be signs of heart disease or other serious medical problems.

In September 2002, my friend Jane found her bunny Remi breathing through her mouth, literally gasping for breath. Jane rushed Remi to her veterinarian, where a large amount of fluid was drained from her chest cavity. Remi was put on Lasix® and spent the night in an oxygen chamber. An echocardiogram the next day confirmed that Remi's heart was enlarged and she was in congestive heart failure. She was sent home with Lasix® and enjoyed another two months with her bonded companion, Biggles2.

Subtle signs that may indicate cardiovascular disease include:

- Change in activity patterns. Rabbits who usually tear through the house may run less or stop to rest more frequently. Climbers may not jump on furniture or other objects as frequently.
- Heavier than normal breathing. This may first appear as panting after exercise and may progress to panting for no apparent reason while resting.
- Changes in eating habits. Sudden reluctance to eat food directly from the floor (or difficulty eating when the head is angled down) may indicate difficulty breathing when the head is in that position.
- Holding their nose up to breathe.
- Difficulty breathing when placed on their back.
- Sudden reluctance to lie flat. Changes in comfortable resting positions may be a sign that your rabbit is having trouble breathing in those positions.
- Bulging eyes. Although all rabbits' eyes bulge when they are stressed, eyes that appear to be bulged constantly may indicate heart disease.

Most rabbits tolerate heart medications well and

can have months (sometimes years) of quality life after being diagnosed with cardiovascular disease. Even those (like Murray) with an initial sensitivity to the medications can do quite well after dosages are adjusted to a level that is both effective and can be tolerated by the individual bunny.

Eye Disease

Weepy Eye

Runny or weepy eyes are not uncommon in rabbits. Sometimes a rabbit's eyes may produce excessive tears (epiphora) without any obvious irritation, but usually epiphora is the result of either conjunctivitis (inflammation of the conjunctiva, or membrane that lines the inner surface of the eyelids) or dacryocystitis (inflammation of the nasolacrimal duct). Exudate may spread infection over the face and jaw, and, if *Pseudomonas* is present, the fur may become tinged bluish-green.

Conjunctivitis is common when the eye becomes irritated from dust, fumes (e.g., ammonia, cedar, or pine shavings), smoke, or a foreign body, making it susceptible to infection by bacteria (often *Staphylococcus aureus,* but also *Pasteurella multocida, Bordetella* spp. and *Pseudomonas* spp., among others). Conjunctivitis may be present without epiphora, and in these cases the vet may test for a deficiency in tear production, which can make corneal ulcers more likely.

A veterinarian may prescribe eye drops or a topical antibiotic eye ointment (ciprofloxacin, gentamicin, triple antibiotic, chloramphenicol), and may sometimes recommend giving the rabbit a course of systemic antibiotics (e.g., enrofloxacin) as well. Care will focus on keeping the eyes clean, giving prescribed medications, and removing any inciting cause (e.g., dusty hay, urine-soaked litter, cedar or pine shavings).

Dacryocystitis can be more difficult to treat. The duct that travels from the rabbit's nose to the eyes follows a rather convoluted path and passes near tooth roots. For this reason, it is common for various tooth problems to cause

Mini lop Amber may be at higher risk of developing dacryocystitis.

partial or complete obstruction of the duct, leading to infection and the discharge of a thick and smelly material from the eyes. Due to the structure of the skull, lops appear to be particularly susceptible to such obstructions. Dacryocystitis can also be the result of pasteurellosis (Chapter 4).

The veterinarian may flush the nasolacrimal duct with sterile water or saline through a soft catheter, but if the cause of the dacryocystitis is an obstruction of some kind, it is likely to recur. For this reason, radiographs may be done to track down the cause. A contrast medium can be injected into the duct in the same way the duct is flushed, allowing the vet to view the position and cause of an obstruction on X-rays. (Note: Flushing is not always successful if the duct is completely obstructed.)

Flushing the nasolacrimal duct without general anesthesia does have the potential to be painful to the rabbit, especially if the blockage is severe or the duct ruptures. Whether to do the procedure with a local anesthetic while the rabbit is awake and under restraint or while the rabbit is under general anesthesia is something your vet may decide on a case-by-case basis. Drs. Jamie and Jason Sulliban explain their differing approaches: Dr. Jamie Sulliban prefers to have the rabbit sedated. "[It] keeps them quiet so I can perform the procedure."

Dr. Jason Sulliban states that if the rabbit is easily handled and has a calm personality he may "burrito" the rabbit and do it with the rabbit awake. If the rabbit is more active, he uses sedation. "The procedure puts a lot of pressure, and the cannula is like a thin-walled blunted needle. I have a concern with the rabbit moving during the procedure and causing trauma."

An ophthalmologic antibiotic ointment or drops (often gentamicin or ciprofloxacin) may be prescribed, often in conjunction with a systemic antibiotic such as Baytril®. Veterinarians disagree on the best method of treating chronic dacryocystitis. Some prefer repeated flushing of the duct, others prefer lifelong systemic antibiotic therapy.

Care

Caregivers will need to give prescribed medications and keep the eye area free of exudate. If the rabbit has a bonded partner, the other rabbit may lick the eye area, keeping it clean. Otherwise, you will need to do this yourself. Wrap a soft clean cloth or sterile gauze pad around your finger and dampen it with warm water or a sterile eyewash such as Opticlear™, and gently wipe off any accumulated discharge. Using your unwashed, uncovered finger to do this could introduce bacteria and/or viruses to your rabbit's eye.

Corneal Disorders

Keratitis is inflammation of the cornea. It can be caused by nutritional deficiencies, infection, trauma, and tear production deficiencies.

Corneal ulcers (ulcerative keratitis). Since the tear film over the eye helps protect the cornea, if there is a deficiency in tear production, corneal scratches that occur from things such as dust particles or a piece of hay may become infected. These may eventually appear as a large yellowish ulcer, and can be very painful to the rabbit. Harcourt-Brown, in *Textbook of Rabbit Medicine,* reports that despite their appearance most cases respond to antibiotic treatment.

Van der Woerdt, author of the chapter "Ophthalmologic Diseases in Small Pet Mammals," in *Ferrets, Rabbits, and*

Rodents: Clinical Medicine and Surgery, describes superficial corneal ulcers that do not usually respond to antibiotic solutions or ointments. Symptoms of these superficial corneal ulcers may include epiphora (excessive tearing), red conjunctiva, and eyelid tics. She recommends treatments such as corneal debridement, grid keratotomy, the use of topical serum, corneal glue, or superficial keratotomy, among others.

Uveitis

Uveitis is the inflammation of the pigmented layer of the eye's iris. This will most likely be observed as a white mass in the iris. Occasionally, an abscess will cause this condition (often in rabbits with pasteurellosis) or it may occur after an injury to the eye by a foreign object. Most often, it is the result of EC. (Serum antibody titers for *Pasteurella multocida* and *E. cuniculi* can be used to differentiate the two.) The protozoan may enter the lens, eventually causing it to rupture. Bacterial infection may ensue.

Removal of the lens is often considered the treatment of choice, especially since rabbits are able to regenerate the lens. If the uveitis is caused by EC, it may also respond to EC treatments. Rarely, if the eye does not respond to medical treatment and is painful to the rabbit, enucleation (removal) of the eye is recommended.

Cataracts

Cataracts may be congenital in rabbits, may result when the lens ruptures from EC infection, may occur with no obvious cause, or may develop as the rabbit ages.[1] Authors of some texts report that cataracts occurring as a result of EC infection do not appear to cause visual impairment or pain. Drops may be prescribed for secondary inflammation. If the cataracts are unilateral (one-sided), the rabbit will still be able to

---

1 Both Kathy Smith and I have noticed that many of the cases of cataracts in older rabbits we have seen or heard of were in black lops. While we have made no formal studies regarding these observations, it would be interesting to us to hear if others have noticed whether any particular rabbit breed or coloration is more likely to develop cataracts.

see enough to get around. At the time of this writing, there is little information available on the cataract removal and its long-term effects.

Glaucoma
Congenital glaucoma may occur in some rabbits, most often New Zealand Whites, dwarf breeds, and Himalayans. Increased pressure may be present very early in life, and the eye soon turns cloudy and the rabbit loses vision. Often, pressure returns to normal as the disease progresses, and no treatment is recommended, as it usually does not appear to be painful to the rabbit. There are topical glaucoma medications, but variable success has been reported for their use in rabbits. Rarely, enucleation is recommended for cases where the rabbit does appear to be in pain from glaucoma.

Hepatic Disease
Excepting hepatic lipidosis, liver disease is not particularly common among rabbits, but it does occur. Any damage to the liver—the organ that detoxifies some compounds and controls the amounts and kinds of many other substances in the blood—is potentially dangerous. Some of the diseases and conditions that may affect the liver are:
- Trauma (fall, predator attack)
- Cancer
- Bacterial or viral infection
- Parasites (coccidiosis)
- Lobe torsion (may occur after unusually strenuous exercise)
- Lipidosis
- Toxic damage

If your veterinarian suspects liver damage or disease, he or she may order diagnostic tests such as hematology, biochemistry (to check liver enzyme levels), fecal analysis, urinalysis, ultrasound, and/or radiographs.

Sometimes elevated liver enzymes may be found in routine blood work done to check for side effects of prescribed medications. These rabbits will usually show none of the usual symptoms associated with elevated levels of the enzymes. This is a fairly common finding with rabbits being given chloramphenicol or any of the bendazoles. Values usually return to normal after the medication is discontinued.

Hepatic Lipidosis

Hepatic lipidosis occurs when fat stored in the rabbit's body is used as an energy source. The process begins when a rabbit does not eat. This results in a reduction in the amount of glucose absorbed in the rabbit's digestive system, and the microorganisms in the cecum stop producing as many volatile fatty acids, which are a major energy source for the rabbit. Hypoglycemia, or low blood sugar, occurs, and fatty acids begin to be accessed from fat tissue. When this fatty tissue is metabolized, organic compounds called ketone bodies are produced. The rabbit's body is essentially "poisoned" by the abnormal amounts of ketone bodies, and the liver is unable to handle the increased fat that collects in hepatocytes (a type of liver cell), eventually leading to liver failure and death if the process is not interrupted. Hepatic lipidosis occurs especially rapidly in obese rabbits (see Overweight, Chapter 3) because the livers of obese rabbits already contain high levels of fats in the hepatocytes. Signs of hepatic lipidosis include:

Heavier rabbits are at higher risk for developing hepatic lipidosis.

- Anorexia
- Depression

- Convulsions
- Death

This process is why anorexia (failure to eat) is potentially fatal to rabbits. *Rabbits must eat!* If they cannot be coaxed to eat on their own, they will need to be syringe-fed (Chapter 2) or given nutrients intravenously. Some veterinarians believe that in the case of a severely anorexic rabbit, it is much more important to get something down the rabbit than to worry about its carbohydrate content, and suggest trying canned pumpkin, baby food preparations of fruits, oatmeal, and/or vegetables (without added onion or sugar), or even a piece of bread or cracker if that is the only thing the rabbit will eat.

Hepatic Coccidiosis

This disease is caused by the protozoal parasite *Eimeria stiedae,* and is more often seen in young rabbits. Although it is not common in companion rabbits, it is being included because it may be found in rabbits who have been rescued from a situation where good sanitation practices were not observed. (The parasite is transmitted through feces, which must be more than two days old to have viable sporulated oocysts.) Symptoms may include:

- Enlarged abdomen from accumulated fluid (ascites)
- Diarrhea (may be blood-tinged)
- Weight loss
- Jaundice (icterus)
- Rough coat
- Lethargy

The prognosis for rabbits with hepatic coccidiosis is usually quite good. The rabbit may be treated with sulfa drugs, clopidol, toltrazuril, or amprolium. Affected rabbits usually survive and eventually become immune, although rarely a rabbit will die from hepatic coccidiosis. There is danger the parasite could be transmitted to other rabbits.

Sanitation is crucial, as the oocysts can remain viable for months.

Harcourt-Brown, in *Textbook of Rabbit Medicine,* notes that the presence of the parasite in the gastrointestinal system interferes with the absorption of fat-soluble vitamins (e.g., A and E) and therefore the requirement for these vitamins is increased in affected rabbits.

Toxic Liver Damage

The liver may be damaged by toxins of various kinds, including:

- Drugs (e.g., NSAIDs, fipronil in flea collars)
- Heavy metals (e.g., lead)
- Mycotoxins (e.g., aflatoxin)
- Phytotoxins (e.g., dieffenbachia, avocado leaves)
- Pine and cedar bedding
- Chemicals (e.g., herbicides, fungicides, fertilizer)

Symptoms of toxic liver damage will vary according to the cause, but may include:

- Anorexia
- Weight loss
- Drooling
- Loss of coordination
- Paresis/paralysis
- Depression

Treatment for toxic liver damage will depend upon the cause. In the case of pine and cedar bedding, the cure can be as simple as removing the bedding. A cause of poisoning may sometimes be deduced by knowledge of a particular item that was consumed (e.g., moldy hay, lead paint, a particular plant). Other times it may be necessary for the veterinarian to run various tests to determine the toxin, including a blood lead analysis, or a test run on the rabbit's food to look for aflatoxins.

Lead poisoning is not as rare as might be expected. In *Notes on Rabbit Internal Medicine,* Saunders and Davies list several items that might be in a rabbit's environment and from which rabbits could potentially consume lead, including batteries, solder (as in a patch on cage wire), lead-based varnish, plaster and putty, the foil covering on wine bottle corks, light bulb bases, mirror backing, costume jewelry, rubberized plastic items (some toys, shoe soles), and seeds intended for planting (might be coated with lead arsenate).

Signs of lead poisoning may include:
- Lethargy
- Anorexia/weight loss
- Enlarged abdomen from accumulated fluids (ascites)
- Rapid breathing (tachypnea)
- GI stasis
- Neurological signs

Lead poisoning is likely to be treated by subcutaneous administration of CaEDTA. If it is diagnosed in time, the rabbit will usually recover.

Care
Home care for rabbits with liver problems will be mostly supportive: giving fluids and medications and syringe feeding the rabbit if it becomes necessary.

CHAPTER 9

ELDERBUNS

Lucile C. Moore

Older rabbits are not unlike older people: they slow down, move a bit more stiffly and carefully, don't see or hear quite as well as when they were younger, like their environment a little warmer, do not enjoy eating as much as they used to, may have problems with incontinence, and their hair thins and turns gray or white. But with a little care, our beloved elderbun companions can continue to be part of our lives for several more years.

Alternative methods of treatment can be particularly help-ful in the care of older rabbits. Acupuncture, Reiki, massage, colors, chiropractic, homeopa-thy—all these and more can help make your older bun's life a little less stressful and more pain-free (see Part II). Shannon Cail made the decision to have acu-puncture treatments for

SnugB, 11 years, still active and in good health.

her rabbit, Bailey:

> The acupuncture treatments were done once weekly, then every 10–14 days. The hour-long sessions consisted of a short exam, relaxing him, then inserting about 20–25 needles into various acupuncture points in Bailey's skin. After the needles were placed, a candle was lit, the lights turned off, and the needles would remain for about 20+ minutes (or until Bailey shook them out). The acupuncture did not cure the kidney disease or arthritis, or slow the decline of old age, but it did help alleviate symptoms and discomfort.[1]

How Old Is an Older Rabbit?

Rabbits may begin to show signs of aging as early as 4–5 years, or as late as 10–12. It depends upon the breed, the general health, and the rabbit's genes. In general, very small and very large rabbits do not live as long as medium-sized rabbits. However, there are always exceptions. Author Nancy Furstinger tells about her dwarf rabbit who lived to the age of 15:

> Cupcake the wonderbun grew her angel wings and flew across the Rainbow Bridge on August 5, 2007, at the amazing age of 15. I rescued her at the age of 11, and she delighted me from the get-go. Cupcake, a black Netherland Dwarf, bonded with Jingle Kringle, a Dutch boy toy who kept her young. She was a character: stamping her tiny foot (which always caused my rottie Splash to scamper), digging humongous tunnels in the backyard, and hopping onto my bed like clockwork at 3 A.M. to bounce on my pillow.

1 Cail, Shannon. 2006. An Extraordinary Journey: A Rabbit's Fight for Survival Against the Odds. *Rabbit Tracks* 3.

Age crept up to Cupcake, as her eyes clouded, her fur lightened, and her pace slowed a tad. She became a bit absentminded, bonier and more vocal (she had an amazing array of chattering and chirping sounds), and I knew she must have a touch of arthritis even though she still ran up the ramp to the second story of her condo. If only she could have delighted me with her antics for another 15 years!

Changes to Make in Diet and Care

Several adjustments are needed in feeding and general care to increase the likelihood of your rabbit growing old with minimal problems. In general, you should:
- Increase fiber
- Be sure adequate liquids are being taken in
- Monitor the rabbit's weight
- Provide adequate calcium
- Watch for urine burn and accompanying risks of flystrike and pododermatitis
- Monitor closely for gastrointestinal hypomotility

Diet is critical because of the older rabbit's decreased activity and food consumption. The combination of these two factors puts the older rabbit at greater risk of gastrointestinal problems, especially hypomotility (Chapter 3).

It is necessary to watch the weight of older rabbits carefully. Some have a tendency to gain too much. This is especially bad for older rabbits, as it will increase the severity of pain from degenerative disease, make urination more difficult, and put additional stress on the heart and other organs. If your older rabbit is gaining weight, a change from alfalfa-based to timothy pellets, or a gradual reduction in the amount given (see weight loss, Chapter 3) can help. The

Fourteen-year-old Abby eats a bowl of slurry.

rabbit should also have unlimited high-quality grass hay, along with safe greens such as curly leaf lettuce, cilantro, and parsley, if he is able to tolerate them. A rabbit's preferences regarding fresh greens may change as he grows older.

Other older rabbits have a tendency to lose weight. If your older rabbit has trouble keeping weight on, you might want to increase the amount of pellets, but only by a tablespoon or so per five pounds of rabbit. Donna Jensen, fosterer and a former chapter manager for the HRS, has cared for many older rabbits who have difficulty keeping their weight up. She makes a special slurry for her rabbits that includes, among other ingredients, Prozyme® and Critical Care®. She feeds them the slurry in addition to their allotment of pellets, greens, and "maybe a blueberry or two." Abby, at 14, is an example of the efficacy of Donna's care.

Calcium content of food for older rabbits is an extremely tricky balance. Older rabbits, especially males, are more prone to develop urolithiasis (Chapter 8). It is now believed there may be a strong genetic component to this condition, and because rabbits excrete any excess calcium consumed, diet is no longer thought to be a major factor. However, some veterinarians still suspect high calcium diets may contribute to the formation of the crystals. Diets too *low* in calcium can cause osteoporosis and predispose your elderbun to bone fractures and tooth problems. See calcium content chart later in this chapter.

Elimination Problems

Older rabbits may have difficulty hopping into their litter

box because of arthritis or other degenerative disease. It can help to cut down the sides of the current litter box, or you can purchase a low-sided or open-front litter box from several rabbit-supply businesses (Appendix III). Older rabbits also need more litter boxes placed in their space, as they may urinate more frequently and not be able to wait long. Make it easy for your elderbun to find a place to urinate appropriately!

Adopting the correct stance for urination can be difficult for rabbits affected with arthritis, spondylosis, and other conditions common to older rabbits. This can lead to urine scald (Chapter 1) and an increased likelihood of maggot infestation (Chapter 4). Keep an eye on the fur around the perineal area, and if you notice it is wet and stained, you will have to take action. First clip the fur and wash the area with a cleanser such as ChlorhexiDerm™ Flush. If you see reddened skin, more drastic action will be necessary to prevent urine burn. Some caregivers of older rabbits who have constant elimination problems take them in to have their hindquarters shaved. This should always be done by a professional because of the rabbit's extremely sensitive skin. It will also lower their heat-conserving abilities, so a rabbit who has been shaved may need warmer bedding or a slightly higher ambient temperature.

If the above tips do not help, consider diapering the rabbit or bandaging the perineal area with a spray or gel bandage formulated to protect skin from urine (Chapter 1). For extreme cases, tail amputation (Chapter 5) may be recommended by your vet as the best solution.

Renal Failure

Kidney failure is common in older rabbits. Rabbits with kidney disease may drink more, urinate more, eat less, have diarrhea, lose weight, become lethargic, and develop gastrointestinal hypomotility. If kidney failure is suspected, your vet may do a urinalysis and ultrasound. The long-term prognosis is not good for rabbits with kidney failure, but their time of quality life can often be extended for several months. Care may involve giving fluids, antibiotics, supplemental nutrition, and a medication such as sucralfate. Stacey Huitikka's 10-year-old Netherland Dwarf, Lucy, needed to be given fluids regularly because of kidney failure. She found that placing Lucy in a high-sided cat bed on the kitchen counter and hanging the fluids from a cupboard hinge allowed her to administer the fluids more easily and helped Lucy feel secure. See Chapter 8 for more information on kidney ailments.

Liver Failure

Signs of liver failure are drinking lots of water, urinating more often and in greater quantities, dehydration, and eating less. Sometimes the livers of older rabbits fail to filter out ammonia, and toxins begin to build up (hepatic encephalopathy). As the toxicity increases, the rabbit may have seizures.

Liver failure, like renal failure, can be slowed through fluid therapy and nutritional support, possibly including herbs. Blood tests will be needed to show how advanced the condition is. Hepatic encephalopathy can be treated by giving the rabbit lactulose three times a day to control the ammonia. Chapter 8 has additional information on liver ailments.

Respiratory Difficulties

Older rabbits may develop problems in both the upper and lower respiratory tract (Chapter 4). Becky Hawley's 11-year-old Netherland Dwarf, Zeus, has chronic sinus problems. He cannot be given antibiotics because of the slowing effect they have on his digestive tract, and Zeus goes through cycles of getting better and worse. But, Becky reports, he has an incredible will to live and is "as happy a bunny as we have."

Teeth

Overgrowth of the incisors and molars is a common problem in older rabbits, as symptoms of lifetime ADD (acquired dental disease) become obvious. Signs of dental disease include: anorexia, drooling, and a rabbit who seems hungry but is reluctant to eat, paws at his mouth, and suddenly changes his food preferences. If you notice any of these signs, you should consider having a dental exam done for your rabbit.

Giving coarser first-cutting hay to older rabbits can help to keep teeth worn down. Maria Perez, manager of the Las Vegas chapter of the HRS, saw a marked reduction in the amount of tooth trimming that was necessary when she began giving coarser hay instead of the softer, more palatable second cutting, or "pretty" hay. However, although this may slow overgrowth, molar spurs may develop despite this precaution. Sometimes, overgrowth of molars may not be noticed by the caregiver until spurs develop and lacerate the tongue or cheeks, at which point the rabbit may become anorexic and develop gastrointestinal problems, and abscesses may form at the site of the ulcerations. Elderbuns should receive full dental exams performed by a vet at regular intervals.

When molar overgrowth does occur, the preferred method of many vets is to burr or file the molars down, although there are also clippers manufactured especially for trimming these teeth. A particular vet may be more expert in one method or another. The molars will need to be redone every four to eight weeks, as will any overgrowth of incisors. See Chapter 7.

Reduced Mobility

Most older rabbits will have decreased mobility. In order to keep the rabbit's spirits up, these locomotion problems will need to be addressed. You may need to alter the elderbun's living area to make it more easily accessible by placing ramps and nonskid mats in strategic places. If the rabbit develops severe mobility problems, consider moving his living space to an area of your house that has more activity so he will not feel alone and abandoned. Melissa Epperson had to decrease the space for her older rabbit, Tyler. She found that Tyler did not mind the smaller area as long as she had plenty of attention and toys. Melissa recommends rotating the toys to reduce boredom, and also suggests making a maze of hiding spaces using cardboard boxes with holes cut out between them.

Some diseases common in old age may eventually lead to paralysis of the hind limbs. If that happens, you may need to make more drastic changes to the elderbun's accommodations. (See Chapter 6 for coping with serious muscle weakness and paralysis in your rabbit, and Chapter 1 for some hints on how to give your rabbit more mobility with slings and carts.) Marion Davis's 11-year-old Dutch rabbit, Radar O'Rabbit, lost the use of his left hind leg, but could still move in a seal-like manner. Marion provided several deep litter boxes lined with thick layers of newspaper and filled with hay, which she changes once a day. Radar loves spending time in his litter boxes, and it cut down on urine-soaked fur, improving the condition of the skin on his lame leg.

Sight and Hearing Loss

Cataracts and glaucoma may occur in the older rabbit. You will notice cataracts as a white or gray area in the eye. Although cataracts can be treated with laser surgery, the cost of the surgery and the difficulty of finding a veterinarian experienced in such surgery usually means cataracts are left untreated. Signs of cataracts may include sensitivity to light, some whitening of the pupil, and, rarely, inflammation of the eye. Glaucoma is also usually not treated in rabbits, although it may be if the condition causes pain. Susan Robbins's rabbit, Rodney, developed glaucoma in one eye. When it did not improve with medication, the decision was made to have the eye removed because of pain associated with the glaucoma. Rodney has been thriving since. Loss of sight from both cataracts and glaucoma is gradual and affected rabbits usually adapt well (Chapter 8).

Dacryocystitis, or irritation of the duct from the nose

to the eye, is also common in older rabbits. Rabbits with an inflamed nasolacrimal duct will have runny eyes (Chapter 8), and may have some crusting around the eye if infection develops. The duct can also become blocked. This condition may require flushing of the ducts and administration of antibiotic ointments. Rabbits being given antibiotic ointments in their eyes can develop dysbiosis if they consume too much of the ointment, so watch carefully for any signs of this intestinal disorder (Chapter 3). Dacryocystitis can lead to conjunctivitis (inflammation of the membranes of the eye). This may be treated with topical antibiotics and NSAIDs.

Elderbuns can also develop masses behind the eye (retrobulbar) that could cause an eye to protrude from its socket. These masses may be abscesses or tumors. Determining the cause of an eye bulging from the socket can be difficult, and in some cases enucleation (removal) of the eye will be recommended by the vet.

Most older rabbits develop some hearing loss, but you will probably not even be aware of it. If you notice your older rabbit is startled when you come up to it from behind, it might be because of hearing loss. Try to remember to approach your rabbit from a direction where he can see you coming, or signal your approach by flicking the lights on and off.

Degenerative Bone Disease

As with older people, most elderbuns will develop some kind of degenerative bone disease if they live long enough. Radiography (X-rays) will be necessary for a definitive diagnosis. Eventually, these rabbits may require quite extensive care, but most of us are so grateful the elderbuns are still with us we are happy to provide it!

Arthritis

Arthritis, an inflammatory condition of the joints, is very common in older rabbits. Several things can help make your

Buster in her prime.

arthritic bun more comfortable. He may like his environment a bit warmer, so you can give him extra bedding and be sure his bed is not damp or in an area with cold drafts. He may need more padding for his arthritic bones, so add a couple more layers to his primary living space, and try some egg-crate foam on the bottom. Chapter 1 has more bedding hints.

Provide easy access to food and water, and always watch the weight of a rabbit with arthritis. Gaining too much weight can elevate the risk of pododermatitis and several other conditions, while losing too much may signal the presence of another disease that will need to be treated. Help the rabbit to move around more easily by providing ramps and encouraging walks, even if you need to use a sling (Chapter 1).

Arthritic buns will need more help grooming, both because they may not be able to bend around to clean themselves and because they are likely to have elimination problems. You will need to feed the bun his cecotrophs if

he cannot bend back to get them anymore. Any rabbit with elimination problems is at risk for urine burn and maggot infestation, so watch for both (Chapters 1 and 4).

Analgesics will be a necessity for a rabbit with arthritis. Many

Arthritis and stenosis afflict Buster.

caretakers have also had good results with alternative methods of pain relief such as acupuncture (Chapter 13). Metacam® is probably the most prescribed medication for arthritic buns in the United States, but sometimes the extent of the pain may require giving opioids. Caretakers who have used both butorphanol and Buprenex® for arthritis pain generally prefer Buprenex® for its longer-lasting effects. They also find it less likely to cause digestive upset. Giving an arthritic bun Adequan®, an injectable medication used for its action in decreasing cartilage destruction and stimulating joint repair, may occasionally be suggested by a vet.

Some caretakers worry about the long-term effects of giving NSAIDs, but you will have to balance your bun's comfort against any potential side effects. Remember too, a rabbit in pain from arthritis is at increased danger of gastrointestinal hypomotility and other digestive disorders. While listed side effects for any medication may in fact occur, it should be recognized that they may not, either. My 90-year-old mother takes over a dozen medications a day, and tells me that if she worried about all the potential side effects she wouldn't have any time left to do anything else. The times she does have a negative side effect she has the medication changed, and you can monitor the effects of medications on your bun and do the same for him.

Some veterinary practitioners claim they have had good results treating arthritic rabbits with glucosamine/chondroitin (sometimes in combination with MSM, or methylsufonylmethane). This is available in a liquid form that is easy to give to rabbits. If you try it, remember to give it for at least two months before deciding if it helps or not, as it may take six to eight weeks before it is effective. Shannon Cail describes her experiences using glucosamine/chondroitin with her rabbit, Bailey:

> My vet was the first one who suggested we try glucosamine/chondroitin for Bailey's spinal arthritis, after diagnosis via radiographs. We could not, at the time, put him on Metacam®

due to his chronic kidney disease. At age 5.5 years old, Bailey was put on 250/250 mg, and thankfully I was able to find it in a local health store in that exact dosage, in tablet form. It took a few days, but eventually Bailey ate it right up. Each morning, he'd be right there begging for his morning "treat." Prior to this, my vet had warned me that it might take eight weeks before we saw any results. And that it did indeed!

After about two or three months it became evident, just by the way Bailey was moving and hopping, that it was working. Bailey was on the glucosamine/chondroitin each day for the next 3.5 years. In 2006 it was clear the glucosamine/chondroitin was no longer working and we then opted for the Metacam®, although I did continue the glucosamine/chondroitin.

Spondylosis

In this arthritic condition, bony protrusions develop on the vertebrae and then fuse over to other vertebrae. It is more common in large breeds and overweight rabbits, but can occur in any older rabbit. This can be an extremely painful condition. A rabbit affected with spondylosis may shuffle instead of hopping, urinate inappropriately, stop grooming himself, or be reluctant to move at all. Signs of extreme pain (tooth grinding, sitting hunched in a corner) may be present, as may incontinence. X-rays will confirm the condition. Pain medication is a necessity. Carprofen may be effective for pain from this condition.

Stenosis

Both spondylosis and spinal arthritis can lead to spinal stenosis, a condition in which a narrowing of the spinal column puts pressure on nerve ends. Treatment will usually consist of controlling pain and addressing loss of mobility. At the time of this writing, spinal surgery is rarely performed on rabbits.

Osteoporosis

Rabbits who do not get enough exercise, or who have inadequate calcium in their diets (may occur in rabbits receiving no commercial pellets in their diet), will be more likely to develop osteoporosis. This is a concern in older rabbits as it makes fractures more likely to occur. If you see no signs of excessive calcium in the diet, give your older rabbit an occasional high-calcium treat such as carrot tops or fresh dandelion greens.

High calcium content foods	Medium calcium content foods	Low calcium content foods
alfalfa	blackberries	apples
broccoli	carrots	bananas
carrot tops	celery	blueberries
clover	Chinese cabbage	cucumbers
dandelion greens	cilantro	grapes
kale	endive	oatmeal
mustard greens	lettuce	peaches
oat hay	oranges	pineapple
spinach	parsley	sunflower seeds
turnip greens	squash	tomatoes
watercress	strawberries	

Table 9.1 Comparative calcium content of selected foods. Calcium content compiled from various sources.

Ulcerative Pododermatitis

Sore hocks are highly likely to occur in an elderbun because of changes in how the weight is distributed on their feet and also because of urine dribble and burn. Check for hairless, reddened spots on your bun's feet a minimum of once a week, paying close attention to the heel area. Chapter 5 has more information on pododermatitis and how to treat it.

Cardiovascular Disease
(see Chapter 8 for more information on heart disease)
Cardiovascular disease is not well-documented in rabbits, but as more rabbits are living longer as indoor companions, more heart disease is being diagnosed. Dr. Jason Sulliban, who sees many rabbits in his Las Vegas practice, comments that in his opinion this is not because more cases of heart disease are occurring, but because more are being recognized. Even so, he believes that cardiovascular disease is probably still being under-diagnosed at this time:

> A rabbit may go in with respiratory problems, and an infection is assumed and the possibility of congestive heart failure is not investigated. As we get better exotic vets with more ability to diagnose, we will be seeing more cardiovascular disease in rabbits.

Dr. Jamie Sulliban, who also treats many rabbits, suggests watching for the following signs, which could indicate heart disease in your older rabbit:

- Change in appetite (this can be a sign of several diseases, including cardiovascular)
- Change in activity level (this also can be a sign of other diseases, but may call for a vet check)
- Exercise tolerance (if the rabbit tires easily it could be a sign of arrhythmia)
- Breathing difficulty (may be a sign of congestive heart failure)

Arteriosclerosis
This is the thickening or hardening of artery walls with its accompanying loss of elasticity. Signs of arteriosclerosis include:

- Lethargy
- Anorexia
- Weight loss
- Convulsions

X-rays will be necessary to confirm diagnosis. Aortic sclerosis does occur in rabbits; most often in New Zealand Whites. Mineralization of arteries has also been reported to occur sometimes in rabbits with very high mineral diets, especially those receiving well water. Rabbits suffering from chronic kidney failure (Chapter 8) may also be more prone to mineralization of arteries.

Atherosclerosis

Atherosclerosis occurs when arteries are blocked by fatty deposits. This is unusual in rabbits, but can occur in rabbits fed high-fat diets. This condition may lead to embolisms if pieces of the fatty plaques detach and enter the bloodstream. Feeding your rabbits a proper diet should avoid the development of this condition.

Strokes

A stroke occurs when blood flow in a vessel in the brain is obstructed. It is rare in rabbits, but does happen. It will be suspected if the rabbit has a loss of function on one side of the body. Rabbits that have suffered a stroke are likely to need fluids and analgesics. They may become incontinent and need to have their bladders expressed, but with supportive care they can sometimes recover function.

Cardiomyopathy (disease affecting myocardium of heart)

This is more common in large breeds, although as companion rabbits live longer it is being seen more often in other breeds as well. Cardiomyopathy may be caused by bacterial and/or viral infection, parasites, vitamin E deficiency, and/or stress. It is not uncommon in older rabbits. Signs may include:

- Weakness

- Lethargy
- Difficulty breathing
- Abdominal distension
- Collapse

An X-ray may show an enlarged heart or fluid. Other diagnostic tests the vet may perform include blood tests, electrocardiography (ECG), and echocardiography. Heart disease may be treated with diuretics, ACE inhibitors (enalapril maleate), and digoxin. Rest is not always recommended because of the need of exercise for gastrointestinal health.

Congestive Heart Failure (CHF)
This is a condition that develops as a result of cardiovascular disease, and is characterized by fluid in and around the lungs, and an enlarged liver (hepatomegaly).
Symptoms may include:
- Rapid heartbeat (tachycardia)
- Rapid breathing (tachypnea)
- Labored breathing (dyspnea)

Orcutt, author of the chapter "Cardiovascular Disorders" in the second edition of *BSAVA Manual of Rabbit Medicine and Surgery,* suggests that CHF should be considered whenever an adult rabbit develops tachycardia or dyspnea. Tests your veterinarian may order if CHF is suspected include radiography, electrocardiography (ECG), and echocardiography. Treatment will focus on controlling fluid retention and improving heart performance. Long-term therapy may include giving such medications as digoxin, ACE inhibitors (e.g., enalapril maleate), and a diurectic such as furosemide (Lasix®).

True Elderbun Stories
Because of the likelihood that everyone with a companion rabbit will eventually face elderbun issues, I thought it would be helpful to include the stories of several older rabbits.

Cocoa (Arlette Hunnakko)

Cocoa is twelve and one-half years old, born on August 9, 1994, from outside dwelling rabbits. I adopted him when he was five or six weeks old. He became my little son and totally bonded with me.

He has always impressed me with his laid-back temperament and loving disposition. He is always generous with affection and bunny kisses, and has never shown any aggression or biting behavior. This is an asset, as he allows me to manipulate, dress, bathe, and do many what he would call strange things to him to help his quality of life.

Cocoa in his younger years.

Cocoa was always very healthy except for a large bladder stone which was removed just before he turned eight years old. I started noticing mobility issues in Cocoa in the fall/winter of 2004: he couldn't stand up to clean his ears without one paw on the floor to keep himself steady and he no longer visited me in bed in the night or jumped on the furniture very often.

The summer of 2005 found him wobbly on occasion with his right hind leg weakening and impeding his movement. During the

Padding setup for pillowcase sling.

fall/winter he was dragging himself and during the following summer he lost most of his back leg propulsion to degenerative disc disease and arthritis; he began taking Metacam®.

Cocoa on a winter walk in his thermals.

By spring—after a short and rather limited success with a handicap cart, I realized I had to do something to help him move around as he was becoming depressed and seemed to be deteriorating. That is when I devised the sling idea by cutting appropriate holes in a pillow case. Cocoa took to it immediately and it improved his overall demeanor. He continues to look forward to his twice daily "sling walk."

During this difficult time, I've learned to appreciate his little life one day at a time, but we look forward to his thirteenth spring when he can once again nibble the fresh grass and feel the warm sun.

Bijou and Dolce (Amy Spintman)

I adopted my first rabbit, Lacey, in 1995, and soon after began volunteering with the San Diego House Rabbit Society. By 1999, Beau, Domino, Cookie, Casey, Burnie, Dolce and Bijou had joined my family and my happy warren of eight was complete (or, as I liked to say, "Eight is Enough!"). Other than the occasional bout of GI stasis and gas, they were all healthy for years. With age, however, that began to change, and several of them developed problems related to arthritis, spondylosis, and/or *E. cuniculi*. I got a crash course in caring for special-needs rabbits, and since my rabbits were relatively close in age, found myself caring for multiple special-needs rabbits at the same time.

At times the work was overwhelming. I think I took better care of my rabbits than I did of myself! Their needs came first. However, what I've gotten from my experiences with my rabbits has made it all worthwhile. I've learned so much from them . . . not just the mechanics of expressing bladders, giving shots and syringe-feeding, but of perseverance, adaptation, and taking life one day at a time.

Bijou

Bijou was the first of my special-needs rabbits. One day when she was five years old, I came home to find her on her side unable to get up. X-rays revealed she had compressed vertebrae in her spine. She never recovered from this, and remained disabled for just over three years until she passed away.

Through experimentation I found that Bijou was most comfortable in a cat-sized "donut bed." I would change her bedding twice a day, give her fluids by syringe since she could no longer drink from a bowl or a bottle, and put her food directly in front of her. She got a butt bath and a massage each evening. Despite her situation, she appeared to be happy—she'd pop up her head when I'd walk in the room, hoping that I was bringing treats, luxuriate in the kisses of Burnie, and give me sweet bunny kisses when we cuddled. It was clear to me that she still wanted to be around, and everyone who met her and spent time with her agreed.

Dolce had arthritis and spondylosis of the spine and progressed to becoming completely disabled. I had borrowed a cart from a friend when Bijou became disabled, but it really scared her, so I didn't get one for Dolce at first.

However, I finally decided to purchase one customized for him, and he loved it! I regret that I waited so long to get it, since by then, his body had already twisted some, and his front legs were starting to atrophy. If I had gotten it sooner, I think it would have slowed the progression of his disability.

Dolce

One thing I learned from Bijou and Dolce is that no older or disabled rabbit is alike. They were most comfortable in a different position, and therefore had completely different setups. Dolce had a lot more front end strength and could hold himself up for a while until closer to the end of his life when his muscles became weaker. Since he could prop himself up, he could drink from a water bottle. However, he could also get himself into more trouble—such as flipping himself over onto his "bad side" and be unable to flip himself back. In some ways caring for Bijou was easier despite the fact that she was more severely disabled; she was limited to her little donut bed, and I didn't have to worry about her getting into bad positions.

After Bijou passed away, I received a note from a friend who said that Bijou and I were a "great team." I hadn't thought of it that way before, but she was right. I couldn't and wouldn't have continued to care for Bijou the way I did if she hadn't been so tolerant of me messing with her so much. She showed her appreciation by giving me kisses (which she never did before she became disabled), and the way she responded to me each time I walked into the room. Her face would brighten, her ears would perk up, and I knew that she was a happy, content little girl. That was all the motivation I needed to continue to care for her.

Bijou's disability inspired me to start the Disabled Rabbits on Yahoo! Groups, which has over 400 members. Even though she's gone in body, her spirit will live on, through the group, and through the rabbits whose lives she touched thanks to what she taught me and what I've been able to share with others.

Muffy

Lest the reader think that all rabbits develop the same problems, meet Muffy. Muffy is one of the first rabbits who came into my life. As he completes his first decade, Muffy, a male mini lop, has shown no signs of aging other than a more stubborn temperament and a rare bout with gastrointestinal hypomotility. He eats well most of the time (including his timothy hay), drinks his water, and does his bunny binkies with as much energy and enthusiasm as when he was two. I'd like to think his easy ascent into old age is due to my careful attention to his diet and care, but in truth I know that at least half is simply good fortune and good genes. Every noon he looks forward to his hour nap with my 90-year-old mother. They curl up together and share their private time.

I say Muffy is "my" rabbit—that is not quite true. After one visit at my mother's house, I was loading up my rabbits to return to my own home. I went in to get Muffy last, and found my mother standing in front of his condo, blocking it. "Muffy is *my* rabbit now," she said quietly and very firmly. So he has been ever since.

Muffy

CHAPTER 10

TRIAGE FOR LARGE-SCALE RESCUES

Lucile C. Moore,
with Debby Widolf, Shelley Thayer, and Sandi Ackerman

Those who are associated with rabbit organizations and rescue groups may be called upon to help in situations where a large number of rabbits need to be captured. When I began writing this book, Debby Widolf, the manager of the Rabbit Department at the Sanctuary of Best Friends Animal Society, suggested that I include a chapter on large-scale rescue triage. I agreed that it was a good idea, but told Debby I would need help in writing the chapter, since I have not had that kind of experience. Debby generously consented to provide some information, and further suggested that I contact Sandi Ackerman in the state of Washington as another person with experience in large-scale rabbit rescue. I followed that advice, and Sandi also graciously contributed a piece based on her experiences.

It should be noted that the information provided in this chapter is for those professionals and volunteers who are associated with sanctuaries, shelters, or other organizations that may be called upon to provide emergency help when many rabbits require rescue in a short time. But I hope it will be interesting for other readers, and much of the information on handling and safety applies to handling rabbits in other circumstances as well.

Preparing for Rescues

Any person or organization involved in sheltering rabbits should be prepared to give help if called upon to participate in the rescue of a large number of rabbits. Such situations may occur when a hoarder situation is discovered by authorities, when rabbits are dumped, when a natural disaster occurs, or any of many other possible scenarios.

Some minimal equipment for use in such situations should be on hand, and a plan for capturing, treating, and sheltering the rabbits should be in place. It is a good idea to have meetings with volunteers in order to set up such plans, and prepare handouts that will be ready should such an emergency occur.

General Emergency Triage

When an organization faces a large-scale rescue of rabbits, rapid decisions must be made as to which rabbits should receive emergency medical care first. Dr. Susan Keeney offered the following general guidelines for determining which medical conditions should be addressed first in emergency situations:

1) Cardiovascular and respiratory emergencies.
2) Injuries causing serious bleeding.
3) Intestinal ailments, because they can rapidly go toxic. Administer fluids, keep the rabbits warm, and force feed if necessary.
4) Bites, less serious bleeding, and other conditions requiring medical attention.

Volunteers aiding rescue efforts should receive instruction in recognizing the signs of each and directing the rabbit's handler to the appropriate medical personnel participating in the rescue.

I am grateful to Debby Widolf and Shelley Thayer for sharing the following excerpts on capturing and handling feral rabbits from the recently completed rescue manual compiled by Shelley Thayer, *Field Operations Handbook*. Debby Widolf's section on rescue procedures and safe handling provides an excellent summary of how to prepare for and conduct a large rescue:

Rabbits
Rescue Procedures and Safe Handling
Debby Widolf

Overview
Rabbits are sensitive creatures. Unlike a dog or cat, they do not "cry" when frightened or even badly hurt. Special care is needed when dealing with a rabbit.
- Rabbits are prey animals and are easily stressed
- If panicked, a rabbit will run into walls and fences resulting in serious and often fatal injuries
- A rabbit can die of heart failure if severely frightened

Supplies and Equipment
- Pole net
- Throw net
- Folding day pens
- Shields
- Fence sections (3' high)

Stress Signs, Fear or Pain
- Rapid breathing
- Enlarged eyes
- Shaking
- Screaming
- Tightening into a ball
- Teeth grinding
- Thumping feet—warning

Before the rescue begins.

Medical Warnings, Injuries

If a rabbit is injured or appears ill, stabilize it to prevent shock.

- Wrap the rabbit in blankets to minimize further injury during transport.
- Keep the rabbit warm.
- Use blankets, a hot water bottle or if a micro-microwave is available, use a "snuggle safe."
- Cover the carrier and put the rabbit in a quiet place.
- Seek medical assistance.
- If an injury is obvious, (broken bone), give a pain medication if available.
- Metacam® or aspirin if medical care can not be obtained in a short time.
- If the rabbit has a rabbit buddy, keep them together if at all possible to reduce stress.

Safety

- Rabbits can bite and scratch when frightened.
- Wear protective gloves and long sleeves.
- Be alert to fast-moving back feet.

Approach

- NEVER chase after a rabbit.
- Walk slowly as you approach.
- The rabbit will eventually slow down or stop.

Capture

- Rabbits want to run for cover.
- Open doors to crates and place food inside.
- The rabbit may run inside, especially if you limit their territory.
- Quickly close the door.
- Work as a team.
- Approach with an open day pen or fencing (works well and is less stressful).
- Corral the rabbit.
- Step slowly inside the fenced area and pick up the rabbit.
- Place in a carrier.

- Corner the rabbit.
- Use a pole net or throw net to capture.
- A blanket can also be used to cover the rabbit.

Rabbits everywhere.

- Wrap the blanket around the rabbit and pick it up.

Handling

Rescued rabbit rests safely in temporary housing.

- Do not struggle with a wildly frightened rabbit.
- It is better to lower yourself to the ground and release the rabbit and try again.
- Rabbits can break their backs if dropped or mishandled.
- NEVER pick a rabbit up by the ears.
- Place the palm of your hand under the rabbit's tummy and lift straight up.
- Cradle in your arms, tucking the rabbits head under/or in the crook of your arm (covering the rabbit's eyes).
- The rabbit can "hide" in this position and will hold still.
- ALWAYS support the rabbit's back and hindquarters.
- Keep the rabbit close and snuggled against your body.
- Speak softly and stay calm.
- Keeping the rabbit's eyes covered helps to calm them.
- Putting the rabbit into a box or crate rear first results in less struggling.

Transport

- After placing the rabbit in a carrier, partially cover it with a towel or blanket.

- This will help the rabbit stay calm.
- Keep rabbits away from barking dogs or loud noises if possible.
- Transport inside the truck cab if room allows.

Once the rabbits have been captured, the organization in charge of the rescue will need to have procedures in place for processing the new rabbit arrivals. The following is an excerpt from Shelley Thayer's section on intake procedures:

Rabbits
Intake Procedures
Shelley Thayer

Overview
Rabbits' intake procedures are similar to other rescued animals, with a few exceptions. Most notable is that rabbits, unlike dogs or cats, will not whine or cry when they are hurt. For this reason, special care must be taken to insure that rabbits are inspected thoroughly, especially on the underside.

Rabbits are fragile and sensitive creatures that can literally die of fright, so following proper handling procedures is crucial to their well being. When frightened, rabbits may panic and run headlong into a fence or side of a carrier. This too is dangerous, as they have a fragile skeletal structure and can break their backs or legs.

Procedures
Arrival from Intake or Medical
When a rabbit arrives from intake, or medical, intake personnel should adhere to the following procedures.

Check basic information on the rabbit to insure

that existing intake form is correct. Include in your check:

- Where the animal was found
- What were the circumstances (i.e., other animals found with it, found inside house, or outside, etc.)
- Microchip found or already inserted

New Arrival

If an animal has not gone through intake, begin the process. Follow the guidelines listed below.

Reno after Best Friends Animal Society and volunteers' effort.

Safety

USE CAUTION when handling rabbits as the back feet move quickly and the nails can make deep scratches. A calm environment is always best, but if not possible, try and retain a calm demeanor.

Handling

Place the palm of your hand directly under the bunny on its tummy and lift straight up. Pull the rabbit close to your body, covering the rabbit's eyes with your arm while tucking its head under the crook of your arm. This allows the rabbit to "hide." Always support the legs and back.

Intake Protocol

- Wear a new pair of gloves or sanitize hands between every animal handled.

- Perform a basic physical examination on the animal.
- Check sex—male or female (rabbits can be difficult to sex—ask for assistance if needed).
- Check if neutered or intact.
- Look for wounds.
- Check for discharge from eyes or nose.
- Try to determine age (if experienced).
- Check female patients for possible pregnancy *before* administering medications.
- Medications are given on an individual basis based on the veterinarian's health assessment.
- Record date and any treatments/meds given.

Sandi's bio reads: "Sandi Ackerman began her involvement with rabbits almost 20 years ago with the acquisition of Duster, an angora rabbit. Duster taught her that rabbits are intelligent, delightful, social animals with a mind of their own. After Duster, people began calling Sandi to take their unwanted angora rabbits and she quickly had 16 rabbits in every room of her home. Sandi feared she was about to turn into a hoarder and must stop taking in rabbits. A few weeks later she learned of a newly formed organization in California called the House Rabbit Society. Members rescued rabbits, but found homes for them so that they could rescue more. This was what Sandi hadn't realized she was looking for, and has happily rescued rabbits and found them homes ever since."

Sandi is the founder of the Washington chapter of the House Rabbit Society (1989); Best Little Rabbit, Rodent, and Ferret House (dba HRS, 1996), a public shelter open for adoptions six days a week; and Rabbit Meadows Sanctuary (1996), a sanctuary for feral rabbits that currently houses just over 300 rabbits. She *has been involved in multiple rabbit rescues, which involved trapping from 52 to 452 rabbits in each effort.*

Trapping and Triage—Feral Rabbits
Sandi Ackerman

Dealing with feral rabbits is a specialty in and of itself. This article is written strictly for organizations doing large scale rescues of feral rabbits who have been living in parks, golf courses, neighborhoods and the like. Not to imply that rescued feral rabbits will have their medical needs ignored, it is reasonable to state that not every rabbit will have the opportunity to be examined by a veterinarian due to the large numbers involved. Therefore, please keep in mind

Trap setup

that we are trying to provide a set of proven guidelines to mitigate potential problems and concerns.

To Reduce Stress Avoid Touching the Rabbits
- Trapping should be done without picking up the rabbits
- Using flexible fencing for the trap, bait with veggies and fruits. After the trap has been dropped, have one person enter the trap and herd one rab bit into a corner. Place a carrier (with door open) into the corner with the rabbit, and tap the rabbit's hip to move him into the

carrier. Then just close the carrier door and lift the carrier out of the trap. Continue until all the rabbits in the trap have been removed. Then start over.

Handling Needs to Be Done in a Manner That Will Prevent Injury to You as Well as the Rabbits

- Dress with a thick fabric, such as denim, covering your upper body, arms and legs. Wear glasses or goggles to protect your eyes. Gloves are strongly recommended.
- To remove the rabbit from the carrier, reach inside and place your hand over both eyes. Wait a few seconds until the rabbit becomes acclimated to the feel of your hand, then, continuing firm pressure, lift his body off the bottom

Introducing the carrier.

of the carrier with your other hand and smoothly and quickly bring the animal out the door. Tuck his head into the crook of your arm to keep his eyes covered. Practice this removal with a domestic, social rabbit before trapping and triage starts, as it is imperative that you are able to perform it deftly to prevent undue stress to your charges.

The Examination Needs to Be Thorough

- Check the entire body (include under chin, arm and leg pits and genital area) for lumps, bumps, wounds, ulcers, scabs, hair loss, or other abnormal findings.

- Open lips to check front teeth for malocclusion. Abnormalities in the shape, angle, or texture of the incisors are most commonly indicators of more serious skull or cheek-teeth problems.

Almost there.

- Look at the nose, checking for discharge and that there is equal air flow from each nostril. Noses can be wet from stress breathing. If you see discharge or a wet nose, check the inside of the front legs. Look for crusts, debris, or localized changes in color of hair from previous nose wiping. This may indicate an ongoing respiratory problem, and the possible need for antibiotics, antifungals, dental treatment, or other therapies.

- Check the eyes. A small amount of clear, watery discharge is normal from stress, but any white, yellow, or green discharge, or discharge only in one eye should be a cause for concern. Pull back the eyelids and look at the conjunctiva (the white portion of the globe); normal eyes have few to no small, thin straight blood vessels.

Diseased eyes will have a red conjunctiva, large concentrations of blood vessels, or enlarged, twisted blood vessels. Any of these symptoms indicates a need for veterinary intervention.

- Wounds: Scabs are common from healing wounds, but check under the scab or scar, feeling for abscesses. If you are unsure, you should pick the scab away to determine if there is fresh skin or exudates (pus), and to speed healing.
- Abscesses: Rabbits with possible abscesses require verification that you're dealing with an abscess and not a tumor. An 18–20-gauge needle attached to a syringe can be inserted into the lump and aspirated to draw out fluid. You will observe exudate entering the syringe, or it may flow out the hole left by the needle when it is withdrawn. Do not attempt to aspirate any masses that are deeper than just under the skin. If you cannot confirm an abscess, the rabbit should be examined by a veterinarian.

  Unlike domestic rabbits, which should always be seen by a veterinarian, a large feral rabbit rescue project usually requires a different strategy to treat abscesses. Antibiotics may be injected directly into abscesses. I have found that bacteria found in feral rabbits are (usually) sensitive to penicillin. Injecting penicillin into abscesses for one week will usually show a decrease in the size of the abscess, indicating that the antibiotic is effective. If the area increases in size or does not begin to reduce, then add another antibiotic such as gentamicin or enrofloxacin to the treatment protocol. It is best, however, to send a sample of the bacteria to the lab to identify which antibiotics will be effective prior to treatment.

Long-acting penicillin (benzathine penicillin combined with procaine penicillin) can be obtained without a prescription.[1] Injecting directly into the bacteria allows the antibiotic to begin working locally without going through the bloodstream and having to enter the encapsulated area.

- Broken bones (legs, feet, hips, toes at odd angle): If you know of a fracture that occurred during capture, or if a bone is found to be exposed or a limb is obviously "flopping," the rabbit should be taken immediately to your veterinarian for treatment. Allowing unstable fractures to remain can have life-threatening consequences in rabbits.

  Many feral rabbits our organization has rescued have been found to have "old" breaks that have already healed. We eventually have all of these rabbits radiographed to verify that the bones have already healed, but during the initial triage, we do not rush these rabbits to our veterinarian. We have found it more effective to observe the rabbit for a time and to watch for concerns when we suspect the injury is old.

- Ear wounds: Many feral rabbits have torn ears. During the exam you should feel under the skin for abscesses, but usually ear injuries do not require treatment.

- Ear mites, rabbit lice and fur mites: These parasites can all be easily eliminated with one dose of Revolution® (a prescription item obtained from your veterinarian). Ask for the largest dog size (2.0 ml) and extract the medication with a 1 cc syringe/ needle. (Each tube of Revolution® contains the same mg of medication per cc.)[2] You can then remove the needle and administer the medication from the syringe, using the dose you and your veterinarian have calculated for the average size rabbit in the colony.

  If Revolution® is too expensive for your budget, you can purchase ivermectin (a non-prescription item[3]), but ivermectin requires multiple doses, 7 days apart. This means you'll have increased handling of the feral rabbits, and overdosing can cause significant neurological problems.

Quarantine

Quarantine is possibly the most important procedure you can follow to not only identify animals with health concerns in the captured population, but also to keep your established population within your sanctuary healthy. We recommend quarantining for 2 months before introducing/mixing with other rabbits in an existing sanctuary. The following should be basic minimum guidelines followed for all animals in quarantine. Personnel who handle, treat, or clean quarantine animals should not go into non-quarantine areas until they have showered and changed clothes and shoes. Healthiest animals in quarantine should be handled, fed, and cleaned before less healthy animals ("clean to dirty" philosophy). Staff should wear disposable plastic gloves and disposable shoe protectors. Both should be changed between pens.

- Animals with similar conditions/symptoms should be housed adjacent or together and away from other animals to prevent transmission of disease.
- As fecal parasites are among the most transmissible and hardest to identify in otherwise healthy animals, fecal samples should be analyzed at least three times while animals are in quarantine.
- Any rabbits who appear to be in worsening condition should be kept separate to be examined by a veterinarian.
- Any rabbit who dies while in quarantine should be given a full necropsy, with possible histopathology, by a qualified veterinarian within 24 hours. Refrigerate, but do not freeze, the body.
- No rabbit should leave quarantine and be admitted to a known healthy population until he is disease-free for at least 30 days, or 60 days post capture, whichever is greater.

Deadly Parasites
- Two potentially serious parasites that feral rabbits may be infected with are *Encephalitozoon cuniculi* (*E. cuniculi*) and *Baylisascaris procyonis* (raccoon roundworm, aka cerebral larval migrans).
- Although there is a blood test for enceph-

alitozoonosis, the result of that test only indicates exposure and is not an indicator of an active disease. (There is ongoing research to establish a new test that will identify active encephalitozoonosis disease. Check with your veterinarian to determine if that test is available.) Observing the feral colony prior to trapping is an appropriate way to learn if either of these parasites will be a problem. Symptoms of these two parasites are similar. Watch for rabbits who appear to have balance problems such as tipping over when sitting/standing up on their back legs; falling over when grooming; the inability to access cecal pellets; stumbling; head tilt; and walking in circles.

- When these symptoms are observed, our organization does a "pre-trap" of 10 rabbits. There are other causes for these symptoms besides encephalitozoonosis and cerebral larval migrans. Therefore the rabbits should be examined by a veterinarian experienced with these diseases. After a problem is confirmed, you will want to have a serious discussion with your veterinarian and your rescue organization to determine what should be done with these rabbits who are symptomatic.

Hard Decisions

If you observe that 10% of a 500 feral rabbit population shows symptoms, you need to consider whether or not you will be able to care for a minimum of 50 or more sick rabbits, and treat them individually. You also need to keep in mind that additional rabbits will likely show symptoms (new cases) during the quarantine period if these diseases are endemic in your population.

- Rescue and triage is designed to help the greatest number of rabbits possible. If you try to burden your organization with too many sick animals, you can easily spread your organization too thin to adequately care for the healthy individuals. It should be decided ahead of time if there is a need to set up a small private area, such as a van or tent, for euthanization to be performed during triage. Obviously, this should be discussed and arranged with your veterinarian in advance. By humanely euthanizing the terminally ill individuals, it may significantly help the remaining 400–450 of the 500 rabbits your organization can reasonably attend to. On the other hand, if your rescue is of a feral colony of 50 rabbits and there are "only" 5 sick rabbits, your organization's decision may be to care for all of the sick rabbits.

- In any case, immediate triage is primary to the success of any feral rabbit rescue, followed by appropriate treatment, monitoring, and quarantine. Without these processes in effect, you will only be adding more difficulty and increase your chance of failure.

1 Pen-g www.RevivalAnimal.com
2 Revolution® 40–85-lb. dog tube contains 240 mg of selamectin in 2.0 ml of liquid. A 5-lb. rabbit would be given 0.25 ml on the skin on back of his neck. (One tube will treat 8 5-lb. rabbits.)
3 1% Ivermectin www.Revival Animal.com

Thank you to Adolf Maas, DVM, of Avian and Exotic Animal Hospital, Bothell, WA, for his editing assistance.

PART II

ALTERNATIVE
HEALING METHODS

CHAPTER 11

AN INTRODUCTION TO ALTERNATIVE TREATMENTS

Kathy Smith

I was introduced to the world of alternative (also called holistic) medicine by the late great King Murray. Three months after he joined our warren, Murray developed a myriad of health problems, including chronic/resistant infections, molar spurs, and recurrent bouts of GI upset. Two years later I had the dubious honor of being the second highest spending client at Lakewood Animal Health Center, where my wonderful traditional veterinarian, Dr. Noella Allan, works.

Around the time Murray began having problems, my husband George noticed a news story about a local holistic veterinarian, Dr. Randy Kidd. I made a note of the name and several months later heard it again when I was volunteering with the local House Rabbit Society chapter. I scheduled an appointment for Murray and began taking him for regular treatments. I am convinced that Murray was able to spend almost five years as my companion and teacher in part because of combining Dr. Kidd's alternative techniques with Dr. Allan's skilled traditional care.

It is no coincidence that Murray's positive response to alternative treatments led me to find a wonderful human doctor who combines traditional and holistic treatments in her practice—my doctor's name happens to be Jane Murray.

Energy work now plays a huge role in maintenance both for my own health and for the health of the rabbits who share my home. While some people still think of alternative techniques as "New Age WooWoo," acupuncture, chiropractic, and many forms of energy work are becoming more widely accepted for both humans and animals.

Traditional medicine focuses primarily on logic and science; a few special traditional practitioners acknowledge that medicine is as much art as science. Many alternative modalities (e.g., chiropractic, acupuncture, massage) also require extensive training in physiology; the most skilled alternative practitioners rely on intuition in addition to technical training, especially in selecting and applying treatments.

Traditional medicine is more narrowly focused on the part of the body with the (current) problem. If symptoms

At an early age, Murray introduced me to the benefits of combining alternative and traditional therapies.

are treated without determining their true cause, traditional treatments can sometimes drive the disease deeper into the body. Alternative treatments are often described as holistic because both examination and treatment focus on the patient as a whole. Most alternative modalities share the belief that disease is caused by some type of imbalance in the body and by restoring balance they help the body heal itself.

Alternative treatments are *not* a substitute for traditional care in cases of injury, infection, or life-threatening conditions where proven treatments are available. Alternative treatments are most helpful in:

- Maintaining health by keeping the body's systems balanced
- Supportive care and/or reducing the side effects from traditional treatments
- Offering treatment options for conditions such as cancer where traditional treatments are prohibitively expensive, harsh, and/or unproven
- Providing comfort and helping to ease end-of-life transitions

CHAPTER 12

INTERSPECIES COMMUNICATION

Kathy Smith

One of the greatest challenges in veterinary medicine is that the patient cannot directly tell the doctor where it hurts. Around the time we were discovering Murray's myriad of chronic health problems, my friend Kim Meyer was taking her first class in animal communication. She needed "practice" subjects and I volunteered Murray. The results were astounding.

Murray's health problems always began with loss of appetite regardless of the underlying cause. His molar spurs were severe and he was particularly sensitive to mouth pain. For a while he was having his molars filed under anesthesia

Murray provided my introduction to the world of interspecies communication. Even I didn't need a translator to understand this message: "Cranberries. NOW!"

every two to three weeks. Dr. Allan and I were excited when we stretched the time to eight weeks. However, at one point

Murray stopped eating only five weeks after having his teeth done, and told Kim his mouth hurt. Dr. Allan was both disappointed and skeptical when I gave her the message. We both thought, logically, "But he was doing so well and it has only been five weeks." However, when a thorough physical showed no other problems, Dr. Allan

Kim Meyer helped April Jones understand that Bunnibun's reluctance to eat hay was caused by tooth problems.

decided to check his teeth under anesthesia. Sure enough, there was one large spur that had already bruised the mouth. Once the spur was gone, Murray immediately started eating normally.

In 2003, Kim Meyer spoke to April Jones's rabbit Bunnibun who was not eating as much hay as usual. Kim's dialog with Bunnibun shows how communication can help pinpoint veterinary problems and prepare the rabbit for the reality of what will be done to fix it, providing both honesty and reassurance. We join the dialog when Kim begins asking about health issues:

KIM: "And no health issues your mom should be aware of?"

BUNNIBUN: "Like what?"

KIM: "Teeth, toes, stomachaches, things like that."

BUNNIBUN: "Well, sometimes my teeth kind of hurt. They pinch. I don't know why that is. But it isn't all the time."

KIM: "Is that why you don't eat so much hay anymore?"

BUNNIBUN: "It pokes me, and it hurts. I guess

maybe it was about the time my teeth started pinching. Can she get that fixed?"

KIM: "Yes, the vet would have to file your teeth down."

BUNNIBUN: "File them? Put their fingers inside my mouth? Ewwww!"

KIM: "You wouldn't be awake for it, they would make sure you were asleep while they were doing it."

BUNNIBUN: "Um, OK, then my teeth would feel better?"

KIM: "Yes, they would."

BUNNIBUN: "Well, then let's do that. I don't like my teeth to pinch. It hurts."

KIM: "I will let her know."

Like many of us, April uses professional communicators to keep the patient informed and gauge symptoms, response to treatment, and find out what else can be done to make the rabbit more comfortable. The dialog with April Jones's rabbit Xander during his treatment for head tilt shows just how grateful some rabbits are for this opportunity:

KIM: "Hi, Xander. This is Kim."

XANDER: "You're going to help me feel better?"

KIM: "I don't know if I can do that, but I can give information to your mom so she can tell the vet exactly how you are feeling."

XANDER: "That would be good. I am very dizzy, and I don't like it. I feel disoriented."

KIM: "Do you know what exactly is happening?"

XANDER: "Just that I am dizzy."

KIM: "Well, you have some infection that

is affecting your balance, so that you do feel dizzy and you may be nauseous too."

XANDER: "No, mostly dizzy. How do we make it go away?"

KIM: "The vet is having your mom give you an antibiotic, and also an antiparasitical in case it's caused by parasites."

XANDER: "So she is covering all the bases."

KIM: "Yes, she is. She wants you to be better just as much as you do!"

XANDER: "Yes, she seems very upset that she can't do anything more for me."

KIM: "I have had bunnies with the health problem you have before, and we humans feel very useless because we can't just wave a magic wand and make you all better. We don't like to see you in pain."

XANDER: "Good, I don't like to see me in pain either! So, what else can I tell Mom?"

KIM: "Anything you like."

Xander appreciated Kim Meyer's honesty explaining that recovery from head tilt would be a slow process.

XANDER: "OK. I would like to snuggle with my buddy, but I don't think she wants to. If Mom can arrange that so my friend is OK with it, I would like that."

KIM: "I will tell her that. What else?"

XANDER: "Don't pick me up, it makes me really dizzy!"

KIM: "But she has to give you the medication."

XANDER: "Oh. Well, I don't know how she can do that without picking me up, but she's smart. She can figure it out."

KIM: "She may have to pick you up, but she tries to make sure that she won't let you fall."

XANDER: "OK. But I get really dizzy then."

KIM: "I know. I am sorry. Is there anything she can do to make you more comfortable?"

XANDER: "Just make me less dizzy. That will help."

KIM: "I will ask. I know there is medication she can give you to make you less dizzy; I don't know if she is using it."

XANDER: "Good. If I can have that, and my friend, I think I will be OK. Now how long 'til everything works?"

KIM: "It could be several weeks."

XANDER: "Oh. Not good. No faster?"

KIM: "Probably not. But your mom and the vet are doing everything they can to make you better as soon as possible."

XANDER: "OK. I like you. You tell me what is going on, and don't tell me it'll be all better right away. Tell Mom that."

KIM: "I will. Anything else you would like to tell her?"

XANDER: "That I am glad I live with her. She takes good care of me and gives me lots of love. I like the attention."

Communicator and Reiki practitioner Janie Landes shares her home with bunnies and volunteers her time at The Rabbit Habit, a nonprofit, no-kill shelter in the Philadelphia area. She shares stories of how her communication skills helped two foster rabbits.

Levi was being fostered for The Rabbit Habit by one of its members. His foster mom contacted me to do a communication for all her bunnies, including Levi. When I communicated with Levi he was showing his mouth was very painful. I relayed the results of the communication and I was told that Levi had just stopped eating and she was afraid he was in stasis and had an ear infection because he was tilting his head to one side.

With the information I gave her, Levi's foster mom went to her vet to have him checked. The ears were fine, but the vet confirmed that his molars were not normal; however, he did not feel that it was enough of a problem to cause him to stop eating. He did not want to do the

Janie Landes helped Levi's foster mom convince the vet that his molar spurs were severe enough to keep him from eating.

dental procedure and wanted to wait till Levi was no longer in stasis.

I checked in with Levi again and I was still getting that his teeth were very painful and that was why he was not eating. The vet agreed to do the dental work at Levi's foster mom's urging. The day after the procedure Levi went home and the first thing he did was dive into his food and eat!

Since then Levi has undergone several dental procedures and the vet has also discovered the roots are overgrown as well. Levi, however, was lucky to find a permanent home with his foster mom!

I have had several rabbits who, like Levi, stopped eating because of tooth problems that did not appear that severe during a physical exam. Like humans, individual rabbits have different levels of tolerance for discomfort. It is important for caregivers to know that even with the best veterinarians, we sometimes have to advocate for our rabbit based on intuition and our knowledge of what is normal for him or her.

Janie's communication with Mia, a rescue living with Rabbit Habit founder Kerry Stewart, demonstrates how communicators often really do feel the animal's pain:

Mia was a foster bunny at The Rabbit Habit and Kerry was concerned with how Mia was acting. She was not eating and she was laying on her side not moving. She was not acting the typical way a bunny with gas or stasis acts.

Kerry took her to the emergency vet as it was after hours. They told her that they thought Mia was blind and had a brain disease. Kerry did not feel comfortable with the diagnosis or the treatment they wanted to do. She contacted me to communicate with her and

**With the help of Janie Landes,
Mia communicated that she had
severe gas pain, not brain disease.**

she did not give me any background information other than she was not feeling well.

I spoke to Mia and this is what I told
Kerry: "I have bad pain in my stomach/dia-
phragm area, right under my breastbone. It
goes straight across. It hurts to the point it is
hard to take a full breath and it is easier if they
are shallow breaths. It radiates around and
across my back. It is not sharp stabbing pains
and I don't feel like someone is sitting on my
chest like I do with heart problems. It feels
more like hard to take a full breath because if
I do it the pains get worse. It feels like when
[rabbits] have gas really, really bad. I am not
feeling anything else but that. It is worrying
her and scaring her."

I could feel that Mia was much more
dramatic about gas pain than the usual bunny.
Kerry treated her for gas and stasis and the next
day she was eating and acting almost herself
again. Oh, and Mia was definitely not blind.

Interspecies communication is telepathic in nature.
Most communicators believe this is an ability we are *all* born

with, but is conditioned out of us at an early age in Western society. In addition to providing communication services, many communicators offer training (live classes, instructional audio/video courses, and/or books) to help interested individuals reconnect with this natural ability.

Opening yourself to the possibility of directly communicating with your rabbit will greatly enhance your relationship with him. Communication helps identify both physical and emotional issues at an early stage, making it easier to maintain both health and acceptable behavior. In his book *Kinship with All Life: Simple, Challenging, Real-Life Experiences Showing How Animals Communicate with Each Other and with People Who Understand Them,* J. Allen Boone explains that the key to establishing this connection is building a *level* bridge between yourself and a member of any species, thus allowing two-way conversation. Such bridges are remarkably easy to build if you approach your rabbit with respect, acknowledging that you have as much to learn from him as he has to learn from you. Mr. Boone goes on to explain that when the interspecies communication bridge fails, it is almost always because the human has changed the slope of the bridge so he is looking down on his (inferior) animal companion.

Another important factor in effective interspecies communication is the human's ability to focus. Both physical illness and stress can interfere with your ability to communicate. I have worked with a number of professional communicators, and all have a strict policy that they will not attempt a session if they are ill. It is a good idea to apply this same rule to serious communication efforts with your own animals.

A good way to begin establishing communication with your rabbit is to set aside a time each day to spend with him. Pick a time when you are most likely to be relaxed and when you are not likely to be interrupted (immediately after meditation is a good time for those who meditate). Before joining your rabbit, sit quietly and take a few deep breaths. Then, explain what you are planning to do and ask his permission to spend time with him. If you get a strong "not now" or "leave me alone" message, you should respect your rabbit's wishes and try at a different time (or skip a day). Otherwise, get down on his level, continue to breathe deeply, and let your mind drift. Let your intuition guide you: lie still, stroke your bunny, or engage in a favorite form of play. Note anything that "comes to you" as a possible message from your rabbit. When it is time for you to return to your chores, thank your rabbit for spending time with you and gently disengage. Most of us wouldn't hang up in the middle of a phone conversation with a friend, so don't abruptly end a session with your rabbit. Write down any messages or other intuitive impressions you got during your time with your rabbit. This will help you recognize repeated messages or patterns of behavior that may be significant.

Many people who actually *do* communicate with their rabbits downplay their ability because the communication does not fit into the mental/verbal model of human communication. In addition to words and thoughts, interspecies communication may include images, smells, sounds, textures, or simply a "knowing." When I contacted Brenda Holden, fosterer with the Minnesota Companion Rabbit Society (MCRS), about her experiences caring for Fawn, a rabbit suffering from megacolon, Brenda did not speak of communication per se, yet she started her e-mail with a statement that immediately touched me as a clear, though possibly unacknowledged, communication:

> A major part in treating it (we think) is stopping issues before they start. If she smells (toots) we quickly give her simethicone. If she lets you pet her ear when it is straight up, she is in pain and she gets some pain meds. When not in pain she will not allow you to pet her ears that way.

Even if you are developing your own communication skills, you may want to consult a professional communicator if your rabbit becomes ill—especially if the two of you have a particularly deep emotional bond. It is not unusual for a professional communicator to consult a colleague in such cases. In times of crisis, either fear or hope can cloud your ability to "hear" what your rabbit is saying. Because rabbits are very sensitive, they will pick up on your worry and stress and may try (out of concern for you) to conceal information that you may need in order to get them proper treatment.

For those who have just faced or are about to face the loss of a beloved rabbit, I highly recommend communicator Penelope Smith's latest book *Animals in Spirit*, which celebrates the connections, like mine with King Murray, that transcend death and may go back many lifetimes. As I was reading Dawn Baumann Brunke's story about her conversations with a friend's cat named Rooskie, I had one of those "Aha" moments regarding something that I knew was true, but had never really understood. In some cases, I have had more than one communicator talk to an animal, since each individual communicator gets a different piece of the puzzle. I had often wondered why these communications all "ring true," yet provide very different (yet rarely conflicting) pieces of information. I contacted Dawn to ask if she would elaborate on that subject for this book and she replied:

> Just as we all relate to the world in a slightly different manner, communicators receive, interpret and translate information from animals in slightly different ways. Some communicators deal with a lot of behavior issues, so they are quick to tune into the behavioral mode of animals and express it as such. Other communicators are sensitive to thoughts, feelings and impressions; thus, they are likely to be responsive to these aspects of an animal's life. Still other communicators are intrigued by spirit levels and enjoy tuning into the "big picture"; for those people it is easy to tap into an animal's spiritual presence in the world

and express this in larger, spiritual terms. This is why three different communicators may receive three different views when they communicate with the very same animal. For me, this is part of what makes animal communication so rich with insights.

Let's not forget that consciousness is incredibly fluid! We all attune to different levels of consciousness with different people at different times. For example, sometimes we are just chatting with a friend while at other times our connection with that same friend suddenly deepens enough to trigger tears or causes us to see things in entirely unexpected ways. So, too, with animals, we may connect in one way to discuss food or walk time, or we may abruptly shift in our sharing of consciousness to explore all kinds of other things—including the deeper mysteries of life.

Every communication is a relationship. As such, our talks with animals are dependent upon the level of trust, honesty, appreciation, and respect that we are willing to bring to that relationship. We can tune into animal consciousness on very physical, mental and emotional levels as well as relate to that animal's "higher self," to the larger group voice of its species or its totem, or even to the "medicine" teaching it carries

Myrrh enjoyed playing after recovering from a severe case of GI pain.

as an aspect of its greater spiritual being. In short, the exchange of thoughts, ideas and experiences with animals is as open as we (and they) are willing to be.

For those who prefer a more physical analogy, these varied perspectives can be compared to the differences you observe when taking photographs from different angles: they simply show different aspects of a complex, multidimensional individual.

All communication (including human) is "filtered" through the experiences and current mindset of the parties involved. The best communicators convey thoughts and words with as little personal interpretation as possible. Myrrh had a special connection to my intuitive friend Karen, who rescued him from a meat farm near her. As a baby he had sustained internal injuries leaving adhesions that caused normal fecal pellets to create a pyloric obstruction. He had several painful episodes before the one that caused his death. The first began with excessive interest in chewing willow followed by a dangerous drop in body temperature. The message Karen received from Myrrh was "I have blue inside me." Once she passed along the message, we began discussing whether he might have eaten something dangerous and blue-colored, but there was nothing blue in his room. Then suddenly I understood his reference to "blue" as symbolizing the extreme cold he felt inside. Communicators often convey a verbatim message that makes no sense to them, but totally makes sense to their client.

Interspecies communication is also an important tool during medical treatments and when it is time for end-of-life decisions. I have always taken time to explain to my rabbits what I am doing to them and why. I tell each one that I am willing to do whatever is necessary to help them continue their time with me. I have always tried—with varying degrees of success—to listen to (and respect) their desires regarding treatment. When Smokey was diagnosed with cancer, he made it very clear that he was willing to try anything to stay with me; so we did aggressive surgery and chemotherapy. A month later, when Choca Paws was diagnosed with a sinus abscess, he let me know that he was tired and ready to move on. Murray ran from me when it was time for his medications, but took them willingly. He had been with us more than three years before giving me a bunny kiss—while he was getting sub-Q fluids. Murray was also very good at letting me know when medications (narcotics) did not agree with him or when a conservative (low) dose of a medication was still too high for him.

I have chosen Dante's story to end this chapter because it illustrates so many aspects of interspecies communication.

On the first Friday night in July of 2007, my friend Karen was riding her horse (in West Virginia) and received a message from Dante telling her his head hurt. Karen was *positive* the message was from Dante. He contacted her using his "signature song," the 1964 Petula Clark song "Downtown" . . . with "Dante" replacing "Downtown" in the lyrics. Karen cut her ride short and hurried home to call me. I assured her Dante was acting fine, but promised to make a vet appointment for him.

Years before, Murray had convinced Dr. Allan that animal communication had some merit. Still, she raised her eyebrow when I told her Dante was acting fine and we were there *only* because of Karen's phone call. However, she wasn't far into her exam when she found a huge ear abscess. Dr. Allan exclaimed, "Wow! This takes animal communication to a whole new level for me!"

Dante's abscess was stubborn. It required multiple flushes under anesthesia, saline flushes at home, and twice daily treatment with antibiotics. Unlike some bunnies who develop a bond with their caregivers, Dante hated the attention. At one point I very clearly heard him say, "I wish I'd never gotten hold of Karen." When I told Karen, she assured me he didn't mean it.

Four and a half months (and many hundreds of dollars) later—on the day after Thanksgiving—Dante abruptly stopped eating. He retreated to the far side of his room, faced into the corner, and refused to budge. This time, I very clearly heard the words: "I'm done!" I assumed that Dante had given up. I called Dr. Allan, reported what had happened, and told her I planned to stop *all* medication. I put a SnuggleSafe® next to him for warmth, then kissed him and told him I loved him. I promised him that if he would start eating again he could live the rest of his life on his terms—no doctors, no drugs, no handling. I scheduled a vet appointment for Monday, assuming it would be for euthanasia if he survived the weekend.

For the next 48 hours I checked on him every few hours, expecting each time to find him gone. I told him I wanted him to live, but it was his decision. I kept food near him and made sure the SnuggleSafe® stayed warm. Around 9:00 Sunday evening I heard him drinking from his bottle.

Dante always used music to make his connection with my friend Karen.

I offered him a small bite of apple, which he sniffed warily and then decided to eat. He lay in the middle of his room for a while before retreating back to his corner.

When I got home from work Monday, he was marginally better. I considered canceling his vet appointment, but intuition told me he might have molar spurs. I lay on the floor with him, nose to nose, and asked his permission to take him to have his teeth checked and filed if necessary. I promised no needles and that I would allow no other treatment. He nudged me, signaling his consent. Dr. Allan did find spurs. She wanted to give him fluids while he was under but I said no—I had promised him—and she understood.

Two weeks later Dante was eating normally and *playing* for the first time since July! I was sure the abscess was still there. The corresponding eye had started oozing, so I asked his permission to clean it up—and this time got a definite "Don't touch me!" answer. I honored my promise and left him alone. On New Year's Day, he rewarded my patience by coming over and asking me to pet him! On January 7, I noticed how beautiful and sleek his coat looked—better than it had looked in years. The evening of January 8, he eagerly ate his apple. When I woke up on January 9, I found him lying peacefully in the middle of the floor. He looked so comfortable and happy that it took several minutes for me to realize he was no longer breathing.

CHAPTER 13

ENERGY MEDICINE

Kathy Smith

Energy and Vibration

Energy and vibrational practitioners share a lot of underlying principles and methods. They focus on the patient as a whole and consider themselves a channel for, rather than the source of, healing powers. Healing sessions begin with a conscious connection to divine energy, an explicit statement of the *intent* to heal, and a direct request for guidance in correctly identifying the source of the problem and properly channeling healing energy. Most end their healing sessions by giving thanks for the guidance they received.

It is important to understand that healing is a process and does not always equate to a "cure." Energy and vibrational

Apollo, who was rescued from a WV meat farm, asked for orange furnishings to help him trust his new family and become more social.

healers consciously accept the reality that traditional doctors face (and fight) every day—that they are *not* in control of the outcome of their healing efforts.

Energy and vibrational modalities are generally non-invasive. Unlike many traditional treatments, in *most* cases treatment based on misdiagnosis will have no effect rather than having a negative effect. Known exceptions to this statement will be noted in the sections below. In general, treatment choices that stimulate growth (e.g., use of the color green) should *not* be used if cancer or infection has been diagnosed or is suspected, since they stimulate growth in all types of cells, including bacteria and cancer.

Energy

We are all energy beings. Although energy medicine is considered "New Age" by many, Western science acknowledges the electromagnetic nature of life. In her book *Hands of Light: A Guide to Healing Through the Human Energy Field*, Barbara Ann Brennan presents a compelling scientific basis (especially in the field of physics) for the results many of us have seen from energy medicine.

Even people who are skeptical about energy healing agree that we are deeply affected by the energy of those around us. We all know people who light up the room by entering it—and others who light it up by leaving. Rabbits are extremely sensitive creatures. One of the most important things you can do for your rabbit's well-being is to be aware of the energy you expose him to.

The first step is to become *conscious* of our own moods and the surrounding energy they create. A great place to start is by making an effort to smile and find something nice to say to each person you interact with. You will probably be rewarded with more pleasant encounters and better service. Notice when you are having negative thoughts or feelings (anger, fear, frustration, worry), acknowledge them (it is unrealistic to expect them never to occur), and replace them with a positive thought. You'll be amazed at how this simple practice will change how you feel and how your rabbit reacts to your presence. Also, be aware of the energy of your guests and how your rabbits react to them. There is a direct correlation between the guests my rabbits seek attention from and those whose visits energize (rather than drain) me.

Energy is fluid. Energy medicine is based on the idea that when the flow of energy is blocked in some way, disease results. Healing consists of locating and clearing the block, which allows energy to flow normally again and restore balance to the body.

Chiropractic and acupuncture/acupressure, addressed in the next section because they should be practiced only by trained professionals, both deal with blocked energy flow. Chiropractic treatment is based on the theory that misalignment of the spine restricts the flow of impulses (a form of energy) from the brain through the spinal column to vital organs and tissues. Acupuncture and acupressure are based on the flow of energy along meridians in the body. Chiropractic treatments—generally considered "quackery" 50 years ago—are now covered by many human medical insurance plans. Acupuncture, too, is gaining more and more acceptance in mainstream human medicine.

Chakra and aura energy are still considered "New Age" concepts. Chakras are centers in the body through which energy enters and exits. The aura is the electromagnetic field that surrounds the body. Energy and vibrational healing are often focused on the chakras and/or the aura. This type of healing can be done without direct contact with—or even close proximity to—the physical body.

Vibration

In her book *Animal Healing and Vibrational Medicine*, Sage Holloway explains, "Vibrational medicines are remedies and technologies which carry high-energy frequency. This frequency invites the individual's energetic field to resonate at this higher vibration. This balances and heals the energy system out through the physical body, integrating the whole being."

Color, crystals, flower essences, and sound are all examples of vibrational healing techniques. They can be used alone (for emotional and minor physical issues) or with traditional treatments. They can be used individually or in combination with each other. As you read through the next few sections, notice which approaches you have a natural affinity for and start with those. There will be a natural synergy between you, your rabbit, and the approaches that appeal to you.

Homeopathic remedies also have a vibrational component; however, because they are given orally they have the potential for interacting with food, herbs, and pharmaceutical products. Homeopathy will be discussed in Chapter 16.

Energy Healing

Energy healing techniques involve channeling energy from the universal life force through the practitioner, with the intent of healing the patient. For in-person sessions, energy is usually directed toward the patient through the hands of the practitioner, often without touching the body.

Energy healers (including my own) are often guided to direct energy to a different part of the body from what might be expected based on listening to symptoms. This is because an energy block in one part of the body can produce symptoms in a completely different area. The most skillful practitioners trust their intuition rather than sticking to a cookbook approach to treatment.

While multi-year, in-depth training programs are available for energy healers, the most readily available form of energy healing is Reiki. Reiki is a Japanese practice for channeling life force energy discovered in the 19th century by Dr. Mikao Usui. Connection to Reiki energy is initiated through complex Japanese symbols that are drawn (physically or mentally) as part of the treatment.

All certified Reiki practitioners have been trained and attuned by a Reiki Master. Practitioners with only Level I training must have physical contact with the patient. Level II training includes distance healing. Level III Reiki Masters can teach and attune others. Classes are available in many parts of the country. Reiki I and II are often taught together in an intensive weekend course. Training includes introduction to techniques, personalized attunement to the Reiki energy, practice sessions (where you give and receive treatments), and introduction to the Reiki symbols.

I recommend Reiki I/II training to anyone who is interested in energy healing and has access to a class. For me, the experience of becoming attuned, feeling the energy flow, actually giving treatments, and feeling my classmates' response created a spiritual imprint that I can return to when necessary. If you find you don't really "connect" with the symbols (as was the case for me), you will find you still have a new and recallable connection to a wise and infinite source of healing energy.

In their book *Animal Reiki*, authors Elizabeth Fulton and Kathleen Prasad offer the following caution when working with small animals: "When Reiki begins flowing from your hands, it can feel too intense for these little creatures, and they may become uncomfortable or feel coerced into the treatment." Ms. Prasad, who also developed "The Animal Reiki Code of Ethics," emphasizes asking permission to perform Reiki and *always* respecting the animal's decision. She also allows the animal at each session to decide whether physical contact is wanted.

Kerry Stewart, founder of The Rabbit Habit, a rescue group in the Philadelphia area, shares a remarkable story and photo taken near the end of foster bunny Flurry's life. Kerry describes the events just before the picture was taken:

> She [Flurry] was somewhat lethargic, not eating, and not herself. Janie Landes, who also does Reiki, had just finished a Reiki session with Flurry, and left the shelter to go home. I gave

Flurry romaine to try and encourage her to eat. She had not eaten on her own in several days, but suddenly began to devour the lettuce.

When I took the photo, I saw nothing unusual with my eyes, nor through the camera's view-

The camera captures Reiki energy entering Rabbit Habit foster bunny Flurry's body.

finder. But when I downloaded it on my computer, a bright, split light appeared. Ironically, when Janie does Reiki, she visualizes the light of God going through her head, down her arms, into her hands, which are cupped on the animal. The Reiki really helped her with the bout of gas. She felt SO much better, and was livelier than I had seen her for a long time.

Note: It is best to remove jewelry before an energy healing session if you are unfamiliar with crystal energy (see section on Crystals below) since the vibrational powers of both metals and stones may be included in the session.

Color

One of the simplest and least expensive ways to use vibrational energy is through color. In his book *How to Heal with Color,* Ted Andrews describes several ways to offer color therapy, including colored fabric, water, light (colored bulbs are recommended instead of filters for use with rabbits), or simply through visualization and breath. Although I don't recommend the use of candles with animals, Mr. Andrews's method of combining geometry with candles inspired me to begin combining geometry with crystal arrangements as discussed in the next section on crystals.

Some rabbits have expressed strong color preferences to me (through intuitive friends and professional communicators), usually requiring the purchase of new towels and/or rugs for their rooms. Others seem less affected by the color of their surroundings. Offering your rabbit a selection of colored cloths in a patch of sunlight allows him to choose the treatment he needs—or none at all. *Note:* Do not leave your rabbit alone with fabrics of any kind if he has a tendency to chew cloth.

Princess Pandora prefers the soothing qualities of her glacier blue towels.

The following is a guideline that can serve as a starting point for color therapy. Remember that individuals will have different preferences for colors and shades. Trust your intuition to lead you to appropriate answers even when they seem to contradict what is listed. Your intuition may be attuned to the problem's root cause, which may be different from what you *think* it is!

- *White* is cleansing and purifying. When a rabbit is ill and I'm unsure of the cause, I always begin by visualizing him surrounded by white, healing light.
- *Black* is a protective color that can be used to ground and calm extremely sensitive animals. Black should be used sparingly, but can be quite useful immediately following a

traumatic experience.

- *Red* is stimulating. It increases strength and can be used to help raise body temperature. Red should be avoided in rabbits suffering from fever.
- *Orange* helps stimulate feelings of sociability and helps eliminate negative energy. It can assist stomach and intestinal processes, specifically helping with food assimilation. Too much orange can affect the nerves.
- *Yellow* helps balance the GI and urinary tracts. It aids digestion and helps with anorexia. Yellow stimulates enthusiasm for life and helps in treatment of depression. Too much yellow can cause nervousness.
- *Green* balances energies, soothes the nervous system, calms inflammation, and stimulates growth. It is useful in treating cardiac conditions and autonomic nervous system disorders. Brighter greens leaning toward blue are powerful in healing most conditions. *Note:* Because it stimulates growth, *green should never be used* to treat animals with cancer or any type of tumor.
- *Blue* is cooling and relaxing. It can help reduce fever, strengthen the respiratory system, and ease loneliness. Too much blue can lead to lethargy.
- *Indigo and deeper shades of blue* strengthen the immune system. These colors can be effective in treating ailments in the eyes, ears, nose, mouth, sinuses, and lungs. Too much indigo or deep blue can cause depression.
- *Violet* is good for cancerous conditions and infections. Blue-purple tones can be used to shrink tumors and ease inflammation. Arthritis can be eased by violet light that leans

toward blue tones. Too much violet can lead to depression.
- *Pink* stimulates the thymus gland and the immune system.

To achieve balance, colors can be used with their complementary color: Red is balanced by green, yellow by violet, blue by orange, and black by white.

Crystals

Since childhood, I have been fascinated by gems, minerals, and crystals. As I have grown spiritually, there has been a change in which stones I am most drawn to. When Murray died, he sent me an amber bracelet through communicator Kim Meyer. Since then, I have found amber to be one of the most powerful healing substances in my home.

Crystals should be cleansed (to remove accumulated negative energy) before their first use and after any intense healing session. Depending on the stone, this can be done by holding it under running water, burying it in sea salt, or smudging it with the smoke from incense. *Note:* Some stones can be damaged by exposure to water and/or salt. Ask about care of each crystal/stone when you purchase it.

After their initial cleansing, crystals should be charged (to fill them with positive energy) before using them for healing. Charging is done outdoors and can be initiated by

Murray introduced me to the healing properties of amber.

sunlight, moonlight, or the energy from a thunderstorm. Crystals require periodic recharging, but most do not require this after every use. Trust your intuition to tell you when and how crystals should be charged.

There are many ways crystals can be used in the healing process. You can hang a piece of jewelry containing a stone (or stones) on or near your rabbit's cage. Always make sure these are hung safely out of reach. Be conscious of the powers in both the metals and stones of any jewelry you wear during Reiki or other energy healing sessions, since this energy could become part of the treatment session.

Raw specimens and smooth stones can be used as decorative accents in your rabbit's room. Trust your intuition to tell you when stones need to be moved, swapped out, rearranged, or recharged. If you are dealing with a particular physical or emotional issue, you may want to use several carefully chosen stones in an arrangement around your rabbit's cage . . . or you may prefer to set up an altar and arrange the stones around his picture and/or a lock of his hair.

Geometrical arrangement plays a role in vibrational medicine. Your intuition will help you determine the best arrangement based on the number of crystals you feel are needed and whether the issue is physical, emotional, or both. The basic candle layout patterns outlined in *How to Heal with Color* by Ted Andrews can be adapted for use with crystals as well.

- The *triangle* amplifies, increasing the power of the individual crystals.
- The *square* stabilizes the entire physiological system while applying energy of the four crystals used. This arrangement is useful when the issues are primarily physical but may involve multiple body systems.
- The *cross* balances the energy of body, mind, emotion, and spirit while applying energy of the four crystals used. This arrangement is useful when it is suspected that issues are

both physical and emotional or when they are primarily emotional.

- The *pentagram* grounds and strengthens the energy of the individual crystals and engages the patient's spiritual energies to assist with the healing process. This arrangement can help reawaken your rabbit's will to fight an illness.
- The *six-rayed star* links body, mind, emotion, and spirit in a way that encourages healing at all levels. This arrangement creates a protective shield during the healing process.
- The *seven-rayed star* balances all the chakras and amplifies the healing energy of each individual crystal. This arrangement can be used periodically for health maintenance by choosing one stone that resonates with each of the chakras.

The book *Crystal Healing for Animals* by Martin J. Scott and Gael Mariani provides a comprehensive list of crystals, with healing qualities, indications for use, and chakra resonance for each. It also discusses making and using liquid crystal essences. Below is an abbreviated list of crystals and some of their more useful applications for rabbits.

- *Amber:* Though not technically a crystal, amber is a stone with powerful and diverse healing properties (perhaps because of the way ancient wisdom has been locked into it). Amber detoxifies, dispels negative energy, and boosts immunity. It helps with bladder, digestive, and respiratory problems. When used regularly, it strengthens the entire system.
- *Amethyst:* This violet/purple form of quartz calms and reduces stress. It can help a rabbit adjust to changes in the household or in

their routine.

- *Aventurine:* This pale cool green form of quartz helps heal emotional scars. It is particularly helpful for rescued rabbits who have suffered abuse or neglect.
- *Black tourmaline:* Helps animals adapt to being part of a human family. Protects them from absorbing stress and negative energy from their human companions. It also helps with skeletal problems.
- *Blue lace agate:* Helps reduce fever and inflammation.
- *Cherry opal:* Aids post-surgical healing and speeds tissue regeneration, especially when combined with rhodolite garnet.
- *Citrine:* This golden-brown or orange-white form of quartz strengthens the immune system and helps protect an animal from negative outside influences.
- *Clear quartz:* Reduces pain and inflammation. Used regularly, it strengthens the immune system and enhances overall vitality.
- *Fluorite:* Strengthens bones and teeth. It increases appetite and improves the body's ability to absorb nutrients.
- *Green jade:* Helps animals acclimate to a new environment. It is also useful for eye and skin problems.
- *Lapis lazuli:* Flushes toxins, encourages absorption of vitamins and minerals, and helps relieve respiratory problems.
- *Malachite:* Eases pain and stiffness and protects against allergens. It may be helpful for rabbits with head tilt since is has been shown to help reduce vertigo.
- *Peridot:* Cleanses toxins and strengthens vital energy.

- *Rose quartz:* Reduces stress and helps emotional recovery of animals with a history of abuse to release resentment.
- *Smoky quartz:* Calms and sedates. It can be held next to an animal in shock while transporting him for emergency veterinary care.

Flower Essences

Flower essences are one of the more common vibrational therapies used by rabbit caregivers. The Bach formula Rescue® Remedy is widely recommended by rescuers and caretakers in books, online articles, and e-mail groups. Rescue® Remedy is recommended for rabbits to calm them after traumatic circumstances, help with adjustment to a new home and/or companion, and relieve tension associated with vet visits.

Rescue® Remedy is comprised of five Bach essences having properties that address problems common to rabbits:

- *Impatiens:* Reduces irritability and agitation.
- *Clematis:* Addresses the "spaciness" that accompanies trauma.
- *Rock Rose:* Helps reduce feelings of terror or fear.
- *Cherry Plum:* Is a remedy for loss of mental or physical control.
- *Star of Bethlehem:* Helps relieve mental or physical trauma.

I both used and recommended Rescue® Remedy before having any understanding of what flower essences really are or how they work. The key to understanding this modality (and others in this chapter) is to begin making the "paradigm shift" from viewing living beings as matter to viewing them as energy. In her article "A Paradigm Shift," Molly Sheehan, cofounder of Green Hope Farm, which makes a line of flower essences, explains:

Though they come in a liquid, Flower Es-

Flower essences helped Meg Brown's bunny Bear through his grief over the loss of his beloved Hoppity.

sences are NOT CHEMICAL. They will not do anything to you in the way that a chemical remedy might kill germs in your system. The liquid in the bottle is a way to store the electrical information of the Flower Essence because liquid holds electricity well. Here's an analogy. The paper that a newspaper is printed on is, to the news, as the liquid a Flower Essence is stored in is to a Flower Essence. Both the paper and the liquid are vehicles for information to get to you.

In her book *Animal Healing and Vibrational Medicine,* Sage Holloway explains the process for creating flower essences as follows: "Peak blossoms are placed in a bowl of pure water and solar infused in morning sunlight or moonlight." She goes on to explain, "What is carried and imprinted into the water is the energetic blueprint of the flower, unified with and activated by the power of the sun or moon."

Because they are vibrational rather than chemical treatments, flower essences can be offered to rabbits in a variety of ways:

- Add a few drops in drinking water
- Apply a drop or two directly to top of the head

- Rub gently on ears
- Add a few drops to mineral water and spray mist into the air for the rabbit to inhale

When you read about flower essences, you will notice a de-emphasis on dosing and amounts, as well as limited concern about choosing the wrong essence. In "A Paradigm Shift," Molly explains:

> When you offer your electrical system the electrical information of a Flower Essence, your electrical system knows if the information is relevant and helpful to its electrical well-being. It knows what is not needed. Your electrical system evaluates everything from an electrical point of view all day long. It knows immediately what will literally "add to the light of the situation" and what won't. That is why sometimes you may feel an almost magnetic pull to a Flower Essence. Your electrical system is trying to tune into the frequency of the Flower Essence that it knows will offer helpful information but it needs you to come closer to the Essence so that it can read the data.

Caregiver Meg Brown recently used Rescue® Remedy and the following additional Bach flower essences to help her companion rabbit Bear recover from overwhelming grief over the loss of his beloved bunny girl, Hoppity:

- *Honeysuckle:* Helps animals who are having difficulty adjusting to new circumstances.
- *Gorse:* Combats despondency and helps restore vitality; is particularly useful in animals who seem to have lost the will to live.
- *Walnut:* Helps animals adapt to change.

Meg also finds flower essences to be helpful with end-of-life transitions (see Chapter 17).

In their book *Bach Flower Remedies for Animals*, authors Helen Graham and Gregory Vlamis discuss the special role flower essences play in the well-being of companion animals: "Flower essences are important in the treatment of animals because they restore the balance and harmony of an animal's true nature, thereby remedying the disorders and diseases resulting from its distortion by humans."

This statement seems particularly applicable to our companion rabbits. Because they are prey animals, the true nature of rabbits is less familiar to humans than that of cats or dogs and is therefore more likely to be misunderstood or misinterpreted. Flower essences help our rabbit companions share the joyful innocence that is rabbit.

Sound

We all respond to the vibrational energy of sound. Whether it is our favorite music, a loved one's voice speaking soothingly, or sounds of nature, sound can be used to give comfort and effect physical changes like quieting the pulse and reducing blood pressure. Many energy workers (including my own) include sound—toning, chanting, and/or drumming—as part of their therapy sessions.

In the rest of this chapter, Greg Wait, who has studied sound and vibrational healing for over 10 years, shares his expertise in this area of energy medicine, explaining how it applies to our beloved companion rabbits:

Chanting for Your Rabbit's Health

As the rabbit
Offers its light
In each moment

And a mountain
Becomes dust
Over billions of years

Each breath you take
Radiates warmth
From the light of innocence

Rabbits come from and exist in the sweetest essence of life—unconditional offering. In this poem, the rabbit is the metaphor for "offering," like a mother offers to a child, like a guru offers love.

Most bunnies enjoy communicating and interacting with their people in some form. One method to help both you and your rabbit connect in a very profound way is through the practice of intentional vibration, such as chanting or sound healing. It can also help bring light to an area of the body or spirit that needs attention.

Chanting can help bring clarity into a number of situations with your rabbits, from the very simple to the more profound. It facilitates overall health and well-being. The practice can be very useful in gaining awareness of how much intervention is appropriate when functioning decreases. Chanting can also be a great support when difficult questions arise around end-of-life issues.

Your bunny does not need to be physically pres-

**Offering tobacco before chanting
at a transition ceremony.**

ent with you when you chant. Chanting is a beautiful and healing gift that you can offer your beloved friend at home, or when they might need to be away from you at the vet hospital. At a time like that, you may feel that there is nothing you can do to help your rabbit. But there is much you can do. You can set your intention for your rabbit's well-being, and by offering your gift of sound and vibration, you will be helping to bring your rabbit peace and comfort, no matter what the outcome of the vet visit.

Chanting is a method for entering the eternal present moment. It is in the present moment that we can gain clarity in our hearts. It is at this time, when we clear our thoughts, that we can become more mindful listeners. Deep listening is love. Chanting enhances healing by integrating the vibration of love into the physical and mental bodies. Through our senses, every cell is affected. Chanting aligns the physical, emotional, mental, and spiritual as one body in the present moment. This creates an optimum climate for good health. Chanting is like a prayer for health.

Preparation for Chanting
To chant for your bunny, I suggest creating a beautiful environment for a healing ceremony:
- You can chant anywhere. However, finding a quiet place, away from distractions, is often more conducive to focusing. This place becomes a circle of light.
- Create an atmosphere that you feel supports healing. I like to light a candle. You may want to use flowers or any objects that have particular meaning to you and your rabbit.
- Set your intention. Perhaps simply ask for the highest good for your bunny. Some-

times my intention is to shine love on my bunny and around the world. At times, I visualize [Meg's and my rabbit companion] Buster in fields of clover, basking in the sun. She is very happy. Whatever your intention, visualize it. Visualization is very powerful for manifestation.

- If outside, I like to smudge with sage. One metaphor for smudging with sage is cleansing the spirit or etheric body.
- Offer (like bunnies, remember!) a gift to bring in the essence of gratitude. I offer thanks to my spiritual teachers and loved ones who have helped me along the way. I put my hands together in prayer position in front of my heart and bow to them. It is like giving them a bouquet of beautiful flowers.

    Sometimes I offer tobacco or corn-meal. I sprinkle it into the wind or offer it to the earth and sky and the four directions. I use a hand drum frequently when I chant. I put the tobacco and cornmeal on the drum before I start drumming. One metaphor for offering cornmeal is that it feeds the spirits of our ancestors and the earth and sky, the ones who made it possible for us to be here.

Make your chanting practice your own, as simple or as ceremonial as you choose. It may change from time to time. You may want to use a rattle or rain stick, instead of a hand drum or no sound beyond the vibration and sound of your own voice, which is perfect. Your intention is what matters most.

Now, get into a comfortable position, close

your eyes, and turn within. Breathe in and out three to four times, to help relax your body and mind.

Bring to mind the focus of your chanting. I will use Buster as an example.

A Method for Chanting
To gain insight or information on Buster, I start by repeating (vocalizing) the word "Buster" or singing it, emphasizing the vowels. Vowels uncover the power of the word.

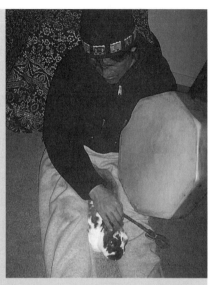

Preparing to drum (actual drumming would not be done this close to a bunny's ear).

Consonants carry that healing power. I chant her name for approximately 20 minutes. **"Buuuu-steeeer."** Chanting energizes a rising tide of physical, mental, emotional, and spiritual pulsation. Your rabbit's name has meaning in the metaphor of the vibration. This meaning will be revealed to you.

Breathing
Breathe in through your nose, and vocalize with the "out" breath through your mouth. When vocalizing the name you are chanting, carry the sound for the entire slow exhalation, then breathe in through your nose and repeat the name on a slow exhalation again. Repeat this process for the entire time you are chanting. Vibration is accentuated by holding the vowel sounds as long as possible. Vowels carry the different levels of meaning. Consonants can be vocalized quickly or even left out. The "in" breath is receiving (light). The

"out" breath is offering (light).

Try to keep your mind free of distractions while chanting. When thoughts arise about the future or past, a method for clearing the mind is to visualize gently putting the thought on a leaf in a river and watching it float downstream and around the bend. You can do this while continuing to chant. By chanting and following the breath we bond all realms of health and love into oneness. A root cause of suffering is separation, or feeling disconnected. By chanting, we are brightening the connection between the earth, sky, our bunny, and ourselves. Suffering is therefore decreased. Potential for joy is increased.

While chanting, please pay attention to what insights, images, or metaphors come into your consciousness. They may come very quickly. One time I had the insight that Buster had no fear of leaving her body. She pictured death as a natural continuation of her life into the spirit world. She saw death as a beautiful process, like the sun rising every day. I wanted to stop chanting and write it down. It was so comforting to me that I did not want to forget it. Yet, my experience is that once you have the image in your mind, it enters your soul and will always be part of you. You will not forget it.

You can chant as often as you like. It will only strengthen your connection to your rabbit. I find chanting to be so powerful and insightful that in the months before Buster's passing, though chanting only a few times, I received many insights that helped her, myself, and Meg. I became more aware of what she wanted us to know.

After chanting, be the witness. Reflect, like the moon reflects off a still pond. Sit quietly and feel the vibration you have become part of. You have made the world a more beautiful place. What images or feelings arise? These may be your answer. Or, insights may come later. You have enhanced your awareness of your bunny. Sometimes answers do not come immediately. There may be a situation that presents itself in the future, and you will just know what the right action is.

Your rabbit's awareness is connected to the first vibration of the creation of the cosmos. They have been living intimately with the cycles of the earth, in vibration, since the first rabbit. It is their survival. People have become desensitized to the natural awareness of life or vibration. By chanting, you reconnect with that original vibration and become more sensitive to it. Healing occurs within that vibration. It is between the pulses of vibration that we can change the fabric of life and promote good health. It is like seeing the first flower of spring. We know that darkness is behind us, light, more flowers, bees, and birds are all ahead of us. Through sound, we have created a new place full of potential for life.

I write my insights from chanting as metaphors in poetry. This is an insight I had while chanting our bunny Charlie's name:

> In white clover
> Bunnies dance
>
> Offering song
> To us
>
> The believers
> That love
>
> Rules
> The world

CHAPTER 14

ACUPUNCTURE AND CHIROPRACTIC

Lucile C. Moore

Both acupuncture and chiropractic are methods of energy healing, but are being included in a separate chapter because of the extensive training required for practitioners. These two modalities can be very effective on rabbits when used in conjunction with traditional veterinary care, but caretakers should be very careful never to allow any but *certified/licensed practitioners* of these methods to treat their rabbits.

Acupuncture

Acupuncture is perhaps one of the best known alternative health treatments, and has been recognized by the American Veterinary Medical Association (AVMA) as an integral part of veterinary medicine. Veterinarians wishing to practice this ancient art can become certified through the International Veterinary Acupuncture Society (IVAS). Never allow your rabbit to receive acupuncture treatments from anyone who does not have this certification.

There is written evidence that acupuncture has been practiced in China for at least 2,000 years, and some experts argue that it has been around for closer to 4,000. Most likely

its roots are in Tao-
ism, which empha-
sizes the balance of
life, epitomized in
the familiar yin-yang
circle of black-and-
white intertwined
commas.

Acupuncture
is a form of energy
medicine. Practitio-
ners of acupuncture

**Acupuncture sessions helped
special-needs rabbit Diego.**

map meridians, or paths, of energy flow through the body.
When the energy flow along these paths is blocked, an imbalance is created, and the acupuncturist seeks to restore
the balance by intentionally affecting specific points along
the pathways, thereby restoring proper flow. This allows the
body to heal.

The needles that are used for acupuncture are very
thin and flexible, and are usually made of stainless steel, cop-
per, silver, or gold. The acupuncturist may vary the substance
the needles are made of depending upon whether a stimulating or suppressing effect is desired at a particular point.
Rarely does the patient evince pain upon the insertion of the
needles. The needles are left in anywhere from 10 seconds
to 30 minutes—the precise length of time depends upon the
particular patient and the condition for which he/she is being
treated. Further sessions may or may not be required. (*Note:*
For some conditions it may take three or four sessions before
improvement is seen.)

Acupuncture has been found to have value in treat-
ing rabbits for pain, arthritis, head tilt, gastrointestinal problems, respiratory disease, and kidney and liver failure, among
other conditions. Many caregivers have found it to be of
particularly great benefit in treating pain in rabbits. It can
be especially useful in those cases where a rabbit has not responded to pain medications or has difficulty tolerating the

NSAIDs and/or opiates often prescribed for alleviating pain.

Donna Jensen, an HRS educator who cares for many special-needs rabbits, has found acupuncture to be beneficial for conditions ranging from a broken back to head tilt. She notes that the effects of acupuncture can be subtle, and that they may be manifested through such things as increased stability and better energy levels. She cautions that one drawback is that acupuncture treatments are often very expensive, and that not everyone will be able to make use of them for that reason.

Shannon Cail tried acupuncture treatments for her courageous rabbit, Bailey, who suffered from several debilitating conditions:

> Dr. Kruse referred us to a wonderful colleague of hers, Dr. Bethany Innis, who also [in addition to physical therapy] practiced animal acupuncture. Within that one week in February, both treatments were started and the difference in Bailey's movement was amazing! He was actually hopping again, to everyone's surprise and delight. I think we were all kind of in shock, to tell the truth.[1]

Jeanette Lyerly also tried acupuncture treatments for her rabbit, who has head tilt:

> We have a 10-year-old rabbit named Luna. In January of 2004, she developed a head tilt and was rolling uncontrollably. She was tested for several things, ear infection, etc., but they were ruled out and she was diagnosed with EC. She had the standard treatment and recovered well. Over the next weeks her tilt gradually went away, and she was left with only the slightest head tilt, which made her look curious about everything.

1 Cail, Shannon. 2006. An Extraordinary Journey: A Rabbit's Fight for Survival Against the Odds. *Rabbit Tracks* 3: 2–4.

Four months later, she had a relapse. Her second recovery was much slower, and for weeks she could not get around. She was unable to get in and out of her litter box, and just walking around made her extremely dizzy. As she was recovering, our vet was working on her acupuncture certification. Luna was one of the first patients to receive acupuncture at our vet's office, Avian and Exotic Animal Care in Raleigh, NC.

Her acupuncture visits began in November 2004 with one treatment each week. After seven weeks, we gradually moved to treatments every ten days, and then every two weeks. She went every two weeks from March of 2005 to May of 2006. At that time, we decided to extend the time between treatments to every three weeks. That is the schedule we are currently on. Our vet will choose her acupuncture points based on feedback from us and from Luna. Sometimes she tells us that on that day she focused on the immune system, the eyes, or the ears.

Over time we have seen a huge improvement in Luna. She has adjusted to the head tilt and is able to get around much better. She began walking again and is now able to run around with some speed. Her stability and balance are much better. She has regained her muscle tone, much of which was lost when she was confined due to rolling, and has good range of motion. She has also gained back most of the weight she had lost. She continues to have some bouts with dizziness, but they are much less severe and much further apart.

In our experience, acupuncture, combined with traditional medication and herbal therapy, has been very beneficial for Luna. While she is not able to do all the things she once could, like jump on the sofa, she does continue to have a good quality of life. For us, that is the best and most important thing.

Kathy Smith, author of *Rabbit Health in the 21st Century,* found acupuncture to be an effective treatment for her rabbit, Murray:

My initial introduction to the power of acupuncture came through Murray. Since my first experience I have worked with two different veterinary acupuncturists (Dr. Randy Kidd and Dr. Pam Truman) treating several bunnies suffering from conditions including arthritis, *E. cuniculi*, and GI issues. All have seemed to enjoy the treatment sessions.

I am fascinated by the intuitive nature of acupuncture sessions. Both Dr. Kidd and Dr. Truman started their sessions by talking to the caregiver. They then focused full attention on the rabbit, talking to them and making a connection before beginning the treatment. The treatment itself consisted of lightly feeling along the energy meridians with two fingers, concurrently feeling the meridians on the left and right sides of the

Murray receives an acupuncture treatment.

body. Indentations on either side of the body indicate points where stimulation with a needle is needed. Very occasionally a rabbit will flinch when a needle is inserted or immediately shake it out. In those cases he will often accept a needle at the same point on the opposite side of the body. More often, if a point really needs to be stimulated the needle seems to be sucked into the body.

Both veterinarians left needles in place for roughly 15–20 minutes. At the end of the treatment they would discover most needles were already loose, sometimes just lying in the fur. On rare occasions when a needle did not seem ready to come out, both doctors would leave it in a few minutes longer, thus allowing the patient (rather than the clock) to control the length of the treatment.

Although acupuncture is usually well-tolerated by rabbits, there are possible side effects. The condition for which the rabbit is being treated may appear to worsen for a couple of days afterwards (although this usually reverses after the second day). Some rabbits may also appear lethargic or sleepy for a few hours after a treatment.

It should also be realized that acupuncture may not have any observable effect at all. Dawn Stuart took her EC rabbit, Espresso, for acupuncture sessions after his disease symptoms had been evident for about six months. She did not see any

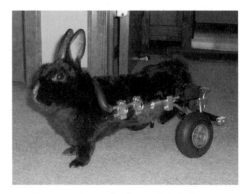

Espresso's caregiver did not see obvious benefits from acupuncture.

definitive results from the sessions, but commented that perhaps if she had been able to start treatments earlier her experience might have been different.

Acupressure

Stimulation of the points along the meridians is not always done by needles. Some practitioners may use lasers, ultrasound, pressure, electrical impulses, or heat and cold. The positive effects seem to manifest whatever the form of stimulation used, and some rabbit caretakers have found other methods of stimulation to be better accepted than the needles by particular rabbits.

Anita DeLelles is a certified Level 1 Small Animal Acupressure Practitioner. She describes the technique and how it can benefit rabbits:

> Acupressure is a gentle, noninvasive therapy based in Traditional Chinese Medicine. It has been used on humans and animals for thousands of years using the fundamental principles of Yin and Yang, the life-force energy that flows through the body, known as Chi.
>
> Acupressure is the art of accessing this energy at acu-points along bilateral pathways or meridians throughout the body. These meridians, and the points along them, link to the body's organ systems both physically and energetically. Disruption in this flow of life-force energy can cause disharmony and imbalance, resulting in illness, weakened immune systems and even injury. By accessing these points, we can influence the energy to that local area or organ system, thereby assisting the body's natural ability to heal.
>
> Rabbits, known for their delicate bone structure and intolerance to invasive therapy, respond well to the light energetic stimulation of acupressure, tolerating longer sessions.

When a certified acupressure practitioner works hands-on, they assess the physical changes at the various acu-point locations. The practitioner can move or adjust the acupressure point work depending on each rabbit's individual response. This makes acupressure flexible, especially for rabbits that may not respond well to being touched in a specific location.

Acupressure can benefit a number of conditions in rabbits, including: respiratory issues; pain management; heart, liver, and kidney issues; and digestive and immune system imbalances. Working in conjunction with good veterinary care, acupressure can benefit rabbits even when an imbalance or illness is not present. By keeping the body in optimal balance it is better able to fight illness and recover from injury. Like a good massage for humans, acupressure is also a source of comfort and relaxation for our rabbit companions, which respond well to regular visits.

Woodrow, a mature, Jersey Wooly rescued male, was diagnosed and treated by a vet for spondylosis and paresis in his hind left leg. He was not able to maintain a consistent hop without falling on his side. After obtaining a full history, an assessment was performed. This included evaluating his coat condition, eating habits, eyes, ears, smell, muscle tone, movement, and, finally, association points, located bilaterally along the

Woodrow (Jersey Wooly in background) has been helped through acupressure.

spine. Taking into account his age and the results of his assessment, the acu-points selected for stimulation focused on bringing energy to his hind, helping to reduce pain and increase mobility in his legs. Other points were also massaged that would tonify and improve the energy to his kidney organ system.

At the end of the first session, after reluctantly submitting to his acu-massage, he hopped off across the room without a missed step. While some bunnies do show improvement after just one session, a more gradual improvement is the norm. Regular sessions by the practitioner and consistent follow-up by the guardian provide the best results. Early assessment is also essential.

Woodrow now has regular sessions, and shows improvement after each visit.

Chiropractic

Chiropractic also deals with blocked energy flow, although in a different way. Reduced to very simplistic terms, it deals with the relationship of the spine to the nervous system. Nerves exit from between the vertebrae in the spine, and the concept behind chiropractic is that any slight change in the alignment of the vertebrae (subluxations) impacts these nerves directly, the effects then radiating out to muscles, joints, organs, and eventually the entire body. Through manipulation of the spine and other techniques, the chiropractic practitioner's goal is to correct these subluxations.

An appointment for your rabbit will most likely begin with the rabbit's case history being taken. The practitioner may then palpate the rabbit, take X-rays, do a neurological exam, and analyze the way the rabbit moves. After the patient is evaluated, the practitioner will perform any adjustments to the spine, joints of extremities, and cranial sutures that he/she feels are necessary. (Note: A chiropractic adjustment is defined as "short lever, high velocity controlled thrust." Because rabbits' skeletons are lighter than those of companion animals such as dogs and cats, it is recommended that caretakers find a chiropractor who has experience treating rabbits.)

King Murray benefited from chiropractic treatment.

Sometimes a rabbit will show immediate improvement, but other times more than one session may be necessary for visible improvement. Occasionally, the animal patient may be tired for up to 48 hours after a treatment.

Kathy Smith, the author of *Rabbit Health in the 21st Century,* took her beloved rabbit King Murray for chiropractic treatment:

> I started taking Murray for chiropractic treatments when it was pointed out to me that when you looked at him straight, one eye was higher than the other. We hoped that correcting this imbalance would also help his teeth wear more evenly. Although chiropractic treatments did not end up helping his teeth, I could tell that combined acupuncture/chiropractic treatments that he received every three to four weeks improved his quality of life and helped him recover more quickly from his frequent dental work. The chiropractic treatments were especially helpful since a lot of physical manipulation was required to position him so Dr.

Allan could file the back teeth.

At each exam, Dr. Randy Kidd would first look at him "straight on" and note if one eye was higher or one bulged more than another. Next he would gently feel along the entire spinal column, noting where adjustments would be helpful. He would perform a few (usually two to four) *very gentle* adjustments then look carefully at the eyes and repeat the process if necessary. He recommended herbs, especially kava kava, to help prolong the effects of the treatments. Sometimes he showed me gentle stretching exercises to use between treatments.

It was a great loss for Murray when Dr. Kidd retired. While Dr. Pam Truman continued his acupuncture, she was not trained in chiropractic work. Because rabbits have such fragile bones, I was not comfortable taking him to a veterinary chiropractor who did not have experience with rabbits.

Chiropractic has been used to treat pain, jaw problems, muscle spasms, and injuries, among other conditions. Talk to your veterinarian about whether your particular rabbit might benefit from chiropractic treatment. As with acupuncture, only a certified practitioner should be consulted. The American Veterinary Chiropractic Association (AVCA) acts as a certifying agency for veterinarians who have undergone the proper training.

CHAPTER 15

HEALING THROUGH TOUCH

Lucile C. Moore

Healing through touch is instinctive. We all do it—we hold, hug, caress, and stroke to comfort and to heal. When we learn to focus that touch and clarify the intent, the healing effects can be very powerful. Not all methods of healing through touch use the same pathways. Some may directly affect the muscles or nervous system; others affect the biofield, or magnetic field, that surrounds a physical body. The three methods of healing through touch presented in this chapter are each designed to promote healing through a different pathway, yet each uses touch in some of their healing techniques.

Massage

It is difficult to think of a more noninvasive and natural method of healing than massage. Think how most animals (yourself included) like to be touched. In essence, massage is intentional, focused touch. Its benefits can range from physical ones, such as increased blood flow, to the emotional benefits that result from being in a state of comfort and relaxation.

Massage is a technique you can learn to do yourself, or you can take advantage of the skill of a licensed practitioner. If you choose to do the latter you may actually end up doing both, for the practitioner may demonstrate basic techniques and give you "homework" to do with your rabbit between professional sessions!

Being the social animals they are, rabbits lend themselves particularly toward the benefits of massage. Even rabbits who do not like being held usually like having their head or ears stroked while they are safely settled on the floor or a chair, and will often tooth-purr as they are massaged. It is a wonderful way to deepen the bond between you and your rabbit.

Chandra Moira Beal, licensed massage therapist and author of *The Relaxed Rabbit: Massage for Your Pet Bunny,* explains the benefits of massage and describes some basic techniques:

> Massage is touch with a healing purpose. I think intention is important and can be a healing force in itself. Massage specifically works the soft tissues of the body, i.e., the muscles and connective tissue, and has adjunct benefits to the circulatory and nervous systems.
>
> On the physical level, it can increase range of motion in the joints. Massage increases circulation of both blood and lymph. As oxygen is delivered to every cell, metabolic wastes are carried away. This is like getting the fluids changed in your car and keeps the body's "engine" running in top form. This in turn keeps immunity strong. Because massage strokes lengthen and contract the muscle fibers, it is like a form of exercise. So rabbits who live indoors or in cages and don't get much exercise can benefit from it as it keeps their muscles toned (it's not a substitute for exercise, though).
>
> On a psychological level, massage helps rabbits let go of emotional baggage by

**Making deep circles over the
large cheek muscle.**

establishing trust with humans through positive touch. Most shelter rabbits are housed
alone (even if they are in a room with other
rabbits, they are in their own cage) so they especially need loving attention via touch. They
may have been abused or neglected in the past
and might equate human touch with pain. Re-
programming them with positive touch can
help them heal from past traumas (TTouch®
is good for this, too). Every living being needs
positive and nurturing touch to survive and
develop normally.

Massage eases stress, which for rabbits can come from traveling, visits to the vet,
changes in the household (new people, new
animals, moving), changes in the environment, late meals, etc. It increases the human-
animal bond, which has benefits for both.
Humans benefit from lower blood pressure,
increased self-esteem, and a host of other documented benefits.

Pressure [in massage] is a subjective
thing, even for bunnies. Some only want light
work; others are okay with deeper touch. Some

want light pressure in one area, but deeper work on a point that feels tense. Humans are the same. In workshops I try to get people to practice on each other first so they can experience both giving and receiving. Maybe we could put this on a scale, with 1 being no pressure at all such as with the resting position. It's just the weight of your hands resting on your bun. A 3 would be about the kind of pressure you'd use to squeeze a cantaloupe to see if it's ripe. A 5 would be the pressure you'd use to squeeze the juice out of a lemon.

A good way to gauge if your rabbit is enjoying the pressure is to watch for feedback signs:

Positive signs
- eyes closing;
- slow and even breathing;
- sighs;
- yawns;
- stretching;

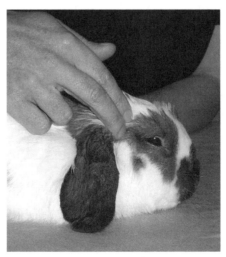

Massaging between Maia's eyes and base of ears.

- snorts;
- falling asleep;
- submissive chin;
- tooth purring;
- licking you;
- flops

Negative signs
- lunging or boxing;
- nipping;
- tail twitching or feet flicking;
- whites of the eyes showing;
- muscles tensing with application of pressure;
- ears flattened with a defensive posture;
- the animal hops away

Effleurage [long gliding stroke] is a good, all-purpose stroke that is like an extension of petting, and the one that bunnies seem to enjoy the most. I would include the head, neck and back. I'd start with long passes down the length of the body, from the nose, over the top of the head, down either side of the spine, and ending at the tail. I try to emphasize to people to make these strokes complete, all the way to the tip of the tail, because that affects something called proprioception, which is how nerve endings tell where we are in space. This gives the bunny a feeling of wholeness, and it feels delicious.

Also, go SLOWLY. Try to go as slowly as you possibly can and see how your bunny reacts. Most really get into it. You'll notice more, too, if you slow down. I'd do several of these strokes, increasing the pressure each time. I'd also work circles around the cheeks and temples, do some petrissage [kneading] around the neck, then massage the ear base and flap.

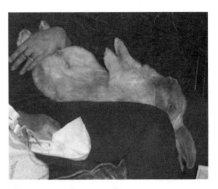

Stormy relaxes after a massage.

Massage also aids peristalsis and elimination, keeping bunny's gut moving. I would emphasize the need for consulting with one's vet first because GI stasis can be complex, and it's a very delicate (literally!) issue. If the vet gives the okay for massage, then I would use about a level 2 pressure (fairly gentle) and stroke in the direction of the colon toward the rectum. Like us, [rabbits] have ascending, transverse and descending sections of their colon. It's important to empty out the descending first, so if that is impacted the matter further up the colon has some place to go. You can work with long, fingertip sweeps down the descending colon toward the rectum. Then work the transverse section the same way, continuing to the descending. Then work the ascending and across the transverse and descending. You can also do small fingertip circles, working in the same order and direction. The technique in my book is good for breaking up and moving gas bubbles along, lifting the belly in a sweeping motion from the center upward toward the shoulders, and working from sternum to tail. These days I try to encourage people to get to know how their bunny's tummy feels normally with some gentle and general sweeping strokes, so that if they do encounter GI stasis they'll know the difference.

I try to emphasize that massage is not a cure-all, and that you should always be aware of your rabbit's health situation, and to refer to your vet with any questions.

Although massage is a very gentle healing method, there are times it is contraindicated. It is not a good idea to massage an animal right after a meal, after strenuous exercise, or if the rabbit is affected by a condition or disease such as high blood pressure, infection, cancer, or diabetes. There are also areas of the rabbit's body the caretaker should avoid: the eyes, area directly over the spine, the kidneys, carotid artery (under the ears, chin, and neck), and femoral artery (inside the thigh).

Healing Touch for Animals®

Healing Touch® is a biofield energy therapy that was developed in the late 1980s. Practitioners use specific techniques to clear, energize, and balance the energy fields around a person, restoring balance and harmony. Carol Komitor applied this holistic energy therapy to animals, and in 1996 founded Healing Touch for Animals® and Komitor Healing Method, Inc. (HTA®/KHM). The techniques of this modality are designed to enhance the healing process and to complement, not replace, traditional veterinary care.

Fifteen-year-old Cupcake (foreground; pal Jingle Kringle behind) benefited from holistic care.

Although this method has primarily been used to treat horses and dogs, it is also very successful when applied to other animals, including cats, birds, reptiles, and small companion animals, including rabbits. HTA®/KHM is compassionate, heart-centered care, and practitioners forge deep emotional connections with the animals they treat. Some issues for which Healing Touch for Animals® techniques might be of benefit in treating rabbits include:

- Anxiety/trauma reduction
- Closer connection to caretaker
- Pain control
- Accidents and injuries
- Cancer
- Euthanasia support

George and Joanne Belev, Reiki Masters/Teachers and Level 4 practitioners of Healing Touch for Animals®, have found this modality to be particularly effective when dealing with abused and traumatized animals. They volunteered their expertise for Homeward Bound Dog Rescue of New York, a nonprofit dog rescue organization:

As you could imagine, most of these animals suffer from abuse, abandonment, and other traumas. The Healing Touch for Animals® techniques used included trauma release, which addresses past trauma in the animal. The trauma release technique is done through a conviction of release, not control! The intention of the trauma release is to release any energy held during a traumatic situation through a gentle heart-centered process. The Healing Touch for Animals® practitioner does not need to know the specifics of past trauma for this technique to be effective. We also used techniques that focus on behavioral modification. While using this technique we communicate with the animals (with words or thoughts) what we would like changed. Helping an animal understand his purpose, then being clear with the "rules" will create a loving place to re-pattern undesirable behavior.

HTA®/KHM incorporates many different techniques. George Belev explains tuning fork vibrational therapy:

Tuning fork vibrational therapy is a way to use the tuning forks to create vibration within the physical body through bone conduction or by using the soft tissue and is an excellent application for any physical issue. This technique is facilitated by placing the tuning fork directly on the physical body. The vibrational frequency of the tuning fork creates deep relaxation, through bone conduction, and stimulates the relaxation response to nerve endings, which carry the response throughout the entire body. By helping to provide the correct physiological response to the body, homeostasis is activated and healing can begin.

A colleague requested that I assess her dog Bess. Bess is a 14+-year-old female pit bull, stray. She suffers from old age, chronic arthritis in hind quarters, obesity, terminal heartworm, tumors and growths.

I observed Bess in obvious pain. She had difficulty walking and based on her gait, I sensed that her pain was in her hind quarters/hip region. My energetic assessment indicated that her hind quarters/hip region was compromised. The assessment combined with her physical problem (i.e., chronic arthritis) confirmed that the culprit chakra was the root chakra. The root chakra governs, among other areas, the back, hips, feet and legs. The treatment plan focused on the root chakra and the use of tuning fork vibrational therapy.

I initiated the treatment by giving Bess the awareness of the forks, hearing the gentle vibration, thus taking away any apprehension of having the forks around the head. The "fight or flight" response is calmed allowing the animal to receive the treatment without creating stress. Then I applied the fork behind her withers, directly on the spine. This is the secondary heart chakra point and it will introduce the sound therapy easily into Bess's energy system by bringing their awareness to the tuning forks without creating fear.

I asked George Belev how HTA®/KHM might benefit rabbits.

While these examples are about dogs, HTA®/KHM methods work equally well for rabbits. Some rabbits like to be held so we can work just off the body, and others are skittish so the work is from a distance. I have worked on rabbits in the past using these techniques and achieved comparable results. Trauma-reducing techniques have been particularly effective. While these gentle creatures are sensitive to the energy (due in part to their being prey animals) they accept the flow of energy on their own terms and let you know when the treatment is over.

Readers interested in learning more about HTA®/KHM can contact a certified practitioner or visit the Healing Touch for Animals® website. Workshops are held across the country at different times of the year, and are open to the average animal caregiver as well as energy medicine specialists and health professionals.

Tellington TTouch®

During the 1970s, Linda Tellington-Jones, an expert horse trainer, developed a training method that had astonishing effects on the horse's behavior and health. She, and those working with her, continued to refine and develop the technique over the next several years.

TTouch® can help when one of a bonded pair is lost.

In the 1980s, it was applied to companion animals and to wild animals at zoos and rehabilitation centers. Today, TTACT (Tellington Touch Animal Companion Training) graduates around the world use their skills to promote positive behavior and wellness in companion animals of many species.

TTouch® may look like massage, but the touch is lighter, usually circular, and each spot is touched only once before moving to the next location. TTouch® is designed to work at the cellular level. Practitioners have reported success in using TTouch® to help rabbits with issues of self-esteem, bonding, litter box training, and to help speed recovery after illness.

Certified Tellington TTouch® and Small Animal Massage Practitioner Marnie Black explains in detail how TTouch® can be used to promote your rabbit's well-being:

Tellington TTouch® for Rabbits

Tellington TTouch® is a powerful bodywork method that can help rabbits who are frightened, grieving, or just need more bonding time with their owners.

TTouch® is a gentle method used to quiet and convey body awareness to an animal. Special touches

and wraps direct the animal's body to relax, deepen respiration, and slow the heart rate. In a calmer frame of
mind the animal is better able to cope with difficult or
frightening situations. The animal's confidence increases
and decisions that are superior to fight, flight or freeze
reactions are more likely to occur.

As prey animals, rabbits are sensitive to everything that goes on around them—smells, sounds, predators (even the family dog), and anything that is moving
above them. The rabbit's body is constantly at the ready
to tense muscles, increase respiration, and sprint or fight
in order to survive.

TTouch® is a powerful method and offers many
different kinds of help to all animals. For extensive information about TTouch® and how to find a practitioner see [the listing for TTouch® in Appendix IV].

TTouch® Principles
When using TTouch® on your rabbit, or any animal,
keep these important principles in mind:
- Be relaxed and physically balanced. Take
  a deep breath and release your body's
  tension.
- Envision how you'd like your animal to
  feel as you touch him.
- Carefully follow directions about depth,
  pressure, time, and speed of each touch.
- Spend only 5 to 10 minutes a day using
  TTouch® until the animal becomes
  accustomed to it.

Helping a Shy or Frightened Rabbit
TTouch® can help to relax the shy and frightened rabbit.
To begin TTouch® allow the rabbit to stay in his place of
safety—removing him will only increase his fear. Cover
a wooden dowel with an Ace bandage or other soft ma-

terial. Slowly, and with respect, touch the rabbit in a circle and one quarter stroke wherever he will allow you to touch him.

Use a pressure that is just enough to move the skin below his hair coat but not massage the underlying muscle. After each touch move to a different location. After using this touch for however long it takes to calm the rabbit—sometimes minutes and sometimes a very long time—the rabbit's body will begin to relax. The more relaxed and confident you are the sooner his body will relax. If he begins to move toward you, you are on your way to touching him with your hands.

The Clouded Leopard Touch. When the rabbit is ready to accept touching from your hands, you can begin a TTouch® called the Clouded Leopard. Place your relaxed hand on the rabbit, anchor your thumb gently in one spot and use the other four fingers to make a circle and a quarter. Catch the skin just beneath his hair coat, and don't press into the muscle. Pretend you are moving your fingers on the face of a clock starting at six on the clock. Do a full circle from six to six and then add ¼ more ending at eight or nine on the clock. Remember to move the skin only, not massage the muscle.

The Abalone Touch. If your rabbit is really terrified, gently place a towel over him so that he feels secure. Keep the towel on him and place your hand over a round part of his body, such as his back or hip. Move your whole hand in a gentle circle and a quarter, just enough to move the skin below the hair coat. Each time you've done a circle and a quarter, gently lift your hand off and go to another location.

The Raccoon Touch. Identical to the Clouded Leopard, the Raccoon Touch is done with smaller, even tiny circles (one finger is fine). Rabbits press lightly down on each other's noses to show trust and friendship. You can do the same by using the Raccoon Touch on the rabbit's nose and ears.

Helping a Rabbit Grieving the Loss of a Mate
Rabbits will stay with a mate their whole lives. Their loving attachment is very evident when they lay quietly side by side, touch noses, and groom each other. Only those who have observed a peaceful bonded pair of rabbits understand how deep this attachment really is.

Sadly, when one of a bonded pair dies, the other is left alone still loving and wanting his mate. Grief in a rabbit is a major event, perilous to his health, and requiring extra support from the owner. A grieving rabbit will sometimes stop eating his regular food and hay and quickly become dehydrated and thin. Opportunist bacteria can take over the rabbit's system or a gastrointestinal blockage can form.

It is important to understand that a grieving rabbit needs immediate physical and emotional support. If it is at all possible, allow the rabbit to see that his mate has died. Viewing the body and understanding that his mate did not just disappear can help the living rabbit get through his grief.

To help your rabbit through this difficult time, begin using the Abalone, Raccoon, and Clouded Leopard TTouches all over the rabbit's body. Also, stroke the rabbit's face between his mouth and his ear going in the direction of the whiskers. This area represents the emotional center. The easiest way to do this is to place the rabbit on a table or on your lap, use one hand to hold him steady and one hand to gently stroke his face from his nose to his ear. Change hands. Do this for about five minutes.

A *belly lift* can improve the rabbit's digestion if he is not eating. This technique must be done very gently. Fold a dish towel into a wide flat band. Put the towel under the rabbit's stomach and hold the ends above his back. Take a slow deep breath in and at the same time *gently* lift his stomach with the towel to a count of five. *Do not lift him off his feet.* Hold for a count of five and slowly lower the towel as you breathe out to a count of five.

It is essential that you not just drop the towel, but release it slowly so the rabbit feels secure throughout the whole process. Do the Belly Lift two or three times in a row.

Common-sense remedies are a big part of TTouch®. Consider ways to help your rabbit apart from touches. Be sure to keep all of your rabbit's routines the same; changes can upset his fragile system. Give your rabbit more of your time, such as sitting with him while you read or watch TV. Always check with your vet if you notice any changes in appetite, level of activity, or droppings.

Use Tellington TTouch® on your rabbit at any time. It's a great method to help you and your rabbit get to know each other better and trust one another. It will benefit you just as much as your rabbit. Use it for just a few minutes a day and both you and your rabbit will come to a deep and loving attachment.

As Marnie Black suggests, many people with companion rabbits find TTouch® to be an effective method, both for promoting health and for increasing the strength of the human-rabbit bond. Maria L. Perez, manager of the Las Vegas chapter of the HRS, says that she finds TTouch® has a very strong emotional effect and helps promote circulation. She uses a combination of TTouch® and acupressure on one of her aging buns, Woodrow, who suffers from intermittent hind leg paresis. Maria notes that when the legs begin to weaken and an older bunny is able to hop some days but not others it can be very frightening to the rabbit. She has found that using the combination of TTouch® and acupressure both calms Woodrow and gives him more mobility.

I have also found another touch, the Ear TTouch®, to be an effective technique for rabbits. This touch can be used to promote good digestion and circulation and to reduce stress. Hold the ear gently between the folded forefinger and thumb,

Pixie and Magic enjoy TTouch® sessions.

and then slide from the base of the ear to the tip. After doing this several times, the tips of the fingers are used to make tiny circles at the base of the ear. This touch is greatly enjoyed by several of my rabbits, all of whom settle down and tooth-purr while I do it. Some practitioners claim that touching the tips of the ear may help bring an animal out of shock.

For some specific case studies on TTouch® and rabbits, visit Eugenie Chopin's website (listed in Appendix IV). Readers interested in learning more about this gentle but extremely effective modality can purchase DVDs and books or attend workshops, which are held in many metropolitan areas throughout the year.

CHAPTER 16

ALTERNATIVE SYSTEMIC TREATMENTS

Kathy Smith

This section combines Western herbs, Chinese herbs, and homeopathy because all are given systemically and thus have the potential to interact with each other, with foods, and/or with Western pharmaceuticals. This possibility does not necessarily mean that treatments should never be used together—interactions can be positive, negative, or neutral. It does mean that such modalities should not be mixed without professional guidance.

I have personally used Western herbs, both alone and in conjunction with Western pharmaceuticals. Western herbs may be familiar to us as cooking herbs, and many (though not all) can easily be found in a fairly natural form. Allopathic veterinarians who question the value of alternative treatments may be comfortable with having their clients use a few Western herbs along with Western pharmaceuticals. Information on herb/drug interactions in humans is being collected and reported in the *Physicians' Desk Reference (PDR) for Herbal Medicines*.

When I first began researching the use of Chinese herbs for this section, I naively asked, "What is the difference between Western herbs and Chinese herbs?" After only a little research, I realized a better question would have been, "What is *not* different?" Frequently Chinese herbs are plants unavailable in the western hemisphere. They are used by practitioners who have been trained in the philosophy and practices of Traditional Chinese medicine (TCM), which focuses on the whole patient (even the entire household), often finding the root cause of the problem in an unexpected place.

Because Western and Eastern approaches work in such distinctive ways, it is important to only combine them systemically under the guidance of a veterinarian who has been trained in both healing philosophies. Used together wisely, combined techniques can be remarkably effective by using the Western approach to manage acute symptoms, thus buying time for the Eastern approach to facilitate healing. It should be cautioned, however, that using the two techniques together without this understanding may cause two costly approaches to simply cancel each other out.

Western Herbs

While Western herbs are often discussed in terms similar to Western pharmaceuticals—listing specific conditions they treat—it is interesting to note that many of them influence more than one major body system. Thus they can often tar-

**Teddy had been attacked by a dog.
He had a severely injured eye and part of
his scalp was missing when he came into
foster care with The Rabbit Habit.**

get a specific symptom and, at the same time, target a root cause even if that is in a different part of the body.

My initial introduction to treating rabbits with herbs was in the mid-1990s, when it was suggested that a combination of echinacea and goldenseal might help with my first gray lop, Smokey's, recurrent ear infections by boosting the immune system. My instructions were to open a capsule, mix a specified portion with water, and administer as a medicine. Smokey was not impressed and I quickly abandoned the idea because the stress of forcing him to take another medication far outweighed any benefit he might receive from taking the herbs.

Deborah Miles-Hoyt is a professional herbalist who lives with companion rabbits and shared her vast knowledge of medicinal herbs with me when I wrote the 2nd edition of *Rabbit Health in the 21st Century*. Ms. Miles-Hoyt explains that many good herbalists today avoid using capsules, which often have little medicinal value. She explains:

> Many are standardized to a particular phytochemical, often removing or neglecting the other phytochemicals in the plant, which work synergistically with these and make them more effective than they are when used alone. It is also virtually impossible to judge the freshness and quality of herbs within the capsules.

With my next gray lop—His Royal Highness King Murray—I had the good fortune to work with veterinarian Randy Kidd using a variety of holistic modalities. From the beginning, Dr. Kidd recommended finding herbs in their most natural forms—fresh whenever possible. Naturally, that wasn't an option with the very first herb he prescribed for Murray—kava kava, which is grown only on a few South Pacific islands. When fresh was not a practical option, Dr. Kidd suggested the seeds, dried leaves, or chopped roots be purchased in bulk and *offered* rather than forced. His experience was that most animals would willingly eat herbs their bodies needed—and that this was particularly true for rabbits and other herbivores. This approach has worked well with my bunnies over the years. Most who have needed herbs have viewed them as treats rather than as medicine!

Herbs can be purchased in bulk at many natural foods stores. Most of the herbs sold under the Frontier brand are organic and if not they will be clearly labeled as such. If you cannot find bulk herbs locally, Herbs Roots and Barks LLC (formerly Oldtime Herbs) is a family-operated mail-order herb retailer in south central Kentucky. They offer quality herbs—by the ounce or by the pound—at a competitive price and have fast and friendly service. When ordering by mail, it is good to keep in mind that a pound of seeds or roots will be a significantly smaller volume than a pound of dried leaves, so order accordingly. Roots are available in two forms—chopped or powdered. Unless your rabbit has severe teeth problems, he will probably prefer the chopped root.

Ms. Miles-Hoyt dries and powders most of her own herbs and makes all her own tinctures. She prefers tinctures because they can be made when the herb is at its peak and kept for long periods without losing potency. Ms. Miles-Hoyt

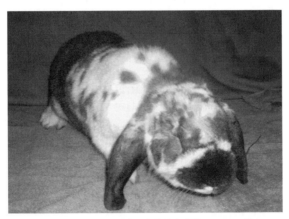

Teddy was treated with bicillin as well as herbal wound cream and eye wash formulated by Deborah Miles-Hoyt. His eye was too badly mutilated to be saved, but his scalp healed completely.

also works with caregivers to develop special formulas to address each individual case. She describes these as "combinations of herbs that work synergistically together to address the cause and alleviate various symptoms." She goes on to explain that she prefers a balanced mixture of herbs because "single herbs can rarely address all the system needs of an illness. It's like expecting your nutritional needs to be met by eating only one food."

My primary veterinarian, Dr. Noella Allan, is more comfortable with a conservative approach to herbs, preferring to introduce only one or two at a time. She cautions against introducing too many new things (herbs and/or food) at one time, especially in the case of an ill rabbit who is already being given several drugs. Both Dr. Allan and Ms. Miles-Hoyt agree that before treating with herbs it is important to have an accurate diagnosis and to work with your veterinarian to check for interactions with any prescribed drug treatments.

As basic rabbit medicine is helping our companion rabbits live longer, healthier lives, cancer is a disease that is being seen more frequently. Since most traditional cancer treatments are unproven for rabbits and may be harsh (making them unsuitable for a rabbit's delicate body), expensive (making them unfeasible for most caregivers), or both, I asked Ms. Miles-Hoyt if she would share her experience with herbal cancer treatments. She replied:

> For cancer, the best thing to do is clean the system, and especially the bloodstream. For this, I use a formula with the following herbs: burdock root, chaparral, red clover, graviola, echinacea, poke root, astragalus, Oregon grape root, green tea, *Quassia amara*, milk thistle, yellow dock, goldenseal root, dandelion root and cayenne.

The rest of the section on Western herbs discusses herbs that I have personally used on my own rabbits to maintain or restore health in the body systems (or specific conditions) listed. At the end of each section, I have invited Ms. Miles-Hoyt to list any additional herbs that she would normally include in her formulas for those conditions.

Liver Health

I have used herbs as the only treatment for several rabbits with one or more extremely high liver values but no clinical symptoms of liver disease. In all cases their values returned to the normal range after being offered a mixture of the following herbs for two to four weeks:

- *Dandelion root*—A liver tonic that gently encourages bile production.
- *Burdock root*—A nutritious liver tonic that also helps clean/build the blood and also has anti-inflammatory qualities.
- *Milk thistle seeds*—Stimulates growth of new liver cells and can help reverse liver damage.

I mix the three together in roughly equal parts and offer one tablespoon (per rabbit) once or twice a day as a treat. After liver values return to normal, I often continue to offer the mixture once or twice a week for liver maintenance.

Ms. Miles-Hoyt also recommends the use of wormwood, an herb that acts to kill parasites that can reside in the liver, weakening this vital organ.

Holly (left) had extremely high liver enzyme values after treatment with chloramphenicol. Both she and brother Theodore eagerly devoured milk thistle seeds and dandelion and burdock roots, and Holly's liver values have returned to normal.

Urinary Tract Health

Herbs can be useful in maintaining urinary tract health. Parsley (both the milder curly variety and the stronger Italian or flat-leaf variety) and dandelion leaf are enjoyed by most rabbits when offered in salads. Both act as diuretics and can strengthen kidney function.

Burdock root and milk thistle seeds, which both help strengthen the liver, also help with urinary tract conditions. Burdock root is useful in cases of inflammatory kidney or bladder disease. Milk thistle assists with removing ammonia from the blood and helps protect the kidneys.

Mature astragalus root (at least three years old) strengthens kidney function and is both antibacterial and anti-inflammatory, making it particularly useful in treating urinary tract infections. Uva ursi leaves are a urinary antiseptic and have been eagerly devoured by several of my bunnies during urinary tract infections.

Ms. Miles-Hoyt adds:

Cranberries, dried or fresh, are willingly eaten by rabbits and are good for *preventing* bladder infections rather than curing them. Pumpkin seeds, also a favorite of rabbits, help stop the formation of kidney stones and sludge, while marshmallow root's slippery nature lubricates inflamed mucous membranes, making stones and sludge pass more easily. It is also beneficial to give herbs that increase circulation within the kidneys, like ginkgo biloba, and those that reduce blood pressure, like hibiscus flowers, to rabbits that are suffering kidney failure.

GI System Support

Herbs can be useful in preventing digestive upset and in treating early signs of discomfort from minor gas attacks. The herbs discussed in this section should *not* be substituted for a vet visit in cases of GI upset that are severe, appear to be worsening, or last more than a few hours without significant improvement.

The following herbs may help maintain or restore GI health:

- *Fennel* reduces gas and may help increase appetite.
- *Ginger* improves digestion.
- *Papaya* (fresh or dried without added sugar) stimulates appetite and aids digestion. Carefully check the label on papaya tablets before feeding to your rabbit. The main ingredient in many brands is sugar, not papaya!
- *Parsley* relieves gas and stimulates normal GI activity. It is easy to find it fresh in regular grocery stores and most rabbits enjoy it.
- *Peppermint* helps relieve gas and is a digestive aid. *Note:* Peppermint may counteract the effects of some homeopathic remedies.
- *Spearmint* relieves gas and colic. It is similar to peppermint but is milder. Some rabbits who don't like peppermint may enjoy spearmint.
- *Thyme* eliminates gas and helps expel some intestinal parasites.

Ms. Miles-Hoyt recommends the following additions:

- *Wild yam* is a soothing antispasmodic, which eases the cramps and pain that can accompany gas.
- *Chickweed* acts as roughage and also lubricates the digestive tract, helping relieve stasis.
- *Marshmallow root* helps lubricate the intestinal tract, easing stasis.

It is good to know which of the above herbs your

rabbit truly enjoys as those will be the best to offer if you suspect a minor GI upset. If your rabbit turns his nose up at a favorite herb, it may be a sign that the problem is no longer minor and a vet visit is needed.

Immune System

Several herbs can be offered to boost immunity in rabbits prone to infection or may be recommended by your veterinarian to be given in conjunction with antibiotics to fight active infections.

- *Echinacea* has antibacterial, antiviral, and anti-inflammatory properties. It should not be given continuously (discuss the best schedule with your veterinarian). *Note:* Echinacea may also interfere with steroids being used in the treatment of cancer.
- *Goldenseal* has anti-inflammatory properties. It is high in berberine, making it effective against a broad spectrum of bacteria, fungus, and protozoa. It is endangered and therefore expensive and even the cut version of the root is quite powdery in texture, which may make it less attractive as a treat.

Mithril enjoys parsley and dandelion (when available) as part of his daily salads.

- *Oregon grape root*, like goldenseal, is high in berberine and is recommended by some veterinarians because it is gentler to the GI tract than goldenseal. Rabbits who have rejected the more expensive goldenseal have

eagerly devoured Oregon grape root.
- *Mature astragalus root* (at least three years old) stimulates T-cell activity and interferon production and raises white blood cell counts.

My youngest bunny, Mithril, who had a severe respiratory infection when he came to me, appears to be susceptible to recurrence, especially when we have drastic weather changes. If he starts sneezing a bit, I offer him some echinacea, which he eats from my hand as a treat.

Pain/Inflammation

As a rabbit ages, he may develop conditions such as arthritis that result in chronic pain. Ms. Miles-Hoyt offers the following suggestions:

> Yucca root brings pain relief and reduces the inflammation of arthritic conditions. Meadow-sweet eases rheumatic pain without upsetting the digestive tract.

Both willow and birch are often recommended for bunnies to chew for pain relief. While both are considered safe for rabbits, it is important to note that if a rabbit shows excessive interest in chewing either, it may be the sign of an underlying medical problem.

One night several years ago my beloved bunny Myrrh was showing a special interest in chewing a willow tent (which had been one of his toys for several weeks). I thought it was "cute" until the next day when I found him lethargic and hypothermic (body temperature was 96°F). Although we nursed him through this episode, he died at less than a year old. Necropsy showed an adhesion where the stomach empties into the intestine. The adhesion had trapped a normal fecal pellet, causing a blockage.

Since Myrrh's death, I have talked to several other people who report similar experiences with willow. It is difficult to say for sure whether unusual interest in willow always signifies an underlying problem or whether, in some cases, ingesting too much can actually create a problem (see Acute Bloat and Blockage, Chapter 3). Willow does contain the glycoside salicin, from which the body can split off salicylic acid, the basis of the therapeutic effects of both willow and aspirin (which also has recognized blood-thinning properties). To be safe, I now offer willow toys to my bunnies only during supervised play time and if someone shows more interest than normal, I schedule a vet visit.

Chinese Herbs

Just as use of Western herbs requires some basic understanding of physiology as well as the plants used, use of Chinese herbs requires an overall understanding of the philosophy and principles of Traditional Chinese Medicine (TCM) as well as an understanding of the herbs themselves and how they work in the body. One of the most important aspects of TCM is that practitioners look at the entire body/mind/ emotional/spiritual being before reaching a diagnosis and deciding on a treatment plan. In many ways this process is more complex than the narrow focus of Western medicine, which often targets only a single part of the body.

In veterinary TCM, the initial conversation with the caregiver (both current symptoms and medical history) and examination of the animal will be an involved and detailed process. Be sure to mention all concurrent symptoms, no matter how minor or unrelated they may seem to you. It is these details that often lead to an accurate diagnosis. In addition, think back carefully (keep a diary, if possible) of when you first noticed the symptoms and how they ebb and flow. Think of season, weather factors (temperature and/or humidity), and time of day as well as any changes in household routine, no matter how minor they seem to you.

The focus of TCM is on creating balance and harmony. For the purpose of diagnosis, body systems are paired (yin/ yang) and associated with the five elemental energies: wood, fire, earth, metal, and water. By looking at the patient as a whole and looking at all signs and symptoms, both major and minor, a practitioner of TCM has a better chance of correctly identifying the root cause of the problem so it can be addressed. In *A Handbook of Chinese Healing Herbs*, author Daniel Reid offers the human example of high blood pressure and/or rapid pulse. In Western medicine these would be diagnosed as heart problems and treated accordingly. In TCM, the cardiovascular system is associated with yin and fire energy while the kidneys are yin coupled with water energy. Depending on other symptoms reported, a TCM practitioner might conclude that the problem that appears to be with the heart (yin/fire) is actually cause by a deficiency in the kidneys (yin/water), which allows the heart's fire to rage out of control. By treating the deficiency in the kidneys, the heart symptoms will naturally subside.

Chinese herbs are classified (and associated with the five elemental energies) as bitter (fire), sweet (earth), pungent (metal), salty (water), and sour (wood). They are also categorized by their influence on the balance of yin and yang.

Yin herbs are said to:
- Cool the system
- Slow down internal energies
- Sedate vital organs

Yang herbs are understood to:
- Heat up the system
- Accelerate internal energies (such as metabolism)
- Stimulate vital organs.

Herbs are further classified as cold/cool or hot/warm according to degree of influence on the yin/yang balance.

There is no simple "cookbook approach" to use of Chinese herbs. Successful diagnosis depends on proper identification of the body system pair that is out of balance and proper identification of whether the root cause is with the more or less obvious organ system. While accurate diagnosis requires a trained veterinarian who asks the right questions, it is equally dependent on a caregiver who is willing to answer all questions openly and completely even if they seem irrelevant.

Because of the difference in how Chinese herbs and Western pharmaceuticals approach illness and treatment (holistic vs. body-system focused), it is recommended that the two approaches be used together only under the supervision of a veterinarian who is fully trained in both approaches. If you are lucky enough to have access to such a practitioner, the synergistic effect of combining the two may be helpful, especially in cases where a Western pharmaceutical cure has not been found (EC, for example).

Jeanette Lyerly describes the combined treatments that have been used for Luna, her 10-year-old rabbit who has had head tilt caused by EC for four years:

> Her treatment has been a combination of traditional and herbal medications. Since she is tilted, she had been having trouble with recurring ear infections in her "down" ear. This is part of what she is taking the Chinese herbs for.
>
> The herbal remedies are compounded for us at the vet's office. The ingredients are mixed together, and then they flavor the mix for us, well really for our bunny Luna, with apple flavoring. We get a solution in a bottle to give to Luna, rather than the original plant. I believe that at least some of the herbs are powdered, since we have to shake the bottle well before taking out the dose. We give the herbal by mouth using a small syringe. Luna likes the medication since it is flavored, and thinks that it is a treat. If you don't hold on she will take the syringe away from you. We also feed regular herbs (parsley, basil, thyme, cilantro, sage, oregano, mint and dill) as part

of Luna's daily salad. As I understand, some of the Chinese herbal formulas do contain more than one ingredient, though I do not know if that is true in general.

Our vet has combined the use of herbal and traditional medications in Luna's treatment. When Luna had a relapse from EC, she was given the traditional fenbendazole, but was also prescribed *Artemisia annua* (not a Chinese herb, but our first experience

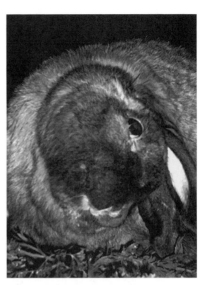

Chinese herbs combined with acupuncture and traditional treatments have helped Luna enjoy life despite EC-caused head tilt.

with an herbal medication). She was also on a steroid anti-inflammatory for a time and was prescribed milk thistle for liver support. For her recent ear infection, she has been taking an oral antibiotic, along with the Chinese herbals "Damp Heat Ear" and "Wei Qi Booster," and an herbal ear drop. The Damp Heat Ear and Wei Qi Booster are prepared as one, so we only have one dose to give. The Damp Heat Ear is to help clear her ear, the Wei Qi Booster is for immune system support, and the herbal ear drops are a topical antibacterial.

Dr. Christine Eckermann-Ross, Luna's vet at Avian and Exotic Animal Care in Raleigh, NC, explains how she uses Chinese herbs in her practice:

Many of the plants are the same, but some are not found typically in "Western" herbal medicine. The same Chinese medicine principles of treatment are applied to herbal therapy and acupuncture, and when I use these herbs, I combine this treatment philosophy with the knowledge we have of the biochemistry and physiologic effects of the herbs. "Western" herbal medicine tends to be more focused on using the same plant to treat the same syndrome or symptoms. In Chinese medicine, similar symptoms may be treated with slightly different formulas depending on the patient's constitution, environment, etc.

Because of the complexity of TCM, I recommend only using Chinese herbs that are dispensed by a veterinarian trained in this modality.

In describing her experience with an earlier episode of head tilt with Luna, Jeanette Lyerly points out the importance of remaining in tune with your rabbit's reactions to treatments and working closely with your veterinarian to make adjustments accordingly:

Luna had also taken a Chinese herbal formula in the past called "Stasis in Mansion of Mind." That one was during her very slow recovery from EC, and she took it for 30 days. Our vet prescribed it because she had evidence that it had helped other pets with similar balance and neurological issues. Since all these formulas are flavored for Luna, she has never minded taking them. Some of them she has seen as a treat, and gets annoyed if you are late with it (there is no mistaking disapproval from a head-tilt bunny). We did have an herbal eye drop for a few days to help with irritation in the "down" eye, but Luna would get upset when we gave it to her (she doesn't generally mind eye drops of any kind). When we reported this side effect to our vet, she changed Luna to a regular pharmaceutical eye drop.

I also asked Jeanette to comment on the effectiveness of Luna's treatments and she replied:

As to the effectiveness of the herbal treatments, together with traditional medicine and acupuncture therapy, I think that both we and our vet would say that these treatments have helped Luna live a longer and happier life. She has lived with this condition for about four years, and she is able to run, play with toys, enjoy her salad, and settle down for some quality petting. She does have some recurring problems with her down eye and ear, but she continues to be stable and have a good quality of life. While this ear infection has been very stubborn, it is getting better, and Luna has avoided having to have ear surgery at the age of 10. We are always concerned about her ability to fight off infections after all she has been through (two bouts with head tilt and EC), and are happy to try formulas that will support her system without causing any harm.

I was extremely impressed with how Dr. Eckermann-Ross responded to my question about how she assesses the risk of interaction when using Chinese herbs with Western pharmaceuticals:

I do use herbs and pharmaceuticals together in some cases. I do have references that cite the known herb-drug interactions, so I consult those. In addition, groups such as the Veterinary Botanical Medicine Association and Chi Institute of Traditional Chinese Veterinary

Medicine are constantly gathering data from practitioners' experience and observations, so our databases are growing all the time. I also get updates from the NIH Complementary and Alternative Medicine website, which is updated monthly. So, while sometimes we do things empirically, we really do have a lot of resources to help make sure that we are doing things safely.

Homeopathy

Homeopathy is based on the concept that minute doses of a substance that would cause a symptom in a healthy patient can be used to treat the same symptom in a sick patient.

For those of us used to Western pharmaceutical treatments, one of the hardest homeopathic concepts to grasp is that an infinitesimally small amount of a substance is actually used in the remedies. Potencies are most often denoted in centesimal dilutions (1/100th stages), denoted with a lowercase *c*. A 30c potency indicates a substance that was diluted one in a hundred (one drop substance to 99 drops water), 30 times (mathematically giving a dilution of 10^{-60}). Typical homeopathic potencies are 3c, 6c, 12c, 30c, or 200c.

Remedies are created by "serial dilution" of the substance with succussion (vigorous shaking) performed at each step. In *The Homoeopathic Treatment of Small Animals: Principles and Practice,* Christopher Day explains the process: "Succussion is carried out at each stage and it is this which seems to release the curative energy of the substance to imprint in the 'memory' of the water structure, while the successive dilution removes its toxic or harmful effects." In this way, homeopathic remedies are similar to flower essences and are often viewed as energetic rather than systemic treatments.

Note that the repeated dilutions actually create a *higher* potency remedy (though that may seem counterintuitive to those of used to dealing with Western pharmaceuti-

When Sonata had a urinary tract infection, Evonne Vey worked with Dr. Newkirk to develop a treatment plan that included homeopathy.

cals). It is also important to understand that potency of a homeopathic remedy does not equate to strength of a traditional drug but rather how it acts. Many homeopathic remedies are biphasic, meaning they have opposite effects depending on potency, providing stimulation in one case and suppression in another.

Although it may sound, from the paragraphs above, that homeopathy will not interact with other therapies, this is not always the case. In his chapter "The Relationship of Homeopathy to Conventional Medicine and Diagnosis," Day mentions that corticosteroids and, to a lesser extent, antihistamines may "block" homeopathic remedies. Also, some homeopathic practitioners recommend the use of homeopathic phosphorus for rabbits who have had any procedure requiring anesthesia because it speeds the process of clearing the anesthesia from the system. These examples demonstrate the *potential* for "interference" between homeopathic remedies and Western pharmaceuticals. When using homeopathic remedies with any other systemic therapy, it is wise to have their use overseen by a practitioner who understands all modalities being used.

In homeopathy, as in Traditional Chinese Medicine, diagnosis depends on more than identifying symptoms, applying a disease label to them, and prescribing the usual treatment. In fact, reaching an exact clinical diagnosis is less critical in homeopathy than identifying all pieces of the puzzle. As part of a homeopathic consultation, you will be asked many questions about your rabbit in addition to his current symptoms: medical history, environment, relationships to other family members, habits and routines, personality, and attitude. You will also be asked which conditions (foods, temperature, humidity, light, etc.) aggravate the problem and which make it better. Nothing is irrelevant. Indeed, the "key" piece of information that identifies the correct treatment to a homeopathic practitioner is often a detail that would never have been mentioned to a traditional veterinarian.

Two important factors influence a practitioner's choice of high- or low-potency remedies. The first is the patient's overall condition: high-potency doses may be contraindicated in the elderly or in those already in a weakened state. The second factor is the homeopath's level of certainty about the remedy. A high dose of the correct remedy attacks the disease directly and can be expected to cure the condition. However, a high dose of a "close" or an incorrect remedy will most likely have no effect at all. On the other hand, a low potency of the correct remedy will also attack the disease directly but may not have enough "force" to completely cure (depending on the strength of the disease itself) or may take much longer to effect a cure. A low potency of a "close" remedy may "chip away" some of the symptoms, often modifying the disease and occasionally curing it (usually only if the disease state is, itself, weak).

In their section on homeopathy, the WildAgain Wildlife Rehabilitation, Inc., website offers the analogy of finding the right homeopathic remedy to using the right key to start your car. The right key (correct remedy)

Evonne Vey used *Arnica montana* and **Hypericum** to speed Ragtime's recovery after having molar spurs filed.

starts the car easily. A key for another make of car (completely wrong remedy) will probably not even go in the ignition. A key for a different car of the same make (close remedy) may go in the ignition, but still won't start the car—and it does no good to try to force it. One must go back and find the right key.

Homeopathy recognizes that each patient is unique and individuals react differently to both the underlying disease state and to the treatments given. While traditional practitioners are often surprised when a patient fails to respond to a treatment or has an adverse reaction, homeopathic practitioners recognize these as individual differences that must be adjusted for.

Before using homeopathic treatments, it is recommended that you consult with a veterinary professional who is trained in homeopathy. Although it is great if someone is available locally, it is not absolutely necessary. Artist Evonne Vey, who lives in Maryland, explains how she works with Dr. Mark Newkirk, a homeopathic veterinarian in Margate, New Jersey:

> When a rabbit presents with a condition that requires veterinary attention, I take the bunny in [to a local veterinarian] for tests and radiographs (if necessary) and then consult with Dr. Newkirk regarding the diagnosis and a home care plan.
>
> For those times when emergency care is not readily available, I keep homeopathic remedies in my emergency first aid kit, including:
> - *Arnica montana:* Minimizes bruising, bleeding, initial shock; especially valuable after dental work and surgery.
> - *Cantharis:* Aids cystitis and painful straining on urinating.
> - *Hypericum:* Dulls the nerve/pain sensation from an injury to the extremities, toes, ears, or tail.

- *Ignatia:* Calms agitation from abandonment, bereavement, or loneliness.
- *Magnesium phosphate:* Reduces radiating pain, abdominal pain, cramps.
- *Pulsatilla:* Excellent remedy for any congestion-type disease; good for new mothers, nursing, and parenting.
- *Silica:* Aids the body in expelling superficial foreign bodies (splinters, thorns) out of the skin; cleanses the blood; helps promote healing of fibrous or scar tissue.

Evonne also recommends keeping the following homeopathic remedies on hand to offer either individually or together at the first sign of GI upset:
- *Carbo Veg:* This remedy calms gas in the stomach as well as bloated abdominal fullness and colicky pain.
- *Hydrastis:* Is helpful to a bunny who has a

Piccolo also received treatment with *Arnica montana* and Hypericum after having surgery to amputate his right back leg, which was badly broken when he was rescued and had failed to heal.

sore stomach and is loathe to eat food.
- *Lycopodium:* Helps lower gas and bloating.
- *Nat Mur:* Relieves burning gas, throbbing stomach pain, white mucus and constipation.
- *Nux vomica:* Helps relieve abdominal discomfort and gas.

Evonne explains how she administers homeopathic remedies:

> I generally use 30c for all these remedies, but a lower dose will work too. I either dissolve single remedies (or combination remedies together) in a little water or juice and syringe into the bunny every 15 minutes or until I see relief.

Like caregivers who administer simethecone in the early stages of GI upset, Evonne watches carefully for signs of improvement and is prepared for a vet visit if the condition fails to improve or worsens.

DEATH AND RECOVERY FROM GRIEF

Lucile C. Moore

There is no topic that is more personal and more diffi-cult than death. Each of us brings his or her own faith background, personal experiences, and emotions to the issue. There are no right and wrong answers; I can only share my personal views and the views of others in the hope they may help someone facing the same issues.

Natural Death and Euthanasia

Whenever I can—when the rabbit is not suffering excessive-ly—I prefer to allow my rabbits to die naturally, at home, in familiar surroundings and encircled with love. This is not always possible, but I believe it is possible more often than people realize.

I acknowledge there are times the physical pain and suffering of a loved companion animal makes euthanization the more humane choice. I have chosen it many times for companion animals myself, especially in my younger years. But now I am older, I am more cautious in making that de-cision, for how often is it made for the mental comfort of the person rather than the physical comfort of the compan-ion animal? We live in a culture that is, by and large, un-easy with death. We don't even like to think about death, since it reminds us of how near it is and how real it is, and we certainly don't want to watch it happen. I believe this mindset may occasionally lead people to euthanize animals who could otherwise have died in relative comfort at their home, in familiar surroundings.

Losing a rabbit friend is always difficult.

Another circumstance that may occur is when the caretaker becomes so upset at seeing their beloved rabbit companion suffer that the decision to euthanize is made too quickly, at a time when in fact there may yet be days or weeks of reprieve from pain and suffering. Anyone who has spent time around those with serious illness knows there are ups and downs. The decision to euthanize may be made at a down time, when in fact there may yet be more "up" times ahead. And perhaps the *rabbit* still wants to live, and shows it by exhibiting a strong fighting spirit. Maybe the time left is only a day, or a week. But as Angela Percival, who has experienced being with rabbits during both natural death and euthanasia, so well expresses it: "Thinking in terms of days or weeks doesn't have any meaning when you are living day by day with a human or animal headed toward the bridge."

It should also be recognized that euthanasia, even when done after administering a sedative—*as it always should be*—is rarely stress-free. Donna Jensen, an experienced fosterer who cares for many older rabbits and sees death often, prefers to let her rabbits die at home surrounded by love whenever possible. "Unless they are suffering," she adds. She points out that the trip to the vet to be euthanized is stressful in itself, as is the insertion of the IV or injections at the office. Sometimes, a veterinarian may agree to come to a person's home to perform euthanasia. This can be less stressful on the rabbit, given it allows him to die in familiar surroundings.

Kathy Smith, author of *Rabbit Health in the 21st Century,* has a slightly different perspective:

> My father spent the last 18 months of his life in a nursing home, slowly losing both his physical and mental abilities. I know he suffered during that entire time, though he was both stoic and upbeat. Even during the last week of his life, when things were really bad, if someone asked him how he was his answer was always "fine." In that way, he was very much like a bunny!
>
> I do not even consider euthanasia for a rabbit unless s/he has a terminal disease like cancer, pain that cannot be adequately controlled, and/or a debilitating condition that is progressing rapidly or has already seriously impacted quality of life (from the rabbit's perspective). Age *can* be a factor, especially when an older rabbit with a chronic, progressive condition develops an acute secondary condition.
>
> When the decision comes from the heart, I personally believe that euthanasia can be the final—and greatest—gift we can give our animal family members. Especially with prey animals, you may not be 100% sure it is "time" until you have waited too long (as I did with Smokey). We cannot always control the attachments of other family members (or even ourselves) that may bind their spirits to a body they need to leave. Making that final trip to the vet because it is what is best for *them* can be a supreme act of love, especially when we

are not sure we can go on without them.

Because euthanasia is such a huge topic to any person with companion animals, I wanted a professional's view. I spoke with Lezlie Sage, adoption program administrator at Best Friends Animal Sanctuary, and a certified interfaith chaplain. Lezlie frequently counsels those facing dilemmas such as euthanasia. "In this culture we are taught that taking a life is the ultimate immoral act," Lezlie explains, "yet we are also taught that a good person will not let an animal suffer. For animal lovers, this can set up a deep internal conflict, especially when you consider that, for many of us, our pets are family. We look at our human family members suffering and know that in those cases it is not acceptable to terminate life. You can see the potential problem here."

Lezlie emphasizes that determining whether to euthanize, or when to euthanize, should always be made with the animal's comfort in mind. She notes that sometimes natural death can be frightening and painful, but agrees that in cases where pain can be eradicated with medication, an animal could be allowed to die naturally. More often, she believes, it is a case of recognizing the point at which euthanasia should be elected. Personally, Lezlie does not like to opt for euthanasia too soon, and comments on her experiences with people in hospice: "Many times people reach faith-affirming understanding or revelations in the final moments of life. It is presumptuous to assume that we understand the internal lives of other species. Who are we to deny them the possibility of a total life experience?"

Lezlie commented that at the Sanctuary they take the correct timing of euthanasia very seriously indeed, and often have long discussions with many caregivers during the process. "You need to watch for the sign that *they* are ready," Lezlie emphasizes. "The vital energy shifts as the end nears. There will be a sense of shutting down and disengagement. At that point there are usually only days or hours of life remaining."

Sharing the Transition

While I was in the process of writing this chapter, a much-loved rabbit companion of one of my contributors crossed the bridge. I was struck with the beauty of the last days they spent together. Meg Brown and Greg Wait were able to do what chaplain Lezlie Sage advises—that is, to recognize when the disengagement from this life was beginning, ease the path by euthanization, and honor the rabbit in a creative manner:

> On Memorial Day, 2007, my husband Greg and I helped our beloved bunny, Buster, who we often affectionately call "Bussy," ease out of her earthly body. We were able to be fully present with her, as she gently moved from one world to the next, with dignity and grace.
>
> After eight wonderful years as a free-range rabbit, due to progressive stenosis and arthritis of her lumbar spine, Buster was no longer able to hop or even scoot by late March of 2007. We set her up in the kitchen, making a "cozy nest" of thick fleece for her to rest on. Her body was partly under a willow tent tunnel, her head and shoulders "peeking" out.
>
> At first, we couldn't imagine that Bussy would be happy, having lost so much physical ability and having her space so suddenly and drastically limited. But she surprised us all (even herself) with her adaptability to going

Young Buster

with what "is."

We told Buster that it was perfectly okay for her to leave her body whenever she was ready. We wanted her to know that it was all acceptable and we would be with her as her body moved closer to the end of its life. Buster stopped eating on the Thursday before Memorial Day. I syringe-fed her from that day through Sunday morning.

On Sunday, we knew that Bus was getting ready to leave her body. She did not seem uncomfortable or in any kind of distress. She seemed very tired, but peaceful and at ease. We told Bussy's friends that she would be leaving her body on Monday. She received visitors and many beautiful e-mails, which I read to her. Many people also lit candles to help bless Bus on her journey. We spent one last "family night" with our girl. The following day, Memorial Day, we helped Buster to gently and peacefully leave her body.

We began the day by lighting a candle in honor of Bussy's journey. Our dear friends

Buster, elegant in her cozy nest.

Sandi, Gucci, and Armani lit three candles for Buster. The first candle was in honor of Bussy's life, the second in remembrance of her passing, and the third in celebration of her new forever-healthy light body.

Greg needed to work for a few hours, so Buster and I had some alone time together. I sat close to Bus most of the day. There were times of silence, being present with her, my hand stroking her soft furry body, or my head resting against hers, as I told her about this very special day, and how we would all be together as she left her body, to go toward the light.

I told Buster that her dad and I would miss her luxurious body and soulful eyes, but that we knew it was time for her spirit to be free of its earthly body. I thanked her for living with us for over eight amazing years and for teaching us so much about what is truly important in this life.

I gathered all of Bussy's photographs, going back to her early years. With each photo, I reminded both of us of funny, adventurous, and mischievous things she had done and quiet times we had spent together.

At 3:30 P.M., I held our beloved friend Buster Bunny as the first dose of the pre-sedate was administered. She rested on my lap atop the soft fleece and the beautiful colored cloth (blue, white, and gold), with prayer ties surrounding her body.

Bussy did not get sleepy right away. It was about four hours from the time that Buster received the first pre-sedate, to the time that her heart stopped. It felt perfect, though. She was totally peaceful. Her presence helped us to feel the perfection of the moment.

Watching Bussy cross over was a bittersweet teaching in impermanence. We sat together in silence, Bussy's lifeless body on my lap. There were no words for the magnitude of those moments.

Greg read a poem that he'd written for his "best girl":

Buster by Greg Wait

From before time began
Buster was in every sunrise
that ever was

And now
she is in every sunset
that will ever be

Like the medicine wheel
we rise to fall
to rise again

This is what she sang
while I was petting
her amber red fur:

In tracks of dancing light
beauty carries the up above
and down below
in time
so that all beings
might be placed
in radiance.

We laid Buster's dear body on prayer ties, then offered songs, prayers, and chants as we watched her ceremonial fire. We sat in silence for a long time, breathing and remembering, as Bussy's sacred fire rose.

Memorial table

That night, I set up a beautiful memorial table for her. On it, I placed one of our favorite photos of her, a small bag of her golden-red fur, a strand of prayer ties that we had made during the day, a copy of the poem that Greg had written for her, a plant, and a candle. We will keep the table set up with remembrances of Bussy always.

Taken Unaware

Not everyone will have the opportunity to celebrate the crossing of a life as beautifully as the above. As a person who lives in the country, I see death frequently, often in its harshest forms. Yet, I am still not always comfortable with this aspect of life. It can be very difficult to cope with unexpected death, especially when it takes one of our beloved rabbit companions. In a worst case scenario, we may even have to watch a loved one suffer physically as death comes.

I lost my first companion rabbit to acute bloat and blockage while I was on the telephone trying to find a vet with rabbit experience (my regular vet did not have weekend hours) who would see my rabbit very early on a Sunday morning. The death was not an easy one—rabbits dying from the complications of serious digestive ailments usually convulse in the final stages, and my rabbit did. He suffered, and was in great pain. The only aid he had during his final time was my physical presence and that of my friend's, and I can only hope he at least felt the love we felt for him.

Memorial garden

If you experience a sudden loss like this, it may be a good idea to seek help from family, friends, or a professional. And remember to be kind to yourself. We make the best decisions we can for the care of our rabbits with the information we have at the time. A sudden death is not your fault.

Depending upon your faith background, prayers, meditation, burying the rabbit, planting flowers in a memorial garden, posting a tribute on a rabbit site, donating to a rabbit charity, or remembering the rabbit in writing or artwork may help ease the sorrow and pain.

The One Left Behind

When one of a bonded pair or group of rabbits dies, the surviving rabbits may show signs of grief and depression, even as a human would. Rabbits are extremely social beings and the ties they forge with other living beings can be very strong. For this reason, any survivor should be watched closely for several weeks for signs of anorexia or depression that could potentially lead to gastrointestinal problems and other illnesses. Try to spend time with any survivors, talking to them and giving them extra little attentions. Nontraditional treatments such as flower essences may be very helpful during this time (see Part II).

The traditional wisdom is that a surviving rabbit should be paired with a new one as soon as possible. This may in fact work well in some cases. However, rabbits are as much individuals as humans, and not all survivors will welcome a new companion right after the death of their old one, particularly if the bond was an especially deep one.

When Meg Brown and Greg Wait's companion rabbit Hoppity died, the survivor, Bear, was grief-stricken and went into an obvious depression. Believing that Bear might welcome the company of one of the other rabbits living in the household, Meg tried to introduce Lola. The normally sweet Bear reacted by trying to bite Lola and showed other signs of distress. Lola was removed from the room, and Bear soon calmed down. Bear, like many people, needed time to grieve before he was introduced to potential new mates.

Afterwards: Coping with the Loss

The great sorrow of losing a beloved companion and member of one's family is that your life will never be the same again. It cannot be. Someone who was a part of it on this earthly plane is gone and will not be back in that form. This has to be faced, and it can be very difficult. That is not to say the intense sorrow will not ease, or your life will not be happy again and your memories positive—they can and will be, but your life won't be the *same,* not ever again.

I have found four special difficulties when losing rabbit companions that I have not found to exist—at least not as acutely—when losing other companion animals. The first is that many people, even those with other companion animals, do not understand deep grief over the loss of a rabbit. Another is that, because the average person does not have much knowledge of a rabbit's needs and has to actively seek the information, a person may learn after a rabbit's death that there was a simple thing that could have been done to save his life, or at least to give the rabbit a chance of surviving. This situation can lead to feelings of extreme guilt. A third difficulty I have found is peculiar to those who adopt special-needs rabbits or who simply adopt many rabbits. In these situations, several deaths may occur in a year, leaving the caretaker feeling that they are drowning in death. The fourth issue is that if a person chooses to adopt special-needs rabbits (or other special-needs animals), they may not live as long as those with normal health, even if they receive the best of care.

I spoke to Lezlie about these issues. "The degree of loss experienced is proportionate to the investment of the heart, not the species," Lezlie stated emphatically. "If a person views her rabbits as children and has put that emotional investment into them, the loss will be relative. If your pain is not understood by a person who you approach for support, seek those who do empathize instead," she advised. She further commented that continuing to return for understanding to a person who cannot or will not give it only intensifies feelings of heartache and loss. She suggested that the support of different people in your life may be helpful for different situations.

"The degree of loss experienced is proportionate to the investment of the heart."

Regarding the issue of guilt, Lezlie emphasized the need to be compassionate to ourselves. If in fact a person makes a mistake and a rabbit companion dies because of it, Lezlie offers the following suggestions: "First, go with your initial emotions. Don't back off from the negative feelings surrounding the death—especially grief. Mourning is a healthy and natural response to loss and should not be stifled. If you are unable to get through the feelings by yourself, seek help—whether from a professional or friend. Unending grief and guilt can be detrimental if it goes unchecked. Then examine what went wrong and be proactive in your own special way. You can honor the rabbit you lost creatively, such as through poetry, art, or the construction of a sacred space for cherished mementos. Identify the problem that led to the rabbit's death. Then resolve to educate yourself about rabbit care so you will never lose one through ignorance. Finally, be honest with yourself—do you truly want to try living with another rabbit, or are they perhaps not right for you? There are other ways to care for rabbits than by adopting them into your home. You can further their cause through educating others, raising money, and advocacy."

Next I asked Lezlie for her advice to caretakers who have lost several beloved companions in a short period of time. "Compound grief can be very difficult to get through," Lezlie stated. "Depending upon the temperament and sensitivity level of the person, it can even lead to post-traumatic stress disorder. Although some people are able to survive such times by themselves, I would strongly suggest seeking guidance for dealing with multiple loss situations.

"People caring for special-needs animals need to be realistic with their boundaries and expectations," Lezlie advised in response to my last question about the shorter lives of some special-needs rabbits. "If the rabbit is terminally ill, the fact needs to be faced—don't assume that you will be able to miraculously save him. Decide how much of 'you' will be taken with him when he goes. Be prepared for the loss, but realize that anticipatory grief can drain you as well. You will need to replenish yourself constantly so you can still be an active caregiver. Take time for yourself: read, take walks, and talk with friends. Look at the toll that caring for special-needs animals can take—do you need to reconsider? Recognize your sensitivities and limitations. If you don't, it can lead to burnout and then you can't help at all. And remember, when you are giving love to any being, the here and now is the only guarantee."

Stephen F. Guida, a volunteer with Brambley Hedge Rabbit Rescue, has this thought on losing special-needs rabbits: "When they die prematurely, you feel pain every bit as much as if they lived to be 10 years old. I myself have gotten a great deal of comfort knowing that whatever time they were on Earth, I made their life as comfortable and enjoyable as I possibly could. I consider caring for a special-needs animal a great privilege in life, and the joy and affection they bring to you outweighs the pain of losing them much too soon."

Beyond Grief

Every so often, a person is profoundly moved simply hearing about another's experience. This happened to me and several other rabbit caregivers to whom Meg Brown and Greg Wait related their experiences communicating with their rabbit companion, Buster, both during her life transition and before. In the hope of helping others, I asked if they would be willing to share any part of their experience with readers of this book. Their generosity in agreeing to publish these intensely personal communications—especially given that some readers will not understand or agree with their life views—is boundless. I can think of no better way in which to end this book.

Buster
Meg Brown with Buster

Greg and I adopted Buster in 1999. We were delighted and awed by our new little wondrous friend. The three of us bonded immediately, and Bus soon had the run of the place! Like most rabbits, she never liked being picked up, so we spent most of our time on the floor. Right up until the day she left her body, we often called each other to see what Bussy was up to. We would stop what were doing to see a flop, how she was snuggling, playing, or discovering something new.

When Bus was about a year old, we adopted Charlie from the local HRS chapter, having read that bunnies really want a bunny friend. She seemed very happy and was getting a great deal of attention, but we didn't want to be selfish, if she also wanted a bunny mate.

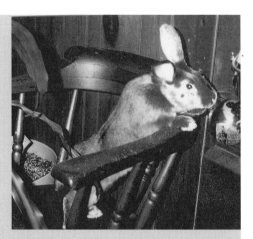

Discovering something new.

We read all of the bonding information we could get our hands on, and then had many unsuccessful sessions with Buster and Charlie. He really seemed to want to be with her. She seemed aloof and much more interested in her humans.

It was at that point when we started speaking with her wonderful animal communicator, Jan Spiers. Bus was very clear that, while Charlie was welcome to live in the same house, she did not want to live in the same space as him. He was much too "needy" for her. Despite reading that one must give bonding time to occur, we decided to listen to what Bus seemed quite clear about. She really did not want Charlie or any other rabbit as a mate. She was quite happy to be a single bun, thanks anyway!

For over eight wonderful years Buster was the head rabbit of Buster's bunny barn, our bunny-filled home. She paved the way for our understanding of rabbits and helped to deepen our compassion and our understanding of impermanence. Buster is my most profound teacher. She feels it is her path to share the bigger picture beyond the raw heartache of physical separation. We offer the following notes from our last few animal communication sessions with Buster and Jan Spiers with open hearts and clear intention in the hope that it may serve to provide comfort and inspiration to those whose beloved friends are leaving their earthly bodies:

(When Jan is speaking, she is "translating," in a sense, what she is receiving from Buster. When Bus is speaking, it is as if an exact quote. But, all of "Jan" and "Bus" are messages from Bus. A few times, Jan will begin in her own words, but that is clear, as she will say something like, "She's showing me . . .")

JAN: Beautiful sweetness from Buster
Intelligent, big life
She likes things her way *(that's our Bussy!)*.
Beneath that, there's an amazing sweetness.

BUS: I feel blessed, cared for.
My body is annoying at times.
I know my body's leaving its connection to life.
Feel gratitude, being cherished, being loved

JAN: She's wanting to hold both you and Greg . . .
your faces . . . looking into your eyes
Wants you to know it's really sweet to be so loved
She's letting it all in, in an even deeper way.

BUS: I am me in a different way than I've been before.
I want you to really know I love you.
Huge thank you for the life you give me and for loving me.

Session with Jan: April 2, 2007

(Our next session with Jan was two weeks later. In the meantime, Bus had become more subdued. . . . Her "affect" had changed noticeably.)

JAN: Buster is much quieter. She's not nearly as

chatty as usual.
Her mind and body are so tired.
Breathing is a little more effortful.
She feels light-headed and a little headachy.
(Bus is now no longer scooting, but lying on her side in the kitchen, under her tent tunnel.)

JAN: How do you feel about how life has changed for you?

BUS: It's a lot of work to be here now. Challenge mentally and physically.

JAN: She is not ready to leave yet. She is very clear about that. *(That surprised us; she's seemed so tired.)*

BUS: Not long, but not now

(Bus was very "quiet" but still eating for about the next ten days. Then, on Friday, April 13, she had a remarkable change in demeanor. She became her perky ole self, curious, interested, and very "present."

Greg was in New Mexico, spending part of the time doing spiritual work with sound and vibration, much of his work focused on Bussy. Also, she started taking flower essences from Green Hope Farm (www.greenhopeessences.com):

***Transition**—For the dying process—both to give physical stamina during the work of dying and to help with the spiritual work done during the last stages of life.*

***Separation**—Caretaker away or at work with the animal home alone. Greg works long hours and then went out of town. Bus is very closely bonded to him.*

***Arbor Garden**—Holds a vibration of Oneness-harmony-grace-and-sanctuary. It is excellent for grief, disharmony, or any situation where we have forgotten our Oneness.*

Bus and I took this every day. I put a couple of drops on Bussy's forehead; she would lean forward and hold her head still, then I'd rub it in. Every time, it seemed she knew that it was good for her and she welcomed the essences into her energy field.)

Session with Jan: April 18, 2007

JAN: Buster feels very different today. After speaking with her the last time, I'm a little surprised that she's still in her body. Something has really shifted for her.

She's in a very pleasant mood. Very alert—"with it" much more so than a couple of weeks ago.

(Jan told Bus that it seemed she was close to leaving her body the last time they talked.)

BUS: I am.

JAN: Buster said that something big has happened since then. She was given a bluish-white ball of energy. She has draped her body over it.

Greg's work, your talking with her, and the essences are all helping her to experience the "bubble."

She is showing me a bright, bluish-white ball of light—so much love and joy.

She is draping her body over it.

She has a "floaty" feeling—elongated.

Buster feels like she's floating on a big ball of love.

Feeling full of joy.

BUS: My body is going to die. I am not.

JAN: Buster is delighted to be here.

When she wakes up from a nap, she sometimes thinks: "Oh, I'm still here. I still have fur."

BUS: That I've had a taste of it for even a moment is extraordinary.

(The "it" meaning where she's going when her body dies)

JAN: She feels an amazing level of support. So pleased and grateful.

BUS: I'm having a really good time.

Everything's good. If you come in and my body
has died. That is perfect, too.

When my body stops, it will be like diving into
light . . . diving into golden light.

*(This is significant, as the flame which helped to carry
Bussy's essence to the cosmos, at one point took the form of
a radiant, golden 20-foot rabbit. I captured a photo of Buster
as this light being.)*

BUS: I feel permission to feel whatever I feel.

I'm floating on a bubble.

I don't feel prey or afraid at all.

I feel really BIG, like a five foot rabbit!

*(That, too, is significant, as Bus needed enough pre-sedate
and the final med for a very large rabbit!)*

A lot has to do with acceptance:

We are born and bodies die.

Appreciate that bodies are born and bodies die.

Very very healing cycle.

It is *not* an "oh no!"

MEG: I'm afraid that I will not be helpful to her if I cry
. . . but I think I won't be able to not cry.

BUS: *(She gives Jan image of her hands on her hips!)*

You absolutely should cry! I would be offended
if you didn't!

Tears are part of it. Gratitude—sorrow, joy—
missing the physical

I know that my body is luscious.

Your body will ache for mine. We got to know
each other—very close.

I would be offended if you don't let yourselves
feel sadness.

Tears have sweet, sweet memories.

Tears are natural.

You will feel "I miss the form."

Touch is special.

What matters when my body dies is the *honoring*.

Feeling the Joy

The enormity of the experience

The enormity of this Big life

Your body is the same. Your chance to say "Yes."

Also in the death of the body, to say "Yes."

That's what matters: Whether the body is offered to earth, ash, sustenance for another body. That is fine, as long as there is honoring.

This is for everything that is living/no difference.

Your Living/my Living/is the same Living.

That's why we can talk. You have a knowing—old knowing of the truth of what I'm saying. Death reminds us. All the same energy.

JAN: She wants you to speak of, "After her body has died" not "After Bussy dies."

The being, Bussy, won't die.

BUS: I love my body. It is feeling toasty and full.

MEG: How does Bus want us to think of her after her body dies, in terms of her place at home here?

BUS: I'm Buster. There's really no need to call it anything.

JAN: Buster's hope is for you to understand what she is telling you today. She really wants you to "get" it. She says it's important for your lives.

Being with (aware of) the Living (Life Force).

BUS: Your connection to me is a connection to something so huge.

All that we see and touch is us also. There is no separation.

That is what my life is about—to be that and help teach that.

Session with Jan: May 24, 2007

(We had a session scheduled for May 30, 2007, but I called Jan to see if we could get a few minutes with Bus, as she had not eaten for a full day and a half, unless syringe-fed. I wanted to check in to see if she was ready to leave, as I was not getting a clear message.

At the time of this session, she was not quite ready. Bus left her body four days later.)

JAN: In the "hello" with Buster, she feels very tired. Her body is so tired. Her connection with her front legs does not extend all the way to her feet. It is symbolic of shifting energy.

She feels like her energy is receding. She feels lighter/resting/comfortable

Syringe feeding has helped her. The oral fluids, especially, helped a lot . . . helped to "wake her up."

She is still happy to be here (in her body).

She feels like her body is dying, though death may take a while yet.

(Four days later, on Memorial Day, we helped our sweet Buster Bunny ease gently out of her furry little earth suit. In preparation for this most special day, I had bought cotton fabric, in the colors recommended in the book, Blessing the Bridge: What Animals Teach Us About Death, Dying, and Beyond, *by Rita Reynolds. The author suggests using blue, white, and gold cotton cloth to assist and comfort animals as they enter the process of the death of the body.*

I cut a large square of each color and draped them over Bussy's tent tunnel. I cut several 3–4" squares of the cloth to use for prayer ties. In making the prayer ties, I took a pinch of tobacco and held it to my heart, as I said a blessing for Bus. I offered the prayer to Father Sky, Mother Earth, and the four directions.

I then placed the tobacco in the center of the small

square of cloth and tied it with a long piece of string, to make a tobacco bundle. I said another prayer, made the offerings, and tied that bundle to the string, a couple of inches from the first . . . and so on until I had a long strand of tobacco bundles, each carrying a prayer for our beloved Bussy.

Buster's tent tunnel draped in colored cloth and prayer ties.

  I held our beloved friend Buster Bunny, as the first dose of the pre-sedate was administered. She rested on my lap atop soft fleece and the beautiful colored cloth, prayer ties around her body. Greg and I sang a Buddhist blessing: "No coming, no going. No after, no before. I feel you close to me, I release you to be so free. Because I am in you and you are in me. Because I am in you and you are in me.")

  (No struggle, no holding back . . . but a floating from one world to the next.)

Session with Jan: May 30, 2007
(two days after Buster left her body)

MEG: How is she? *(Jan was very quiet, longer than usual, when she checked in with Bussy.)*

JAN: Meg, it's hard to put words to it . . . to what Buster is expressing. The best I can come up with is: **RADIANT**
   Incredibly Radiant. Intelligent. But, not in the traditional sense of the word. There's a sharp awareness, almost like it has edges, it is so sharp. By that, I mean there is such acute clarity. Alertness. Awareness. Full. Big words. Big meaning.

BUS: I'm really **ALIVE.** Vigorous **BIG!!!**

JAN: She is so clear . . . so sharp, but in clarity. Heavy. But, not like the heaviness of a physical body . . . a Very, VERY large presence.

So big. So large. An acute awareness.

Buster is really vibrant and resting in appreciation.

She has a FULLNESS of having had a very big physical experience of a lifetime.

She recognizes there was effort in caring for her body. Feels gratitude to you, gratitude to her body. She was along for the ride. Given such an exquisite body and fur.

BUS: I think my body was so pleased to be me. I think my body loved it.

I had a really good time in my body.

I was a chestnut walking full of life (reference to her beautiful red-gold fur color).

JAN: There are so many layers of Bussy coming through. She is talking about her life in the way that you or I would talk about the absolute greatest vacation we had ever been on . . . the sights, the sounds, the feeling of joy.

She's not just remembering her life in her body, she's *feeling* again:

BUS: When my body was big and pretty.

JAN: Feeding the princess . . . not just food, but attention, love, and appreciation.

Buster wants to thank you both for holding the space of the death of her.

It was a full afternoon of leaving her body.

(From the time that Buster received the first pre-sedate to the time when her heart stopped, was about four hours. It was very peaceful, though just not the way that we had thought it would be. She required more medication than what would normally be necessary, in order for her heart to stop. But, it felt so perfect to all of us . . . being with Buster in her process

and trusting the perfection of that process.)

MEG: Why did her body take the time that it did to die?

BUS: You always knew I was a five-foot rabbit!!

Floating

JAN: She's making a joke, but to some extent, that's really true. Her energy was enormous her whole life.

It was the "floating" that allowed her to stay in her body longer. There was a Force of Love present. It made the approach of letting go of the body a much, much easier physical time. The floating. It was like a drug itself.

Buster was very physically comfortable before the death of her body.

BUS: Drugs were offered to my body. They were "gifted." No resistance, but they had to work through and with the larger "drug" of floating.

JAN: As the drugs added up, there was a feeling of: "Oh yeah, I see the support."

Her body accepted the drugs. Nothing was resisted, but it needed to be recognized.

So beautiful to have the quiet time with you and Greg. Not rushing the death of her body at all.

BUS: It is where we came from. Always here. That's floating.

MEG: Did any beings meet you to help you?

BUS: Floating was a huge help.

You want to know if there were any beings who took the form of animals or human, to help me.

There was a small black rabbit, off to the side . . . a friendly little face. Sweet.

I was very aware of a "council" . . . individuals, but no forms, animal or human.

They were light beings!

(I asked Bus about the golden bunny, rising from the fire. I took some photos of the fire, as we cremated her dear little body. One of the photos appears to have a very large golden bunny, facing to the right, with a radiant, golden body. Was it meant for us, as a gift from her?)

BUS: It was that. Even more. It was the dance of all bunny bodies being in celebration.

My body being embraced.

Felt like a joyful song: "Bunnies here. Bunnies there. Bunnies everywhere."

Outlandish joy!!! in the fire and light.

JAN: Recognition of bunnies being loved and celebrated by another species. Humans in the bunny world. Golden light. Celebrating bunny-ness everywhere.

Bunnies dancing everywhere.

Dancing bunnies. Celebration.

BUS: There really are no small things in life.

Respectful treatment of rabbits—all beings—is the key.

MEG: Should we always keep a memorial table set up in her honor?

BUS: Absolutely! Why even have the discussions? Of course!

JAN: She is saying that it is also joyful for us to have her presence move through photos.

Good to look at photos and feel her presence.

BUS: I am here.

MEG: Can Bussy still be present here (in Buster's Bunny Barn) and do the spiritual work that she needs to do?

Bus: Yes. The best way to describe it is that every-thing is here at the same time. Really not an-other place. It's all here. There's no time and space, just a way of trying to organize.

It's all energy and energy doesn't have walls.

Bus: Give Charlie time to adjust. Be extra sensitive with him.

(It was so sweet to hear Bus bring Charlie up, knowing that he would now be living in what used to be her space.)

Jan: She said he'll be smelling her smells. Imprints of her get studied by him. He's processing every-thing.

Bus: He wants to know that he's enough for you. He worries that he won't be enough for you.

Perhaps I overdid it—being sure that he always knew how Big I am.

He has no shoes to fill. Tell him he's a GREAT Charlie.

He's the best Charlie ever!

The way that I am with you will not diminish the way that you are with him. Let him know how happy you are that he is Charlie.

Jan: I know your incredible, raw achy feeling. Life changing . . . deep healing . . . rippling effect of this dramatic experience in your life.

More love just keeps showing up.

Buster feeds into that. The clarity of the experi-ence of your approach to the death of her body came out of you.

A calling. Helping others to know how it can be.

Bus: I am here with you. I will help you.

(We think about Buster a lot and allow ourselves to feel the raw ache of missing her physical presence. We have been changed forever, deeply blessed and inspired by her wisdom

and her pure heart. Our work to help foster awareness and compassion for rabbits and other beings will continue forever in Bussy's memory.)

Rising into the light.

APPENDIX I

TABLES OF SELECTED MEDICATIONS USED TO TREAT RABBITS

Lucile C. Moore and Kathy Smith

Many drug interactions can occur, some beneficial, others life-threatening. Interactions may also occur with herbs and homeopathic remedies. Compounding ingredients such as the drug base tartrate could also potentially affect the rabbit. Never dose a rabbit yourself, and watch for negative reactions to any medication or combination of medications.

Table 1 Selected narcotic and steroid analgesics.

Analgesic	Type	Dosage
buprenorphine Buprenex®	narcotic	.01–.05 mg/kg q6–12h
butorphanol Stadol® Torbugesic® Torbutrol®	narcotic	0.1–1.0 mg/kg q4–6h
dexamethasone	adrenocortico-steroid	0.2–2.0 mg/kg as anti-inflammatory 2–4 mg/kg for shock
fentanyl-fluanisone	narcotic	0.2–0.3 ml/kg
meperidine (pethidine) Demerol®	narcotic	5.0–10.0 mg/kg
nalbuphine Nubain®	narcotic	1–2 mg/kg q4–5h
prednisolone or **prednisone**	glucocortico-steroid	0.5–2.0 mg/kg

Drug dosages compiled from various sources. One kg of a rabbit's body weight is approximately 2.20 lb.; therefore a dose of 3 mg/kg would be 3 mg per 2.20 lb. of rabbit's weight. PO=by mouth, SC=subcutaneous injection, IM=intramuscular injec-

How given	Possible side effects	Comments
IV, SC, IM	May depress respiratory system	May be used for post-surgical pain, pain from fractures. Effective 8–12 hours.
SC, IM, IV	Diarrhea, may depress appetite, GI, cardiovascular	May be used for post-surgical pain, joint pain. Lasts 2–4 hours.
PO, SC	Predisposes to gastric ulcers, slows GI. Do not combine w/NSAIDs	Reduces inflammation and pain in rabbits with tumors, arthritis, and severe ear and eye disease
IV, SC		
IM, SC	Possible depression of GI, respiratory and cardiovascular systems	
IM, SC		Lasts 2–4 hours
IM, SC, IV	May depress GI, respiratory and cardiovascular systems.	
PO, SC, IM	Hyperactivity, swelling, slowing of GI system, gastric ulcers, suppresses immune system. Do not combine w/NSAIDs	Anti-inflammatory; also used for EC, cancer, and as single dose for shock.

tion, IV=intravenous injection, q=every, h=hour. *(Your veterinarian will take factors other than body weight into consideration when determining the proper dosage for your rabbit. Do not attempt to compute dosages yourself.)*

Table 2 Selected non-steroidal anti-inflammatory analgesics (NSAIDs).

NSAID	Dosage	How given
acetaminophen Tylenol®	Not recommended for rabbits	
aspirin	10–100 mg/kg, q8–24h	PO
carprofen Rimadyl®	1.5 mg/kg q24h 1–2.2 mg/kg q12h	PO SC, IV
flunixin meglumine Banamine®	1.1 mg/kg q12–24h	SC, IM
ibuprofen Advil® Motrin®	2–10 mg/kg q12–24h	PO
indomethacin		
ketoprofen Orudis®	1–3 mg/kg q12–24h 3 mg/kg q12–24h.	PO IM
meloxicam Metacam®	0.1–0.3 mg/kg, rarely 0.5 mg/kg q24h	PO
piroxicam Feldene®	0.2–0.3 mg/kg q8h	PO

Drug dosages compiled from various sources. One kg of a rabbit's body weight is approximately 2.20 lb.; therefore a dose of 3 mg/kg would be 3 mg per 2.20 lb. of rabbit's weight. PO=by mouth, SC=subcutaneous injection, IM=intramuscular injec-

Potential side effects	Comments
	Not recommended
Has more potential side effects than most and will increase bleeding	Use in emergency to provide pain relief
Gastric ulcers, kidney impairment	Can be mixed in flavored syrup for giving by mouth, effective against bone and joint pain, not as effective for soft tissue pain
May be contraindicated in digestive disorders because of its negative effect on prostaglandins, which are necessary for cecal production	Good for soft tissue pain
May be more prone to cause gastric ulcers than other NSAIDs	Use only in emergencies.
Inhibits prostaglandin production, may induce hepatic lesions	May be beneficial in spinal injury therapy
Interacts with aspirin, diuretics	
Gastric ulcers, kidney impairment	Lasts 12–24 hours, good for arthritis pain

tion, IV=intravenous injection, q=every, h=hour. *(Your veterinarian will take factors other than body weight into consideration when determining the proper dosage for your rabbit. Do not attempt to compute dosages yourself.)*

Table 3 Selected antibiotics used for rabbits.

Antibiotic	Type	Dosage	How given
amikacin Amiglyde-V®	aminoglycoside	2–10 mg/kg q8–12h	SC with fluids
		2 mg/kg q6h	IM, IV with supplemental fluids
amoxicillin	penicillin related		SC, IM
azithromycin Zithromax®	azalide	7.5–30 mg/kg q24h	PO
ceftiofur sodium Naxcel®	cephalosporin		
cephalexin Keflex® Ceporex®	cephalosporin	15–30 mg/kg q24h	SC
		11–22 mg/kg q8–12h	PO
ciprofloxacin Cipro® Ciloxan®(topical)	fluoroquinolone	5–20 mg/kg q12h	PO
difloxacin Dicural®	fluoroquinolone	5–10 mg/ kg q24h	PO, SC

Drug dosages compiled from various sources. One kg of a rabbit's body weight is approximately 2.20 lb.; therefore a dose of 3 mg/kg would be 3 mg per 2.20 lb. of rabbit's weight. PO=by mouth, SC=subcutaneous injection, IM=intramuscular injec-

Potential side effects	Comments
Toxic to kidneys in dehydrated rabbits. Monitor kidney values.	Broad-spectrum, some anaerobes. No GI absorption. Used for injection into abscess capsule, in nebulizers (IN).
Dangerous by mouth; inject only.	Rarely used for bacteria not sensitive to other antibiotics. High risk.
Diarrhea, especially at higher doses.	Broad-spectrum, many anaerobes. Good bone penetration. Given for infections of ears and urinary tract.
Injection or beads only to avoid potentially fatal side effects.	Effective on *Pasteurella multocida*
Anorexia, diarrhea toxic to kidneys. Fewer side effects when administered subcutaneously.	Broad-spectrum, including anaerobes; penetrates bone. Sometimes effective on *Staphylococcus*.
Anorexia, diarrhea, cartilage damage in very young.	Broad-spectrum. Used for urinary tract, eye, ear, respiratory infections; wounds.
Anorexia, diarrhea, cartilage damage in very young.	Stays in body longer than some fluoroquinolones.

tion, IV=intravenous injection, q=every, h=hour. *(Your veterinarian will take factors other than body weight into consideration when determining the proper dosage for your rabbit. Do not attempt to compute dosages yourself.)*

Antibiotic	Type	Dosage	How given
doxycycline Vibramycin®	tetracycline	2.5 mg/kg q12h 4 mg/kg q24h	PO
enrofloxacin Baytril®	fluoroquinolone	10 mg/kg q12h 5–15 mg/kg q12h	PO SC, IM
florfenicol Nuflor®	chloramphenicol	15–30 mg /kg q12–24h 50 mg/kg q24h	IM PO
gentamicin Gentocin®	aminoglycoside	2 mg/kg q6h 5–8 mg/kg total dose; divided 8–24h	IM/IV SC/IM IN topical
marbofloxacin Marbocyl® Zeniquin®	fluoroquinolone	2–5 mg/kg q6–12h	PO
metronidazole Flagyl®	nitroimidazole	20 mg/kg q12h for 3–5 days	PO
neomycin sulfate	aminoglycoside	30 mg/kg q12h	PO
orbifloxacin Orbax®	fluoroquinolone		
oxytetracycline	tetracycline	50 mg/kg q12h	PO SC, IM

Potential side effects	Comments
May restrict absorption of calcium and drug itself; do not administer while giving calcium.	Broad-spectrum, especially *Pasteurella*, sometimes *Staphylococcus*. Also some fungi. Good penetration of bones and teeth.
Loss of appetite, mild diarrhea, sterile abscesses if injected. Avoid liver-flavored Baytril®.	Broad-spectrum including *Pasteurella, Bordetella, Listeria, Staphylococcus, Yersinia,* but not anaerobes. Can be given for longer time. Also nebulized (IN).
Bone marrow suppression, usually reversible. Possible decrease in appetite.	Broad-spectrum, good penetration. Good for *Staphylococcus* and *Streptococcus*.
May affect kidneys when injected; usually used as topical or in beads.	Used as topical treatment for conjunctivitis, in nebulizers, and in antibiotic-impregnated beads. Not effective on *Streptococcus* or anaerobes. No GI absorption.
Possible cartilage damage in young rabbits.	Broad-spectrum. Used for GI and respiratory infections. Appears a promising antibiotic for rabbits.
Anorexia, weakness, lethargy, toxicity to liver and kidneys	Helps prevent overgrowth of harmful bacteria in intestine; also effective against protozoa. Use with caution.
Toxic to ears and kidneys.	
Anorexia, diarrhea, possible cartilage damage to young rabbits.	Effective *Escherichia coli, Klebsiella,* and *Streptococcus,* among others.
May restrict absorption of calcium and drug itself, do not administer while giving calcium.	Broad-spectrum, especially *Pasteurella*, sometimes *Staphylococcus*. Good penetration of the bones and teeth.

Antibiotic	Type	Dosage	How given
penicillin G procaine	penicillin	20,000–60,000 IU/kg q24–48h	SC, IM
penicillin G procaine w/ penicillin G benzathine (bicillin)	penicillin		SC, IM
sulfadiazine/ trimethoprim Tribrissen®	potentiated sulfonamide*	30 mg/kg q12h	PO, SC
sulfadimethoxine Albon® Bactrovet®	sulfonamide	10–15 mg/kg q12h antiparasitic 50 mg/kg once, then 25 mg/kg per day for 10–20 days	PO
sulfamethoxazole/ trimethoprim Bactrim® Sulfatrim®	potentiated sulfonamide*	15–30 mg/kg q12h	PO
tetracycline Panmycin®	tetracycline	50 mg/kg q8–12h	PO
tilmicosin Micotil®	macrolide		
tylosin Tylan®	macrolide	10 mg/kg q12h	SC, IM

* Various potentiated sulfonamides are sometimes listed together under the term "Trimethoprim/sulfa."

Potential side effects	Comments
Inject only.	Inject only. Use with caution.
Inject only. Decreased appetite, sterile abscesses where injected.	Inject only. Theoretically remains in body longer and penetrates pus better. Give for several weeks.
Occasional mild diarrhea and slight decrease in appetite, but rarely has side effects	Broad-spectrum, including some anaerobes, but not effective for established abscesses. Effective against some protozoa.
Diarrhea	Very effective against anaerobes. Also effective against coccidia.
Rarely; anorexia and mild diarrhea	Broad-spectrum, including some anaerobes. Also some protozoa.
Anorexia. Do not give at the same time as calcium.	Effective against *P. multocida*
Causes fatal diarrhea in rabbits when given by mouth	Test dose of 5 mg/kg should be given. May be used in antibiotic-impregnated beads.
May cause diarrhea in rabbits when given by mouth	Broad-spectrum, anti-inflammatory. Used in antibiotic-impregnated beads.

Table 4 Selected antiparasitics.

Antiparasitic Agent	Type	Dosage	How given
albendazole	benzimidazole	10–20 mg/kg q24h for 5 days (worms)	PO
		20 mg/kg q24h for 4 weeks (EC)	PO
artemisinin	Extract from *Artemisia annua,* sweet wormwood		
cyromazine (licensed UK) Rearguard®			topical
fenbendazole Panacur® Lapizole	benzimidazole	10–20 mg/kg q24h 5 days (worms)	PO
		20 mg/kg q24h 4 weeks (EC)	PO
ivermectin Ivomec®	avermectin (macrocyclic lactone)	0.2–0.4 mg/kg, repeat in 10–14 days	SC
lufenuron Program®		10–30 mg/kg q15–30 days	PO
nitenpyram Capstar®			topically for maggots

Drug dosages compiled from various sources. One kg of a rabbit's body weight is approximately 2.20 lb.; therefore a dose of 3 mg/kg would be 3 mg per 2.20 lb. of rabbit's weight. PO=by mouth, SC=subcutaneous injection, IM=intramuscular injec-

Potential side effects	Comments
May have effects on embryo/ fetus, bone marrow suppression	Used in treating EC, worms. Rapidly absorbed and eliminated from body.
Considered experimental for EC in rabbits	Antimalarial.
	Flystrike (preventative— interferes with life cycle of organism)
Possible negative effects on bone marrow	Used for worms, sometimes for treating EC
	Used for fur mites and flystrike; also EC
Long term effects on rabbits unknown	Fleas, rarely for EC
	Flystrike

tion, IV=intravenous injection, q=every, h=hour. *(Your veterinarian will take factors other than body weight into consideration when determining the proper dosage for your rabbit. Do not attempt to compute dosages yourself.)*

Antiparasitic Agent	Type	Dosage	How given
oxybendazole Anthelcide EQ®	benzimidazole	15 mg/kg (worms)	PO
oxytetracycline	tetracycline		
ponazuril Marquis®	toltrazuril-sulfone		
pyrimethamine Daraprim®		See article by Dr. van Praag www.medirab-bit.com	
selamectin Revolution®	Avermectin (macrocyclic lactone)	6–8 mg/kg	topical
thiabendazole	benzimidazole	110 mg/kg once, then 70 mg for 8 days	PO
		100–200 mg/kg once	PO

Potential side effects	Comments
	Worms, EC
	May be prescribed for EC
Considered experimental for EC in rabbits by some vets	Anti-protozoal used for horses
Considered experimental for EC.	Antimalarial. Used to treat toxoplasmosis in rabbits.
	Used for ectoparasites
	EC

Table 5 Selected medications used for treating gastrointestinal disorders in rabbits.

Medication	Dosage	How given
cholestyramine Questran®	0.5 g/kg q12h	PO
cimetidine Tagamet®	5–10 mg/kg q8–12h	PO, IM, SC
cisapride Propulsid®	0.5 mg/kg q6–12h	PO
cyproheptadine Periactin®	0.5 mg/kg q12h	PO
famotidine Pepcid®		PO, SC
metoclopramide Reglan®	0.5 mg/kg q6–12h	PO, SC
omeprazole Prilosec®		PO
ranitidine Zantac®	2–5 mg/kg q12h	PO
	2 mg/kg q24h	IV
simethicone	20–40 mg per adult rabbit q4–6h	PO
sucralfate Carafate®	25 mg/kg q8–12h	PO

Drug dosages compiled from various sources. One kg of a rabbit's body weight is approximately 2.20 lb.; therefore a dose of 3 mg/kg would be 3 mg per 2.20 lb. of rabbit's weight. PO=by mouth, SC=subcutaneous injection, IM=intramuscular injec-

Possible side effects	Comments
Will dehydrate—give with liquids, at least 20 ml extra oral fluids	Binds bacterial toxins in intestine. May be given to rabbits at risk of developing enterotoxemia.
	For treating GI ulcers, acts by reducing acid
May be contraindicated in cases of intestinal obstruction; possible cardiovascular effects	Intestinal motility drug. May be difficult to obtain, except in compounding pharmacy.
	Appetite stimulant
	For treating GI ulcers, acts by reducing acid
May be contraindicated in cases of intestinal obstruction	Intestinal motility drug
	For treating GI ulcers
	For treating GI ulcers, acts by reducing acid
If preparation contains artificial sweetener, could possibly increase intestinal gas.	To reduce gastrointestinal gas. Mechanical action.
Do not give in conjunction with cimetidine, tetracycline, phenytoin, or digoxin.	A coating medication used for treating GI ulcers. Must be taken regularly. Caution: may interfere with other drugs taken orally.

tion, IV=intravenous injection, q=every, h=hour. *(Your veterinarian will take factors other than body weight into consideration when determining the proper dosage for your rabbit. Do not attempt to compute dosages yourself.)*

APPENDIX II

RABBIT VITAL SIGNS

Kathy Smith,
reviewed by Noella Allan, DVM

	Normal	Monitor closely	Intervention required
Eyes	Bright, clear, no discharge	Occasional clear discharge or slight crustiness	Dull, glassy, or opaque; noticeable discharge (especially green or yellow) or crusted over; squinting
Ears	Pale pink; no wax or discharge	Slight to moderate wax; occasional head shaking or scratching	Red or swollen ears; discharge; persistent head shaking or scratching
Nose	Dry; no sneezing	Occasional sneezing with no discharge; slight clear discharge	Discharge or crustiness; chronic sneezing; stained fur and/or buildup of debris on the forepaws (associated with wiping the nose)
Teeth/ mouth	Pale pink gums; incisors wearing evenly; dry chin	Slight, uneven growth of incisors; slight change in food preferences	Noticeable overgrowth of incisors; broken incisors; drooling or wet chin; bad breath

	Normal	Monitor closely	Intervention required
Fur/skin	Shiny, soft, well-groomed fur; pale pink skin; no sign of "dandruff"; little or no scratching	Fur slightly coarse/dull; frequent scratching; small amounts of "dandruff"	Dull, coarse, or matted fur; bare spots; noticeable flakiness; excessive or frantic scratching; dark pink or red skin; swellings or bumps
Foot pads	Light pink or fur-covered	Dark pink or missing fur	Red, swollen, or open sores
Rump	Clean, dry, and odorless; skin pink under fur	Occasional fecal matter, dampness, or odor	Wet or caked with fecal matter; strong odor
Gait	Free movement, no irregularities	Slight gait change or minor limp	Pronounced gait change to non-weight-bearing; any change in limb's appearance
Fecal/ cecal pellets	Fecal pellets round, firm, uniform size and color; no visible cecals	Occasional "string of pearls" or visible cecals	Small, hard fecal pellets; large globs of fecal/cecal matter (on bunny, floor, or litter box)
Urine	Clear; colorless, yellow, brown, or even orange/ red	Cloudy; slight change in quantity	Visible blood; sand-like deposits or toothpaste-consistency globs; noticeable change in quantity; straining to urinate or abnormal posturing
Body temperature	101°F–103°F	100°F–101°F or 103°F–104°F	<100°F or >104°F

APPENDIX III

TRADITIONAL RESOURCES FOR RABBIT CAREGIVERS

Lucile C. Moore and Kathy Smith

Useful Websites

House Rabbit Society http://www.rabbit.org
Contains many useful articles on rabbit health and care.

MediRabbit http://www.medirabbit.com

Morfz http://www.morfz.com or http://homepage.mac.com/mattocks/morfz
Contains extensive links to rabbit health information and information on veterinarians who treat rabbits.

Rabbitvet www.rabbitvet.net
Maintained by Arlette Hunnakko, this lists vets from around the world who treat rabbits.

Veterinary Partner http://www.veterinarypartner.com

Recommended Texts and Rabbit Books

The Biology and Medicine of Rabbits and Rodents (4th edition), John E. Harkness and Joseph E. Wagner. Philadelphia: Lea & Febiger, 1995.

BSAVA Manual of Rabbit Medicine and Surgery (2nd edition), Anna Meredith and Paul Flecknell (eds.). Gloucester, UK: British Small Animal Veterinary Association, 2006.

Ferrets, Rabbits, and Rodents: Clinical Medicine and Surgery (2nd edition), Katherine E. Quesenberry and James W. Carpenter (eds.). Philadelphia: Saunders, 2004.

House Rabbit Handbook: How to Live with an Urban Rabbit (4th edition), Marinell Harriman. Alameda, CA: Drollery Press, 2005.

A House Rabbit Primer: Understanding and Caring for Your Companion Rabbit, Lucile C. Moore. Santa Monica: Santa Monica Press, 2005.

King Murray's Royal Tail: The True Story of an Easter Bunny, Kathy Smith. Lincoln, NE: iUniverse, Inc., 2004.

Notes on Rabbit Internal Medicine, Richard A. Saunders and Ron Rees Davies. Ames, IA: Blackwell Publishing, Inc., 2005.

Rabbit and Rodent Dentistry Handbook, Vittorio Capello, DVM, with Margherita Gracis, DVM.Lake Worth, FL: Zoological Education Network, 2005.

Rabbit Health in the 21st Century: A Guide for Bunny Parents (2nd edition), Kathy Smith. Lincoln, NE: iUniverse, 2003.

Rabbits Everywhere, Alicia Ezpeleta. New York: Harry N. Abrams, Inc., 1996.

Rabbits: Gentle Hearts, Valiant Spirits; Inspirational Stories of Rescue, Triumph, and Joy, Marie Mead with Nancy LaRoche. Charlottesville, VA: Nova Maris Press, 2007.

The Relaxed Rabbit: Massage for Your Pet Bunny, Chandra Moira Beal. Lincoln, NE: iUniverse, Inc., 2004.

Stories Rabbits Tell: A Natural and Cultural History of a Misunderstood Creature, Susan E. Davis and Margo DeMello. Brooklyn, NY: Lantern Books, 2003.

Textbook of Rabbit Medicine, Frances Harcourt-Brown. Philadelphia: Butterworth-Heinemann, 2002.

Why does My Rabbit . . . ?, Anne McBride. London: Souvenir Press, Ltd., 1998.

Rabbit Shelters and Sanctuaries
The state or geographical area in which the organization is located/based is listed in parentheses, but many of these organizations offer educational programs, adoptions, products, and/or other services beyond their home area.

3 Bunnies Rabbit Rescue (New England) www.3bunnies.org

Adopt-a-Rabbit Program, the Rabbit Sanctuary (South Carolina) www.adopt-a-rabbit.org/

Best Friends Animal Society/Sanctuary (Utah) www.bestfriends.org/
Best Friends Network http://network.bestfriends.org/

Best Little Rabbit, Rodent, and Ferret House (Washington state) www.rabbitrodentferret.org

Brambley Hedge Rabbit Rescue (Arizona) http://bhrabbitrescue.org/

Bright Eyes Sanctuary and Rabbit Rescue (Maryland) http://brighteyessanctuary.org

Bunny Bunch (California) www.bunnybunch.org/

Bunny Magic Rabbit Rescue and Wildlife Rehabilitation (Maryland) www.bunnymagic.org

BunnyLuv Rabbit Resource Center (California) www.bunnyluv.org

Cats & Rabbits & More (California) www.catsandrabbitsandmore.com

East Valley Bunny Rescue (Arizona) www.bunnyrescue.org
Friends of Rabbits (Virginia)

www.petfinder.com/shelters/VA158.html

House Rabbit Connection (Massachusetts and Connecticut)
www.tagyerit.com/hopline

The House Rabbit Network (New England)
www.rabbitnetwork.org/philo.shtml

North Texas Rabbit Sanctuary (Texas) http://ntrs.org/main.html

The Rabbit Habit (Pennsylvania) www.rabbithabit.org

The Rabbit Haven (California) www.therabbithaven.org

Rabbit-Related Businesses

Alison Giese Photo Creations www.alisongiese.com/
Photo greeting cards featuring adorable bunnies (and a few pup-
pies), including a personalized moving announcement and gradu-
ation cards. Those fortunate enough to live in the San Diego area
can also have Alison—an experienced rabbit caretaker and active
member of the San Diego chapter of the HRS—care for their rabbits
at the **Sweet Dreams Bunny Lodge** while they are out of town.
(www.sweetdreamsbunnylodge.com/).

American Pet Diner www.americanpetdiner.com/
Family-owned farm that has been in business for over 25 years
providing healthy hay products and safe treats and supplements
for small mammals. Makers of the nutritional supplement Critter
Be Better®. American Pet Diner markets an excellent mountain
hay that may be more palatable than other hays to some special-
needs buns.

Bright Eyes Pet Photography brighteyespetphoto.com
Private, in-home sittings are offered by this Maryland photography business that specializes in rabbit photos. Ideal for having a
professional photo taken of your special bun (or other companion
animal).

Bunny Bunch Boutique www.bunnybunchboutique.com
Profits from the Boutique help the Bunny Bunch rescue rabbits. Items of interest to those giving special care to rabbits include: a disc heating pad, herb-blended hay, garden treats, and a GI stasis kit.

Bunny Bytes: Outfitters of the Urban Rabbit
www.bunnybytes.com
Many supplies, safe treats, and basics are available. Of particular interest to readers of this book might be the health supplies, a large litter box, and the hay.

The Busy Bunny® www.busybunny.com
Offers many products for rabbits and their human companions. A few of the products that might be of interest to those with rabbits needing special care include herb garden kits (fresh kitchen herbs are helpful treats for your rabbit requiring special care!), herbs in bags, grooming tools, and supplements such as Prozyme®.

Cats & Rabbits & More www.catsandrabbitsandmore.com/
Good educational information is available at this website, and a large selection of toys, treats, and other items are for sale. The bunny-safe cardboard Hopper Hideaway and Cottontail Cottage make wonderful places for that special bun to play and rest. Items of particular interest for those with rabbits needing special care are the blankets, quilts, and "bunny buddy."

Doggon' Wheels www.doggon.net
Carts, diapers, and additional products for disabled rabbits and other companion animals are available.

Harewear http://harewear.tripod.com/
"Buy a shirt, help a shelter bunny!" Carla's beloved rabbit Simon is the spirit behind Harewear. Choose a design (rabbit or other) to be printed on a shirt, tote, or other apparel. Several shirt styles and a wide selection of print designs are available.

K-9 Carts www.k9carts.com
In business for over 40 years, this company makes carts for rabbits as well as other companion animals.

KW Cages www.kwcages.com/
In addition to a variety of cages and condos, KW Cages carries a wide selection of rabbit books, including many veterinary texts. They also carry various health supplies and grooming tools that are useful for giving rabbits special care.

Leith Petwerks, Inc. www.leithpetwerks.com/
Many products for the bunny needing special care are available here, including a 48″ Bunny Abode condo with hinged top, Bene-Bac Pet Gel (probiotic), an assortment of blunt-tipped syringes, and an open-front litter pan (very handy for the disabled or geriatric bun).

APPENDIX IV

ALTERNATIVE TREATMENT RESOURCES FOR RABBIT CAREGIVERS

Lucile C. Moore and Kathy Smith

Useful Websites

Acupressure
www.heartsofire.com

Acupuncture
www.ivas.org
www.natural-animal-health.co.uk

Alternative Healing Practitioners
www.ahvma.org

Animal Communication
www.animaltalk.net
www.animaltranslator.com
www.animalvoices.net
www.spotsaid.com
www.springfarmcares.com

Chiropractic
www.animalchiropractic.org

Crystals and Gemstones
www.crystal-cure.com

Flower Essences
www.greenhopeessences.com

Healing Touch for Animals®
www.healingtouchforanimals.com

Herbs
www.oldtimeherbs.com

Homeopathy
www.ewildagain.org/Homeopathy/homeopathy.htm

Reiki
www.animalreikisource.com

Traditional Chinese Medicine
www.tcmpage.com

TTouch®
www.marnieblack.com
www.ttouch.com
www.ttouch.co.za (Eugenie Chopin)

Recommended Books

Animal Healing and Vibrational Medicine, Sage Holloway. Nevada City, CA: Blue Dolphin Publishing, 2001.

Animal Reiki: Using Energy to Heal the Animals in Your Life, Elizabeth Fulton and Kathleen Prasad. Berkeley, CA: Ulysses Press, 2006.

Animals and the Afterlife: True Stories of Our Best Friends' Journey Beyond Death, Kim Sheridan. Carlsbad, CA: Hay House Inc., 2003.

Animals in Spirit: Our faithful companions' transition to the afterlife, Penelope Smith. New York: Atria Books, 2008.

Bach Flower Remedies for Animals, Gregory Vlamis and Helen Graham. Forres, Scotland, and Tallahassee, FL: Findhorn Press, 1999.

Crystal Healing for Animals (2nd edition), Martin J. Scott and Gael Mariani. Forres, Scotland, and Tallahassee, FL: Findhorn Press, 2002.

A Handbook of Chinese Healing Herbs, Daniel Reed. Boston: Shambhala Publications, 1995.

Hands of Light: A Guide to Healing Through the Human Energy Field, Barbara Ann Brennan. New York: Bantam, 1988.

Hear All Creatures!: The Journey of an Animal Communicator, Karen Anderson. Woonsocket, RI: New River Press, 2008.

The Homoeopathic Treatment of Small Animals: Principles and Practice, Christopher Day. London: Random House UK, 2005.

How to Heal with Color, Ted Andrews. St. Paul, MN: Llewellyn Publications, 2005.

Kinship with All Life: Simple, Challenging, Real-Life Experiences Showing How Animals Communicate with Each Other and with People Who Understand Them, J. Allen Boone. San Francisco: Harper One, 1976.

The Relaxed Rabbit: Massage for Your Pet Bunny, Chandra Moira Beal. New York: iUniverse, 2004.

The Tellington TTouch: A Revolutionary Natural Method to Train and Care for Your Favorite Animal, Linda Tellington-Jones. New York: Penguin, 1995.

GLOSSARY
British spellings given in parentheses

alopecia: hair loss

anorexia: loss of appetite

apical: tip of a rounded structure, as in roots of teeth

ascites: enlarged abdomen from accumulated fluid

aspect: side facing a given direction

ataxia: incoordination, confusion, muscular weakness

azotemia (azotaemia): high urea levels in blood

cardiomyopathy: disease affecting the myocardium, a muscle of the heart

caudal: tail, posterior

cecotrope, cecotroph, (caecotroph): (both accepted spellings) soft, membrane-enclosed rabbit droppings

clinical: disease shows obvious signs and symptoms

comminuted: in small pieces, fracture with more than two fragments

contraindicated: not advisable

cranial: head

dacryocystitis: infection of the nasolacrimal duct

debride: remove unhealthy tissue

distal: far from the point of attachment, opposite of proximal

dysbiosis: pathogenic or other bacteria overproduce in the gastrointestinal tract, negatively affecting the population of "friendly" bacteria. Out of symbiosis.

dysplasia: abnormal growth or development

dyspnea (dyspnoea): labored breathing

encephalitis: inflammation of the brain

endoscope: for visualizing the interior of a hollow organ such as the uterus

exophthalmos: protrusion of eye

femur: thigh bone

granuloma: nodules of localized tissue inflammation

hepatic: relating to the liver

hyperthermia: high body temperature

hypothermia: low body temperature

luxation: dislocation

meninges: membranes that cover the brain and spinal cord

meningitis: inflammation of the meninges

nebulize: make into a fine spray

neoplasia: tumor, cancer

nystagmus: involuntary movement of eyeballs

paresis: slight or partial paralysis

periapical: around the apex

perineal: between the anus and the genitalia

proximal: next to, nearest to a particular structure

quadriceps: muscle at front of thigh that is divided into four parts

renal: referring to kidneys

retrobulbar: behind the eye

sciatic nerve: nerve near hip

septicemia (septicaemia): "blood poisoning," toxicity throughout body from bacteria spreading from local infection via blood

subclinical: no recognizable symptoms present

subluxation: partial dislocation, or misalignment of joint

tachycardia: rapid heartbeat

tachypnea (tachypnoea): rapid breathing

tibia: leg bone between knee and ankle

torsion: twisting and wrenching

vestibular: body's balance system; central cavity of ear

ABBREVIATIONS AND ACRONYMS

ADD: acquired dental disease

AIPPMA: antibiotic-impregnated polymethylmethacrylate

CHF: congestive heart failure

EC: in rabbits, usually referring to *Encephalitozoon cuniculi* or the disease caused by it

GI: gastrointestinal

h: hour

HRS: House Rabbit Society

HTA/KHM: Healing Touch for Animals®/Komitor Healing Method

IM: intramuscular

IN: intranasal

IV: intravenous

LRS: lactated Ringer's solution

MBD: metabolic bone disease

NSAID: non-steroidal anti-inflammatory drug

PO: by mouth

q: every

SC/SQ: subcutaneous

TCM: Traditional Chinese Medicine

URI: upper respiratory infection

UTI: urinary tract infection

CONTRIBUTORS

Sandi Ackerman is the founder of the Washington chapter of the House Rabbit Society (1989); Best Little Rabbit, Rodent, and Ferret House (dba HRS, 1996); and Rabbit Meadows Sanctuary (1996), a sanctuary for feral rabbits. (pp. 270–278, photos pp. 270, 271, 272)

Noella Allan, DVM, Lakewood Animal Health Center, Lee's Summit, Missouri. www.lakewoodanimal.com. (pp. 224, 225, 229, 352, 414, 415)

Vineeta Anand is a Washington-based writer. In 1997, she started Friends of Rabbits, a rabbit rescue organization that promotes a better quality of life for companion rabbits through education and example. She retired from rabbit rescue in 2006 and now enjoys watching and photographing wildlife. (pp. 99–102, photo p. 100)

Chandra Moira Beal is a licensed massage therapist, freelance writer, and author of *The Relaxed Rabbit: Massage for Your Pet Bunny*; she shares her life with her husband and three rabbits (one of them a foster bunny). www.ChandraBeal.com. (pp. 333–337; photos pp. 334, 335)

George Belev has been practicing complementary therapies since 1997. He is a Usui Reiki Master/Teacher, a Shinpiden Animal Reiki Master/Teacher, a Healing Touch for Animals® Certified Practitioner, a pet massage instructor, and a certified Healing Touch® Practitioner. George is cofounder of Wellness and Healing, which offers cooperative, energy-based modalities to people and animals. George regularly gifts his services to various humane societies and rescue groups to help these animals adjust during their time of transition into the shelter and ultimately into their new homes. George is on the board of directors of the Animal Protective Foundation (Scotia, New York), is the certification advisor for Healing Touch for Animals®/Komitor Healing Methods, and is on the advisory and education councils for the International Association of Animal Massage and Bodywork. (pp. 339–341)

Marnie Black is a Certified Tellington TTouch® and Small Animal Massage Practitioner. Marnie works one-on-one with animals on the West Coast, and offers workshops on TTouch® and massage nationwide. She also speaks about the human-animal relationship to groups nationally. See www.marnieblack.com for more about her work. (pp. 342–346)

Betsy Bremer shared a photo of her very special bunny girl, Zsa Zsa, who is part of a family of rescued animals that includes three rabbits and three cats. (photo p. 186)

Diane Brookfield is a Colorado artist who lives in a mountain community with her husband, Bob, and her cat, Lolly Zoomer. (illus. pp. 54, 61, 62)

Meg Brown is a devoted animal advocate with a deep sense of the spiritual nature of all beings. Her primary work focuses on rabbit rescue and education and farm animal welfare. She is an active volunteer with the upstate New York chapter of the House Rabbit Society and North Country Wild Care and is a member of the Bunny Bunch and RabbitWise's Bunderground Railroad. Meg is a licensed massage therapist and has practiced a wide variety of alternative healing modalities over the past 25 years. She lives with her husband, Greg, and 12 family rabbits in their upstate New York home, Buster's Bunny Barn, named after their first rabbit, who continues to be a profound teacher and beloved friend. (pp. 57–59, 374–378, 383–396; photos pp. 40, 57, 58, 59, 60, 249, 312, 374, 375, 378, 384, 391, 393, 396)

Dawn Baumann Brunke is the author of *Animal Voices: Telepathic Communication in the Web of Life* (Bear & Company, 2002); *Awakening to Animal Voices: A Teen Guide to Telepathic Communication with All Life* (Bindu Books, 2004); and *Shapeshifting with Our Animal Companions: Reconnecting with the Spiritual Awareness of Animals* (Bear & Company, 2008). For book excerpts or more information, see www.animalvoices.net. (pp. 293–295)

Mark E. Burgess, DVM, received his veterinary credentials in 1986. He has a special interest in exotic species, and enjoys educating other professionals about exotics through such programs as the Special Animal Medicine courses at Oregon State University's

School of Veterinary Medicine and the Portland Veterinary Medical Association's continuing education series. Dr. Burgess has been recognized for his extensive work with ferrets and also for his work with wildlife. He practices in Beaverton, Oregon, at Southwest Animal Hospital. (pp. 74, 75, 79, 82–85, 187, 199)

Shannon Cail is a graphic designer who has shared her home with beloved house rabbits for over 10 years. (pp. 26, 165, 241, 250, 251, 323; photo p. 215)

Joanna Campbell has had pet rabbits for over 30 years. She got the rabbit bug after a fellow student brought rabbits to class for show and tell. Since then, she has continuously had a variety of rabbits, from dwarves to Flemish Giants. Joanna first became acquainted with the House Rabbit Society in 1997. She went on to become a nationally certified HRS educator, HRS fosterer, and served on the House Rabbit Society board. At the same time, she founded Minnesota Companion Rabbit Society and continues to serve as president of that group. (p. 97)

Kim Jackson Clevenger has had pet bunnies since 1981. She became involved with the House Rabbit Society and rescue work in 1995. She also takes her bunnies on animal-assisted therapy visits to local nursing homes and Ronald McDonald houses. Her husband **Terry Clevenger** married into her rabbit passion in 1987. He most enjoys the visits to the kids at the Ronald McDonald houses. (pp. 173–184; photos pp. 174, 176–179, 181)

Anita DeLelles is a certified Level 1 Equine and Small Animal Acupressure Practitioner with accreditation from the Tallgrass Animal Acupressure Institute. Now living in St. George, Utah, Anita offers acupressure therapy to animals in both southern Nevada and southern Utah. Anita shares her life not only with her husband, Ron, but also with her overly pampered cats and horses. (pp. 327–329)

Margo DeMello, development director of the House Rabbit Society, and coauthor of *Stories Rabbits Tell* (with Susan E. Davis) and *Why Animals Matter* (with Erin E. Williams). (pp. 40–42; photos pp. 41, 42)

Christine Eckermann-Ross, DVM, joined Avian and Exotic

Animal Care in Raleigh, North Carolina, after graduating from North Carolina State University's College of Veterinary Medicine in 2000, where she now serves as an adjunct assistant professor in the Department of Clinical Sciences. She has lectured at professional conferences on avian and exotic animal medicine and acupuncture. She is a certified veterinary acupuncturist and herbalist and has special interests in avian medicine, acupuncture, herbal medicine, surgery, and oncology. (pp. 361–364)

Alexandria (Alex) Fenner, a court reporter who lives with three wonderful house rabbits: Maybelline, Phoebe, and Joey. (p. 50; photos pp. 15, 50, 381)

Peter Franco, PhD, is a research scientist and educator at the Twin Cities campus of the University of Minnesota and a partner in a biotech company. Peter and his wife, Laura, are active in the Minnesota Companion Rabbit Society (Laura is the adoption coordinator), and the couple jointly care for their special-needs rabbits. (p. 211; photo p. 219)

Nancy Furstinger shares her home in New York's Hudson Valley with three treasured dogs and six house rabbits (plus numerous fosters)—all rescues. She is the author of more than 100 books, including many on her favorite topic: animals! (pp. 241, 242; photo p. 338)

Bill Guerrera, DVM, The Animal Doctor, Broomfield, Colorado. www.theanimaldoctor.vetsuite.com. (pp. 48, 49, 56, 142, 149, 161, 213)

Stephen F. Guida is a volunteer with Brambley Hedge Rabbit Rescue. He has shared his home with several rabbits requiring special care. (pp. 17, 18, 159, 204, 382, 383)

Morgan Heller contributed a photograph of her much-loved rabbit, Tasha, who lived to be nine years old. The photo was taken by Morgan's sister, **Gretchen Katzenberger.** (photo p. 193)

Patti Henningsen is Vice President of Fostering and Publishing for Friends of Rabbits, and has been involved with rabbit rescue for seven years. She cares for about 30 rabbits (plus other animals) as part of her Bright Eyes Sanctuary. She has been an animal communicator for five years and owns Bright Eyes Pet Photography, which specializes in rabbit photography. (pp. 134–138; photos pp. 135, 137, 138)

Jim and Brenda Holden are volunteeers with the Minnesota Companion Rabbit Society and share their home with rescued rabbits. (pp. 102, 292)

Arlette Hunnakko lives in Ontario, Canada. She is the bonded human of the 13-year-old bun, Cocoa. Arlette is a member of the Ontario Rabbit Education Organization, and is the webmaster of www.rabbitvet.net. (pp. 36, 256, 257; photos pp. 40, 256, 257)

Donna Jensen has been volunteering as an educator and fosterer with the House Rabbit Society since 1991, and was manager of the San Francisco Peninsula chapter for 10 years. She was also a volunteer with the Peninsula Humane Society for 16 years. Donna cares for about 50 foster bunnies, many of whom are special needs. (photos pp. 24, 78, 131, 134, 243)

April Jones lives in Washington state and got her first bunny, Bunnibun, in 1998. Since that time she has rescued bunnies from Washington, Oregon, California, Maryland, and Michigan. She currently has 18 bunnies. She is the WA/OR state coordinator for Rabbitwise Bunderground Railroad. (photos pp. 284, 286)

Susan G. Keeney, DVM, Diplomat, American Board of Veterinary Practitioners. Owner, Medical Director, Siena Animal Hospital, Las Vegas, Nevada. www.sienapetvet.com: sukeeney@aol.com. (pp. 164, 262)

Rebecca M. Kintner works full time as a special education teacher, but still finds time to volunteer seven days a week at her local rabbit rescue, and to foster rabbits in her home. She has three companion rabbits of her own: Courage, Chance, and Riley. (pp. 69–72; photo p. 71)

William E. Kurmes, DVM, is a 1993 graduate of Colorado State University. He practices in Flagstaff, Arizona. (pp. 108, 199–201)

Janie Landes has been an Animal Communicator and Reiki Practitioner for over 10 years. She feels her life's purpose is to help animals and teach others how to communicate with them. She volunteers her time at The Rabbit Habit, which is a non-profit, no-kill shelter. Besides her work with animals, Janie enjoys reading and creating art. Janie lives in Dublin, Pennsylvania, with her three wonderful bunnies, Isabella, Dodger, and Belle. Visit Janie at www.janielandes.com. (pp. 288–290; photo p. 288)

Ronita (Ronie) Lawrence is an emergency and critical care veterinary nurse and House Rabbit Society volunteer and educator. She has a degree in veterinary technology and completed an externship at the University of Pennsylvania Veterinary Hospital. Her article on Bun-Bun has appeared in the *Southeastern HRS Newsletter*, *Wisconsin House Rabbit News* (December 2005 and March 2006), and in *Smart Rescued Animals* (October 2006). (pp. 38, 39)

Karen Cole Leinenkugel is a children's librarian in California. For many years she and her husband, Ed, have shared their home and love with numerous house rabbits. SnugB is their oldest and dearest bunny friend. (photo p. 240)

Delores Lowis is a rabbit rescuer who shared a photo of her disabled companion rabbit Snowflake with nurse bunny Elliot. (photo p. 25)

Jeanette Lyerly and her husband have had rabbits for more than 10 years. They are both members of the North Carolina Triangle House Rabbits Group. Jeanette is also a rabbit volunteer at the Wake County SPCA. (pp. 323–325, 360–363; photo p. 361)

Joe Marcom, a retired paramedic, is the foster/adoption coordinator for a Houston rabbit rescue group (Bunny Buddies). He has a special interest in injured and special-needs rabbits. jmarcom@earthlink.net. (pp. 152, 153; photo p. 153)

Jodi McLaughlin is a certified massage therapist and freelance writer. She lives in rural Pennsylvania where she volunteers her love of bodywork to lucky goats, pigs, ponies, and her own little family: hubby Rick and house buns Diego and Berry. (pp. 29, 34, 35, 56, 57, 165–168, 170–173; photos pp. 34, 81, 166, 170, 172, 322)

J. Medawar generously contributed a piece on the relationship of behavioral difficulties and physical conditions. (pp. 208–210)

Kim Meyer is an animal communicator, as well as board member and fosterer for Vision Hills Sanctuary in Austin, Texas. Her specialty is rabbits, although she also works with guinea pigs, chinchillas, hamsters, gerbils, and mice. She works to care for the animals by doing computer technical support. (pp. 284–288)

Deborah Miles-Hoyt, Master Herbalist and author of numerous articles about using medicinal herbs with rabbits, has worked extensively with pets, predominantly rabbits, for five years. Her product line is Hoyt's Holistic Herbals for Pets, Potomac Falls, Virginia. DebHoyt@aol.com. (pp. 350, 352, 354, 355, 357)

James K. Morrisey, DVM, Dipl. ABVP (Avian Practice), Companion Exotic Animal Medicine Service, Cornell University Hospital for Animals, Ithaca, New York. (pp. 224, 227)

Jane and Steve Muncy are the proud new bunny parents of Hotots Ranger and Tonto and mini lop Amber. They also share their lives with seven cats, one of whom (Skywalker) thinks it is his duty to watch over the rabbits. (photos pp. 76, 232)

Joseph J. Nobile, volunteer at the Humane Society of Pinellas and the SPCA in Florida, rescues and adopts special-needs rabbits. (photo p. 33)

Missy Ott is a House Rabbit Society educator who has worked with many special-needs bunnies. She lives in Florida. (p. 152)

Maria L. Perez is the manager of the Las Vegas chapter of the House Rabbit Society. She sanctuaries 16 medically compromised rabbits. http://www.bunnyrescuefund.org/. (pp. 17, 18, 111; photos pp. 17, 104, 109, 118, 121, 236, 328, 342, 371)

Theresa Romaldini contributed photographs of her young bunny, Peanut, who was born with severely splayed legs. (photos pp. 16, 161)

Lezlie Sage, certified interfaith chaplain, is an adoption program administrator at the Sanctuary of Best Friends Animal Society. (pp. 373, 381, 382)

Santee Bunny Shelter, an independent rescuer who takes rabbits others have not been able to help and tries to find them proper indoor homes. (photo p. 201)

Sharon generously shared a photo in memory of her house rabbit, Sweety. (photo p. 119)

Molly Sheehan is a co-founder of Green Hope Farm. Their line of non-alcohol-based flower essences includes the Animal Wellness Collection, created especially for "the animals that grace your life." (pp. 311–313)

Julie Sherwin, formerly in the publishing and public relations fields, now works as a wildlife rehabilitator and is the founder of a Wisconsin rescue group for house rabbits, Soulmate Rabbit Rescue. www.linedgroundsquirrels.com/SoulmateRabbitRescue.html. (photo p. 163)

Amy Spintman has been a volunteer with San Diego House Rabbit Society since 1996, and currently sits on their board of directors. In 1998, she started Cats & Rabbits & More, which supports the efforts of shelters and rescue groups by posting their adoptable animals on the website, and sells toys for small animals. She developed the Cottontail Cottage and Hopper Hideaway small animal playhouses, which are sold through the website, rescue groups, and several rescue-friendly retailers. (pp. 55, 56, 257–260; photos pp. 22, 258, 259)

Kerry Stewart has enjoyed the company of her own rabbits since 1991. In 1997, she founded The Rabbit Habit, a domestic rabbit rescue located in southeastern Pennsylvania. Kerry also teaches in a corporate child development center, and in rare downtime, enjoys her home, artwork, crafting, and baking. (pp. 303, 304; photos pp. 290, 304, 349, 351)

Dawn Stuart contributed a photo of her special-needs rabbit, Espresso. (photo p. 326)

Jamie and Jason Sulliban, DVMs, have been veterinarians in Las Vegas, Nevada, for the last eight years. They are actively involved with the House Rabbit Society and NSPCA. The doctors also focus on treating other animals such as dogs and cats and exotic species, including reptiles, birds, exotic mammals, and koi. They currently own and practice at the Aloha Animal Hospital in the SW area of Las Vegas. www.alohaah.com. (pp. 66, 106, 148, 233, 253)

Shelley Thayer is a project specialist for Rapid Response, emergency rescue for Best Friends Animal Society. Her experience includes Hurricane Katrina, Reno Rabbit Rescue, Lebanon Paws for Peace, and many others. Shelley lives with her husband and five special-needs and rescued dogs and cats in Mammoth Lakes, California. (pp. 267–269)

Suzanne Trayhan is the president of the House Rabbit Network and has worked with rabbit rescues for over 13 years. She has written many articles on rabbit care and rescue work. Suzanne currently shares her home with her rabbits Daisy, Hamilton, and Brady, her dog Max, and her husband Gary. (pp. 228, 229)

Evonne Vey is an artist specializing in pet portraits (www.evonnesartcreations.com) whose interest in nutrition and homeopathy led to the formation of The Natural Rabbit e-group. She lives with her husband and seven rabbits, two dogs, five cats (one rescued from Athens, Greece), and many fish. (pp. 367–369; photos pp. 365, 366, 368)

Greg Wait has studied sound and vibrational healing for over 10 years. Much of his work has been through sacred dance and ceremony. He studied intensively with Rick and Elisa Cotroneo through the Experiential School of Sound Healing at the Mica Peace Chamber. The teachings come from the Southern Ute and Picurus Pueblo elder, Joseph Rael, Beautiful Painted Arrow. Greg recently returned from New Mexico, where he studied with Joseph at his Mystery School. Greg is a registered nurse who lives in upstate New York with his wife, Meg, and 12 family rabbits. He enjoys spending time with his daughters, Talara and Sierra, hiking and skiing in the Adirondack Mountains, and practicing Anusara yoga. (pp. 314–320, 377; photos pp. 315, 318)

Debby Widolf has been involved with rescue and education work to better the lives of domestic rabbits for the past 13 years. After leaving a 23-year career as an occupational therapist she is now working for Best Friends Animal Society as manager of the Rabbit Department. She was most recently involved in assessing and consulting on the rescue operation of over 1,200 rabbits from a hoarding situation in Reno, Nevada. Rabbits are her passion. E-mail: debby@bestfriends.org. (pp. 263–267; photos pp. 264, 265, 266, 268)

Barbara Yule is originally from Australia, and has been working in rabbit rescue for over 20 years. She is the founder of the North Texas Rabbit Sanctuary, which is based in the Dallas/Fort Worth metroplex. (pp. 30, 31)

SELECTED BIBLIOGRAPHY

Andrews, Ted. 2005. *How to Heal with Color*. Woodbury: Llewellyn Publications.

Bailey, Ralph. Excision Arthroplasty in a Rabbit. The Rabbit Charity. Retrieved June 14, 2007 from http://web.archive.org/web/20011112010522/http://www.therabbitcharity.freeserve.co.uk/excision.html

Boone, J. Allen. 1976. *Kinship with All Life: Simple, Challenging, Real-life Experiences Showing How Animals Communicate with Each Other and with the People Who Understand Them*. San Francisco: Harper One.

Brennan, Barbara and Jos. A. Smith (illustrator). 1988. *Hands of Light: A Guide to Healing Through the Human Energy Field*. New York: Bantam.

BSAVA Manual of Rabbit Medicine and Surgery. 2000. Edited by Paul Flecknell. Gloucester: British Small Animal Veterinary Association.

BSAVA Manual of Rabbit Medicine and Surgery. Second edition. 2006. Edited by Anna Meredith and Paul Flecknell. Gloucester: British Small Animal Veterinary Association.

Cail, Shannon. 2006. An Extraordinary Journey: A Rabbit's Fight for Survival Against the Odds. *Rabbit Tracks* (3): 2–4.

Capello, Vittorio and Margherita Gracis. 2005. *Rabbit and Rodent Dentistry Handbook*. Lake Worth: Zoological Education Network.

Cheeke, Peter R. 1987. *Rabbit Feeding and Nutrition*. Orlando: Academic Press.

Crossley, David A. 1995. Dental Disease in Rabbits and Herbivorous Rodents. *Periodont* (9). Retrieved July 2007 from http://periodont.spallek.com/peris9.html

Day, Christopher. 2005. *The Homoeopathic Treatment of Small Animals: Principles and Practice.* London: Random House UK.

Downes, Anne. 1999. Rabbits. *Menagerie: The Magazine for Pets & Their People.* Retrieved April 24, 2006, from http://www.menagerie.on.ca/02-99/rabbits.

Ferrets, Rabbits, and Rodents: Clinical Medicine and Surgery. 2nd ed. 2004. Edited by Katharine E. Quesenberry and James W. Carpenter. St. Louis: Saunders.

Fulton, Elizabeth and Kathleen Prasad. 2006. *Animal Reiki: Using Energy to Heal the Animals in Your Life.* Berkeley: Ulysses Press.

Furuoka, Hidefumi, Hiroshi Sato, Midori Kubo, Shigeo Owaki, Yoshiyasu Kobayashi, Takane Matsui, and Haruo Kamiya. 2003. Neuropathological observation of rabbits (*Oryctolagus cuniculus*) affected with raccoon roundworm (*Baylisascaris procyoni*) larva migrans in Japan. *J. Vet. Med. Sci.* 65 (6): 695–99.

Grauer, D., J. M. Kabo, F. J. Dorey, and R. A. Meals. 1987. The Effects of Intermittent Passive Exercise on Joint Stiffness Following Periarticular Fracture in Rabbits. *Clin. Orthop. Relat. Res.* 220: 259–65.

Grest, P., P. Albicker, L. Hoelzle, P. Wild, and A. Pospischil. 2002. Herpes Simplex Encephalitis in a Domestic Rabbit (*Oryctolagus cuniculus*). *J. Comp. Path.* 126: 308–11.

Harcourt-Brown, Frances. 2002. *Textbook of Rabbit Medicine.* Oxford: Butterworth-Heinemann.

Harcourt-Brown, F. M. 2004. *Encephalitozoon cuniculi* infection in rabbits. *Seminars in Avian and Exotic Pet Medicine* 13(2): 86–93.

Harcourt-Brown, Frances. 2005. *Encephalitozoon cuniculi* in Pet Rabbits. *50° Congresso Nazionale Multisala SCIVAC, 2005.*

Harvey, Carolynn. Rabbits: Geriatrics and Chronic Disease. The Rabbit Charity. Retrieved June 14, 2007, from http://web.archive.org/web/20011112010522/http://www.therabbitcharity.freeserve.co.uk/vet-geriatrics.html

Holloway, Sage. 2001. *Animal Healing and Vibrational Medicine.* Nevada City: Blue Dolphin Publishing, Inc.

Janovitz, Evan B., Cindy Fishman, Sarah Zimmerman, and Steve Thompson. 1998. Fatal Human Herpes Simplex Virus Encephalitis in a Domestic Rabbit. *Animal Disease Diagnostic Laboratory Summer 1998 Newsletter.*

Johnston, Matthew S. 2006. Rabbit Emergency and Critical Care: How to Save Them. Conference Notes, Proceedings, 109th Minnesota Veterinary Medical Association Convention, Duluth, MN.

Kanfer, Sari. 2002. Dental Problems in Rabbits. *Zooh Corner.* Retrieved July 2007 from http://www.mybunny.org/info/dental_problems.htm

Keeble, Emma. 2006. Common neurological and musculoskeletal problems in rabbits. *In Practice* 28: 212–18.

Keeble, E. J., and D. J. Shaw. 2006. Seroprevalence of antibodies to *Encephalitozoon cuniculi* in domestic rabbits in the United Kingdom. *The Veterinary Record* 158: 539–543.

Kelleher, S. A. 2002. Dealing with GI Problems. *Seminars in Avian and Exotic Pet Med.* 2(2): 94–101.

Kilgore, Alexandra. 2006. Dental Disease in Rabbits. *Rabbit Tracks* 4: 2–4.

Krempels, Dana. 2007. Runny Eyes, Runny Nose. What Do They Mean? *H.A.R.E. (Houserabbit Adoption, Rescue and Education).* Retrieved July 2007 from http://www.bio.miami.edu/hare/sneezing.html

Krempels, Dana, Mary Cotter, and Gil Stanzione. 2000. Ileus in Domestic Rabbits. *Exotic DVM,* 2(4): 19–21.

Kruse, Astrid M. 2000. Windows to the Bunny Soul: Your Rabbit's Eye Health. House Rabbit Network. Retrieved July 2007, from http://www.rabbitnetwork.org/articles/eyes.shtml

Kruse, Astrid M. 2006. Urinary Calcium and Its Consequences. *Rabbit Tracks* 2: 4–5.

Kunzel, Frank, Andrea Gruber, Alexander Tichy, Renate Edelhofer, Barbara Nell, Jasmin Hassan, Michael Leschnik, Johann G. Thalhammer, and Anja Joachim. 2008. Clinical symptoms and diasgnosis of encephalitozoonosis in pet rabbits. *Vet. Parasit.* 151(2–4): 115–124.

LaBonde, Jerry. 2007. Critical Care and Emergency Medicine for Exotic Animals. Conference notes, Michigan Veterinary Conference, Lansing, MI.

LaBonde, Jerry. 2007. Rabbit Medicine and Surgery: Tips and Techniques. Conference notes, Michigan Veterinary Conference, Lansing, MI.

Lawrence, Ronie. 2005. Just Look for the Sparkle. *Wisconsin House Rabbit News* 12(4): 6.

Lawrence, Ronie. 2006. Just Look for the Sparkle, Part II. *Wisconsin House Rabbit News* 13(1): 3–4.

Ligabue, M., D. Lucchetti, T. Catone, L. Fabrizi, L. Marvasi, and A. Zaghini. 2005. Rapid depletion of marbofloxacin residues in rabbit after therapeutic treatment. *Food Prot* 68(11): 2480–4.

Martinez-Jimenez, D., S. J. Hernandez-Divers, U. M. Dietrich, C. O. Williams, M. W. Blasier, H. Wuilson, and P. M. Frank. 2007. Endosurgical treatment of a retrobulbar abscess in a rabbit. *JAVMA* 230(6): 868–872.

Morrisey, James K. and Margaret McEntee. 2005. Therapeutic Options for Thymoma in the Rabbit. *Semin. Avian and Exotic Pet Med.* 14(3): 176–181.

Oglesbee, Barbara. 2006. *The 5-Minute Veterinary Consult: Ferret and Rabbit.* Oxford: Wiley Blackwell.
Reed, Daniel. 1995. *A Handbook of Healing Chinese Herbs.* Boston: Shambhala Publications.

Rosenthal, Karen L. 2001. How to Manage the Geriatric Rabbit.

Atlantic Coast Veterinary Conference. Retrieved February 17, 2007 from http://www.vin.com/VINDBPub/SearchPB/ Proceedings/PR05000/PR00408.htm

Sanchez-Migallon, D. Guzman, J. Mayer, J. Gould, and C. Azuma. 2006. Radiation Therapy for the Treatment of Thymoma in Rabbits. *J. Exotic Pet Med.* 15(2): 138–144.

Saunders, Richard A., and Ron Rees Davies. 2005. *Notes on Internal Rabbit Medicine.* Oxford: Blackwell Publishing.

Scott, Martin J., and Gael Mariani. 2002. *Crystal Healing for Animals.* Second edition. Forres: Findhorn Press.

Shibuya, Kazumoto, Masanori Tajima, Kazutaka Kanai, Miheko Ihara, and Tetsuo Nunoya. 1999. Spontaneous Lymphoma in a Japanese White Rabbit. *J. Vet. Med. Sci.* 12: 1327–29.

Smith, Kathy. 2003. *Rabbit Health in the 21st Century: A Guide for Bunny Parents.* 2nd ed. Lincoln: iUniverse, Inc.

Smith, Penelope. 2008. *Animals in Spirit: Our faithful companions' transition to the afterlife.* New York: Atria Books.

Tyrrell, Kerin L., Diane M. Citron, Jeffrey R. Jenkins, Ellie J. C. Goldstein, and Veterinary Study Group. 2002. Periodontal Bacteria in Rabbit Mandibular and Maxillary Abscesses. *J. Clin. Micro.* 40(3): 1044–47.

Vlamis, Gregory and Helen Graham. 1999. *Bach Flower Remedies for Animals.* Forres: Findhorn Press.

Weissenbock, H., J. A. Hainfellner, J. Berger, I. Kasper, and H. Budka. 1997. Naturally occurring herpes simplex encephalitis in a domestic rabbit (*Oryctolagus cuniculus*). *Vet. Path.* 34(1): 44–7.

INDEX

Also Available from Santa Monica Press

A HOUSE RABBIT PRIMER
Understanding and Caring for Your Companion Rabbit
by Lucile C. Moore

A House Rabbit Primer is a complete, up-to-date handbook on all aspects of rabbit care for both new and experienced pet rabbit owners.

In *A House Rabbit Primer*, author Lucile C. Moore—who holds a Ph.D. in biology with a specialty in animal behavior—provides pet rabbit owners with valuable information about the total care of their pet. Part one tells owners just what to expect from their new member of the family and gives detailed information on how to house, feed, and train a rabbit. Part two contains a comprehensive medical section. In addition to detailed information on many rabbit diseases, there are tips on creating a first-aid kit for rabbits as well as providing emergency care.

With more and more pet owners choosing to keep their rabbits indoors full time, this informative guide lays out practical information for making rabbits a healthy part of any family.

"This comprehensive manual covers everything readers need to know about keeping rabbits as pets in a well-organized and informative fashion. . . . This book should be required reading for anyone interested in keeping pet rabbits and is recommended for public libraries."   —*Library Journal*

$14.95 • Trade Paper • ISBN: 9781891661501 • 264 pages
5½ × 8½ • Black-and-White Photographs • Pets/Reference

Books Available from Santa Monica Press

The Bad Driver's Handbook
Hundreds of Simple Maneuvers to Frustrate, Annoy, and Endanger Those Around You
by Zack Arnstein and Larry Arnstein
192 pages $12.95

Calculated Risk
The Extraordinary Life of Jimmy Doolittle
by Jonna Doolittle Hoppes
360 pages $24.95

Dinner with a Cannibal
The Complete History of Mankind's Oldest Taboo
by Carole A. Travis-Henikoff
360 pages $24.95

**The Disneyland®
Encyclopedia**
The Unofficial, Unauthorized, and Unprecedented History of Every Land, Attraction, Restaurant, Shop, and Event in the Original Magic Kingdom®
by Chris Strodder
480 pages $19.95

**The Encyclopedia
of Sixties Cool**
A Celebration of the Grooviest People, Events, and Artifacts of the 1960s
by Chris Strodder
336 pages $24.95

**Exotic Travel Destinations
for Families**
by Jennifer M. Nichols
and Bill Nichols
360 pages $16.95

Footsteps in the Fog
Alfred Hitchcock's San Francisco
by Jeff Kraft and
Aaron Leventhal
240 pages $24.95

**Free Stuff & Good Deals
for Folks over 50, 3rd Edition**
by Linda Bowman
240 pages $12.95

Haunted Hikes
Spine-Tingling Tales and Trails from North America's National Parks
by Andrea Lankford
376 pages $16.95

A House Rabbit Primer
Understanding and Caring for Your Companion Rabbit
by Lucile C. Moore
264 pages $14.95

**How to Win Lotteries,
Sweepstakes, and Contests
in the 21st Century**
by Steve Ledoux
240 pages $14.95

James Dean Died Here
The Locations of America's Pop Culture Landmarks
by Chris Epting
312 pages $16.95

L.A. Noir
The City as Character
by Alain Silver and James Ursini
176 pages $19.95

Led Zeppelin Crashed Here
The Rock and Roll Landmarks of North America
by Chris Epting
336 pages $16.95

Letter Writing Made Easy!
Featuring Sample Letters for Hundreds of Common Occasions
by Margaret McCarthy
208 pages $12.95

Mark Spitz
The Extraordinary Life of an Olympic Champion
by Richard J. Foster
360 pages $24.95

The 99th Monkey
A Spiritual Journalist's Misadventures with Gurus, Messiahs, Sex, Psychedelics, and Other Consciousness-Raising Experiments
by Eliezer Sobel
312 pages $16.95

Redneck Haiku
Double-Wide Edition
by Mary K. Witte
240 pages $11.95

**Route 66 Adventure
Handbook**
by Drew Knowles
312 pages $16.95

**Route 66 Quick Reference
Encyclopedia**
by Drew Knowles
224 pages $12.95

**The Ruby Slippers,
Madonna's Bra, and
Einstein's Brain**
The Locations of America's Pop Culture Artifacts
by Chris Epting
312 pages $16.95

**Rudolph, Frosty, and
Captain Kangaroo**
The Musical Life of Hecky Krasnow—Producer of the World's Most Beloved Children's Songs
by Judy Gail Krasnow
424 pages $24.95

Self-Loathing for Beginners
by Lynn Phillips
192 pages $12.95

Silent Traces
Discovering Early Hollywood Through the Films of Charlie Chaplin
by John Bengtson
304 pages $24.95

The Sixties
Photographs by Robert Altman
192 pages $39.95

Tiki Road Trip, 2nd Edition
A Guide to Tiki Culture in North America
by James Teitelbaum
336 pages $16.95

Tower Stories
An Oral History of 9/11
by Damon DiMarco
528 pages $27.95

Vanity PL8 Puzzles
A Puzzle Book Where You Solve the Vanity Plates
by Michelle Mazzulo
96 pages $8.95

**"We're Going to See
the Beatles!"**
An Oral History of Beatlemania as Told by the Fans Who Were There
by Garry Berman
288 pages $16.95

**When Your Rabbit
Needs Special Care**
Traditional and Alternative Healing Methods
by Lucile C. Moore and
Kathy Smith
456 pages $19.95

	Quantity	Amount
The Bad Driver's Handbook ($12.95)	_____	_____
Calculated Risk ($24.95)	_____	_____
Dinner with a Cannibal ($24.95)	_____	_____
The Disneyland® Encyclopedia ($19.95)	_____	_____
The Encyclopedia of Sixties Cool ($24.95)	_____	_____
Exotic Travel Destinations for Families ($16.95)	_____	_____
Footsteps in the Fog: Alfred Hitchcock's San Francisco ($24.95)	_____	_____
Free Stuff & Good Deals for Folks Over 50, 3rd Edition ($12.95)	_____	_____
A House Rabbit Primer ($14.95)	_____	_____
How to Win Lotteries, Sweepstakes, and Contests in the 21st Century ($14.95)	_____	_____
James Dean Died Here: America's Pop Culture Landmarks ($16.95)	_____	_____
The Keystone Kid: Tales of Early Hollywood ($24.95)	_____	_____
L.A. Noir: The City as Character ($19.95)	_____	_____
Led Zeppelin Crashed Here ($16.95)	_____	_____
Letter Writing Made Easy! ($12.95)	_____	_____
Mark Spitz: The Extraordinary Life of an Olympic Champion ($24.95)	_____	_____
The 99th Monkey: A Spiritualist's Misadventures ($16.95)	_____	_____
Redneck Haiku: Double-Wide Edition ($11.95)	_____	_____
Route 66 Adventure Handbook ($16.95)	_____	_____
Route 66 Quick Reference Encyclopedia ($12.95)	_____	_____
The Ruby Slippers, Madonna's Bra, and Einstein's Brain ($16.95)	_____	_____
Rudolph, Frosty, and Captain Kangaroo ($24.95)	_____	_____
Self-Loathing for Beginners ($12.95)	_____	_____
Silent Traces: Early Hollywood Through Charlie Chaplin ($24.95)	_____	_____
The Sixties ($39.95)	_____	_____
Tiki Road Trip, 2nd Edition ($16.95)	_____	_____
Tower Stories ($27.95)	_____	_____
Vanity PL8 Puzles ($8.95)	_____	_____
"We're Going to See the Beatles!" ($16.95)	_____	_____
When Your Rabbit Needs Special Care ($19.95)	_____	_____

	Subtotal _____
Shipping & Handling: 1 book $4.00 Each additional book is $1.00	CA residents add 8.25% sales tax _____
	Shipping and Handling (see left) _____
	TOTAL _____

Name _____

Address _____

City _____ State _____ Zip _____

☐ Visa ☐ MasterCard   Card No.: _____

Exp. Date _____ Signature _____

☐ **Enclosed is my check or money order payable to:**

Santa Monica Press LLC
P.O. Box 1076
Santa Monica, CA 90406